The
Martin
Luther
King
Congressional
Cover-Up

The
Martin
Luther
King
Congressional
Cover-Up
The Railroading of
James Earl Ray

John Avery Emison

PELICAN PUBLISHING COMPANY
GRETNA 2014

The word "Pelican" and the depiction of a pelican are
trademarks of Pelican Publishing Company, Inc., and are
registered in the U.S. Patent and Trademark Office.

Library of Congress Cataloging-in-Publication Data

Emison, John Avery.
  The Martin Luther King congressional cover-up : the railroading of
James Earl Ray / by John Avery Emison.
     pages cm
  Includes bibliographical references and index.
  ISBN 978-1-4556-1910-8 (pbk. : alk. paper) — ISBN 978-1-
4556-1911-5 (e-book) 1. King, Martin Luther, Jr., 1929-1968—
Assassination. 2. Ray, James Earl, 1928-1998. 3. Conspiracies—
United States—History—20th century. I. Title.
  E185.97.K5E45 2014
  323.092—dc 3
                                                          2013051032

Printed in the United States of America
Published by Pelican Publishing Company, Inc.
1000 Burmaster Street, Gretna, Louisiana 70053

To my three grown children, Ave, Jay, and Wes.
And to people everywhere who seek truth, love liberty, and, as Texas
rancher and historian J. Evetts Haley said, "are willing to struggle to
find the one and fight to hold the other."

CONTENTS

Acknowledgments

In humble appreciation, I acknowledge the advice, counsel, and encouragement offered during the writing of this book by my elder friend, John Jay Hooker Jr., who is legendary for the mental exercise of "playing catch." In playing catch, we encouraged each other's thought processes. This helped to frame concepts that contributed enormously to my work. My appreciation to him is expressed with a great deal of admiration and affection.

It is also my pleasure to mention others who were helpful along the way. Donn King, with whom I worked decades ago, lent his expertise in drawing several figures. Brenda Fincher helped me with indexing the manuscript. State senator Reginald Tate arranged a private tour of the location of the assassination, which is now owned by the National Civil Rights Museum in Memphis. Vincent Clark of the Shelby County Archives was helpful in many ways, especially in finding and permitting the use of a number of photographs. Carrie Hagin arranged for J. Tony Serra's comments on the "green bundle" of evidence. The personnel of the US Army Office of the Chief of Military History were graciously and efficiently helpful.

Sean Coetzee, the owner of Prism Forensics LLC of Los Angeles, California, forensically enhanced the audio recordings of the James Earl Ray guilty plea hearing of March 10, 1969.

Tennessee Secretary of State Tre Hargett graciously permitted me to use several photographs from the Tennessee State Library and Archives as well as attempted to get documents owned by the State of Tennessee released from the fifty-year seal by the US House of Representatives. Congressman John J. Duncan Jr., whom I am privileged to call a friend, as well as Congressman Stephen Fincher, wrote letters supporting the release of these documents. Unfortunately, that effort has yet to prove successful.

I wish to thank the personnel of the Gerald R. Ford Presidential Library for finding documents relating to Richard Ober.

The personnel at the offices of the Federal District Courts in Nashville and Memphis were most helpful in finding documents and pointing in the right direction. The office of the Clerk at the US Court of Appeals for the Sixth Circuit, Cincinnati, Ohio, was likewise helpful.

I am honored to have had the opportunity to personally interview or correspond with Gareth Aden, Ronald B. Adrine, Harry S. Avery, William L. "Dick" Barry, James C. Beasley Jr., Peter G. Beeson, Howard Bingham, James A. "Bubba" Blackwell, G. Robert Blakey, Larry Brinton, Hudley Crockett, William Henry Haile, Arthur Hanes Jr., Hal Hardin, John Jay Hooker Jr., Charles E. Koster, Stonney Lane, James H. "Jim" Lesar, Priscilla Post Johnson McMillan, Roy Nixon, William F. Pepper, Gerald William "Jerry" Ray, Samuel H. "Bo" Roberts Jr., J. Tony Serra, Hampton Sides, Stephen C. Small, James D. "Jim" Squires, Joseph Sweat, Reginald Tate, Charles Thone, Mike Vinson, and James Earl Ray.

Finally, the moral support and interest by my friends and family meant more than words can express. I especially appreciate the time that Dr. Robert Bruce Avery took to discuss his father, Harry S. Avery, and to listen to the audiotapes that were given to me by James Earl Ray.

Introduction

This book examines the weak physical and circumstantial evidence against James Earl Ray. It examines Ray's alleged motive to assassinate Rev. Martin Luther King Jr. and dismisses it as inadequate and wishful thinking on the part of both local and federal investigators and prosecutors. It examines the much stronger motive others had to murder King. It examines Ray's ability or lack thereof to commit this crime and describes the extreme implausibility of him doing so without help.

This book also scrutinizes the work of four influential authors who have written about the King assassination, each of whom has assured the public that the government got its man—that James Earl Ray acted alone and there was no conspiracy. These authors and their books are: William Bradford Huie, *He Slew the Dreamer;* George E. McMillan, *The Making of an Assassin;* Gerald Posner, *Killing the Dream;* and Hampton Sides, *Hellhound on His Trail.*

This book examines the historiography of these authors' cases against James Earl Ray. It reveals through the progression of these books the repetition of many unproven, and in some cases specifically disproven, elements of the government's allegations against Ray. Without these elements of the case against James Earl Ray, the government's storyline of Ray as the lone assassin falls apart, as does these authors' credibility. Yet, the same worn-out assertions that are necessary to perpetuate the government's narrative continue to be repeated.

Finally, this book proposes a complete theory of the crime and James Earl Ray's pivotal role as a patsy. It identifies the parties responsible for King's assassination at an organizational level within the CIA.

Please note: this case is *not closed.* There is room for interpretation of the evidence by other thoughtful writers whether or not they agree with some, all, or none of my conclusions. This book is not *the* truth of the case, but I believe it is a *beginning* of the truth that will be refined by

11

others in the due course of history. Thus, it is my hope that this book will shift the subsequent debate about King's murder away from declaring Ray the gunman into asking who killed him and why.

WHERE DOES THIS BOOK FIT IN?

Several authors have previously described credible elements of a conspiracy surrounding the King assassination. Four of the best-known authors who have advanced the notion of a conspiracy to murder King are Harold Weisberg, Mark Lane, Philip H. Melanson, and William F. Pepper. Their works, individually and collectively, make important contributions to our current knowledge about the King assassination.

Harold Weisberg, who wrote primarily about the John F. Kennedy assassination, published the book *Frame-Up* about the King assassination in 1969. This book was re-published in 1971 under the title *Martin Luther King: The Assassination* and was his only major work on the King-Ray case. Weisberg's approach in this early conspiracy book was to cast doubt on everyone around Ray, including the lawyers, jailers, prosecutors, judges, investigators, witnesses, and corrections officials, both in England, where he was apprehended, and in the US. All are painted in Weisberg's rather wide brushstrokes. In spite of this, his book is an important compendium of the documents that surfaced in the early years of the case and has an excellent bibliography to support his work. Weisberg was convinced that there was a conspiracy to murder King and describes Ray's role as a decoy. From Weisberg's temporal perspective of the early 1970s, he views Ray as knowing more than he admitted to and sees the assassination as an unsolved crime. Weisberg did not refine or revisit his view on either point in later works.

Mark Lane's 1977 book, *Code Name "Zorro": The Murder of Martin Luther King Jr.,* which he co-wrote with comedian and activist Dick Gregory, confidently states that Ray was not the assassin. It was republished with some additional material the following year, concurrent with the very beginning of the House Select Committee on Assassinations investigation. Lane's book devotes a great many pages to gaps in the evidence that it claims the FBI and the Memphis police missed. They identify several eyewitnesses or other key witnesses who were in the vicinity of the assassination and not interviewed or simply ignored by the authorities. *Code Name "Zorro"* draws the conclusion that the FBI murdered King on the basis that director J. Edgar Hoover despised King and the civil rights movement. Lane implies that the FBI was behind the shady Raoul character who manipulated Ray with petty crimes and plenty of money.

Philip H. Melanson published two books that touch on the King assassination, articulating what he considers to be a certainty that a conspiracy was at work. The first and most important book, *The Murkin Conspiracy: An Investigation into the Assassination of Dr. Martin Luther King Jr.*, is entirely devoted to the topic of the King-Ray case. Melanson conducted an extensive investigation of Ray's Canadian aliases in the early 1980s and concluded that James Jesus Angleton of the CIA likely supplied them to him. More than any other author, Melanson documents many of the questions about the aliases that were not answered by the FBI or the HSCA. He confidently states in the book that there is overwhelming evidence that a single gunman could not possibly have carried out King's assassination by himself. Like Weisberg, he sees the crime as unsolved. Like Weisberg and me, he believes that Ray knew more than he ever told. Melanson's other book, *Secrecy Wars*, peripherally touches on elements of the King-Ray case, such as Percy Foreman's financial conflict of interest in providing legal representation for Ray.

William F. Pepper was a friend and supporter of King in the 1960s and later provided legal representation to the King family in a wrongful death civil-action suit. His two books, *Orders to Kill* and *An Act of State*, were published in 1995 and 2003 respectively.

In *Orders to Kill*, Pepper's pledge to deliver the whole truth about the King assassination is too ambitious. However, it thoroughly describes the US military's belief that King was a subversive tool of international communism and a grave threat to national security. It also illuminates the CIA's role in the Special Operations Group (SOG) and in Operation CHAOS, a domestic surveillance program. Pepper's effort is far less convincing to identify by name the shady Raoul (spelling varies) character, who Ray claims manipulated and paid him in the months leading up to the King assassination. Pepper claims that the man's real name was Raul Pereira. Whether this was the actual identity of the man, Pepper's better argument is that *a Raoul character existed*, by whatever name, who managed and manipulated Ray. Thus, Ray did not work alone and the government's claim that there was no conspiracy is highly suspect.

In *An Act of State*, Pepper recounts the investigation and progress of the wrongful death civil suit the King family filed in 1998 against Loyd Jowers. Jowers was the owner of Jim's Grill, the restaurant downstairs from the flophouse in the 400 block of South Main Street in Memphis, where James Earl Ray checked in on the afternoon of the assassination. *King v. Jowers* went to court in 1999, and the jury concluded that Jowers and various government agencies at the local, state, and federal levels shared liability for the wrongful death of Martin Luther King Jr. In other words, the only jury ever to consider Ray's case decided that he was the patsy rather than the triggerman.

My book has commonalities with the aforementioned authors. I agree with them that there was a sophisticated conspiracy to assassinate King and that James Earl Ray was not the assassin. Beyond this, there are significant specific differences and emphases among the four of us. Each of these previous books has contributed to the subsequent one, and I would be remiss if I failed to acknowledge that this book builds on their research and revelations.

My book differs from each of the pro-conspiracy books by Weisberg, Lane, Melanson, and Pepper in important ways. I believe that Weisberg overdid it when he attempted to paint everyone around Ray as bad guys. Clearly, there was a lot of fault to be found between Percy Foreman and Judge Preston Battle, and Weisberg was particularly harsh on them. Weisberg was also ruthless toward Ray's first attorneys, Arthur Hanes Sr. and Jr. of Birmingham, Alabama. Yet, the Haneses solidly supported Ray's initial innocence plea and were ready to defend him at trial in November 1968. Weisberg's book was further limited due to timing. Its 1969-71 roll out missed all the facts of the case that were established during the federal appeals process, as well as the HSCA investigation, and the documents released in the 1990s under the Assassination Records Review Board. Thus, Weisberg's book, while important in its day, is now dated.

Lane and Gregory did not develop the full story on Ray's Canadian aliases, nor did they have access to Ray's CIA 201 file (which was not released for another fifteen years), which documented the agency's interest in whether he obtained a full trial.

Melanson's 1989 book *The Murkin Conspiracy* suffers from the fact that the voluminous CIA files on Ray and others involved in the King-Ray case were not released until five to ten years after its publication. If

Melanson had had access to those files at the time he wrote his book, he might have discovered that the CIA had had an interest in whether Ray obtained a full trial. What is more, he might have made the connection between the organization that opened that CIA file on Ray and the Canadian aliases they likely provided to him.

Although much of Pepper's factual investigation of the King-Ray case is convincing at the level of the details, his analysis of the big picture of the assassination is troublesome. I am not comfortable with Pepper's idea that several agencies and organizations, both civilian and military, were involved at the local, state, and national levels of government. I find it difficult to get my mind around any explanation of the King assassination that includes the knowing participation by state and local police, the FBI, and the CIA. That's too large a group to convince me they all had some role in the assassination.

Another early and significant book that raised several troubling, unanswered questions about the King assassination was John Seigenthaler's 1971 *A Search for Justice,* co-authored by James D. Squires, John Hemphill, and Frank Ritter. Squires wrote most of the material in the book that pertained to the King-Ray case. It cannot be said that *A Search for Justice* was one of the pro-conspiracy books, even though it clearly casts doubt on the government's storyline that Ray was the lone assassin. Among the questions the book raises is whether Ray's track record as a bungling petty criminal demonstrates the ability to plan and carry out an assassination that otherwise appeared to be a professional contract killing. Obviously, it did not. It notes that Huie's flip-flop on whether Ray was the killer is significant. Perhaps most importantly, *A Search for Justice* questions Ray's ability to finance his alleged stalking of King, his clean getaway, and his travel through five countries prior to his capture.

A more recent take on Ray's role in the King assassination incorporates elements of the government's storyline as well as elements asserted by the conspiracy writers. Stuart Wexler and Larry Hancock assert in their 2012 book, *The Awful Grace of God,* that Ray probably was responsible for King's murder but most likely assisted by co-conspirators in the White Knights of the Ku Klux Klan of Mississippi. They disagree with the government's storyline that Ray acted alone in the actual murder, yet they also disagree with the conspiracy writers that there was no governmental involvement.

THIS BOOK'S CONTRIBUTION TO WHAT WE KNOW
ABOUT RAY AND THE KING ASSASSINATION

This book contributes to the factual record of the King assassination and the aftermath in several important ways. It also helps to clarify what really happened in Memphis and the consequences as well as why the official explanation is inadequate and inaccurate on many points.

- It expands what we know about James Earl Ray's highly suspicious Canadian aliases. It explains the most likely origin of these aliases and how they relate to Ray's role as a pawn.
- It reveals Gov. Buford Ellington's interest in avoiding a trial due to the state's weak evidence.
- It reveals Governor Ellington's action to stop the only independent investigation of the King-Ray case.
- It expands our knowledge of the CIA's interest in whether Ray obtained a full trial.
- It connects the CIA's 201 file on Ray with the aliases.
- It reveals a web of CIA connections around Ray, including those who imprisoned him, those who wrote about him, and even those who represented him in court.
- It reveals and explains Percy Foreman's deceit in the courtroom, his coercion of Ray's guilty plea, his suborning perjury of Ray's testimony, his lies to the HSCA as to how he got involved in the case, and how all of Foreman's case files on Ray were said to have been destroyed.
- It reveals that the idea to create an unusual and rigorous surveillance system with 24/7 lights and cameras in Ray's cell came from federal, rather than local, authorities. This system deprived Ray of the basic human rights of sleeping in a darkened cell at night or using the toilet without the observation of others, thus diminishing Ray's ability to think clearly and resist manipulation.
- It conclusively proves, through affidavits from officials who were present in the courtroom the day Ray pleaded guilty, that the Shelby County district attorney's office altered the transcript of Judge W. Preston Battle's questioning of Ray. The bogus transcript was used by prosecutors to ensure that Ray's appeals process was doomed to fail. The altered transcript changed the words Ray spoke in

Memphis, putting far more incriminating words in his mouth than those he actually spoke. A federal judge, not knowing the transcript was altered, later described the inaccurate words as "central and determinative" in his decision against Ray's appeal.

- Likewise, it conclusively proves that the staff of the House Select Committee on Assassinations made several additional transcript alterations in its *Final Report* and appendix volumes.

WHY I WROTE THIS BOOK

I wrote this book because I was tired of being lied to by the government, the mainstream news and publishing media, and the sycophant writers who clamor to destroy the truth and accommodate official lies.

Reading their works reminds me of the introduction to the 1960s sci-fi television series *The Outer Limits:* "There is nothing wrong with your television set. Do not attempt to adjust the picture. We are controlling transmission." The Establishment controls most of what you see and hear about the assassination of Martin Luther King Jr., too. It amounts to a semi-official narrative that sanctions a very narrow range of discussion of the case. The CIA even had an in-house joke to describe their control of the news and publishing media. They boasted they were "the mighty Wurlitzer," playing the tune the CIA wanted the public to hear.

The writers who collaborated created a fictitious reality—a false consciousness that G. Robert Blakey, general counsel of the HSCA, bought into and continues to serve decades later—that makes their narrative of James Earl Ray as a "dirty racist" quite believable. These writers ignored evidence that Ray was manipulated to be a pawn and take the fall for intelligence-related organizations, which had their own reasons for silencing Martin Luther King.

This book will adjust the picture.

The
Martin
Luther
King
Congressional
Cover-Up

PART ONE: THE FACTS

CHAPTER 1
Overview

This book is a dissent from the official record that James Earl Ray assassinated Rev. Martin Luther King Jr. in Memphis, Tennessee, on April 4, 1968.

When I use the term "official record," I am referring to the documents compiled by the Federal Bureau of Investigation (FBI); the Memphis Police Department; the prosecutors, criminal trial court, and appeals courts of Tennessee; the federal district courts in Nashville and Memphis; the US Court of Appeals, Sixth Circuit, in Cincinnati, Ohio; the US House Select Committee on Assassinations (HSCA); as well as the Central Intelligence Agency (CIA) and other investigative- and intelligence-related agencies that were released under the Assassination Records Review Board (ARRB). In other words, the official record is the government's account of events regarding the King assassination and subsequent investigations.

The official record holds that James Earl Ray assassinated King because Ray was a violent, Southern racist who was dedicated to the idea of white supremacy and could not tolerate any leader—especially a black one—who would make blacks legally equal to whites. The HSCA *Final Report* nuanced the racial allegations to a limited degree by concluding there was a "possibility" of a paid race-related conspiracy but that Ray nevertheless carried out the assassination alone.

The whole world knows King as a symbol of non-violent resistance, a symbol of the modern civil rights movement, a symbol of peace, justice, and good.

Likewise, James Earl Ray also has become a symbol. He is the visible manifestation of something invisible: the violent, Southern white racism that killed King—at least, this is what we are told.

The official record concludes that Ray accomplished this crime alone and unassisted, without overt help from any accomplice, witting or unwitting. The details of his story and alibi are considered inadequate. Since 1970, this record has been emphatically attested to in mainstream media and publishing houses by a series of authors who have assured the public time and time again that the government had its man, that Ray acted alone, and that there was no conspiracy behind King's murder.

But the government's record is wrong on a great many points, and there are compelling reasons to dissent from its conclusions. The record contains numerous gaps, inadequacies, inconsistencies, factual conflicts, and deliberate, criminal falsifications of evidence. The HSCA had subpoena power from 1976 to 1979 and a staff of lawyers who should have gotten to the bottom of the mystery. Instead, the man in charge of the HSCA staff, Chief Counsel G. Robert Blakey, bungled the investigation, and the cover-up not only continued but also deepened.

After years of review and research, it is evident that James Earl Ray did not fire the fatal shot that killed King. Although Ray was a criminal, he was not a dangerous, violent racist with a motive to assassinate King. In fact, it is strikingly disingenuous to assert that Ray was motivated to murder King, because persons unknown to him may have held a $50,000 bounty on King's life. Yet, this motive is the slender reed the HSCA would have us grasp.

Indeed, Ray was a participant in the conspiracy to kill King—but an unwitting one. He was only the pawn set up to take the fall in order to protect others. Six days before the assassination, the FBI's counterintelligence program (CI) was actively manipulating King and his entourage to stay at the Lorraine Motel, where he was later shot to death on the second-story balcony. The CIA's CI organization picked out Ray as an able patsy for this crime and supplied him with money and clever aliases for nine months prior to the assassination (July 1967-April 1968). The agency's involvement with and manipulation of Ray, as well as the national security threat that the intelligence community believed King posed, points to the CIA as the most likely organization responsible for the assassination of King. It is highly likely that the CIA's number one CI agent, James Jesus Angleton, was the man behind the curtain. The FBI's CI group cooperated but, for security reasons, probably did not know of the plot in advance. Whether the decision came from a higher source than Angleton, we will never know, unless there is a smoking-gun document in the HSCA record scheduled to be unsealed in 2029.

In the late 1970s, the HSCA had the authority and resources to get the story right, but they blew it. Blakey and his HSCA staff had within their hands the power to reveal the truth but chose instead the path of least resistance. Perhaps this was a deliberate choice. Perhaps Blakey's investigation was compromised and manipulated because intelligence-related organizations with motives unknown to him penetrated his staff. In recent years, Blakey has been extremely critical of the CIA's role in his investigation. Was his effort doomed from the start? It may have been.

WILL THE REAL JAMES EARL RAY PLEASE STAND UP?

The real James Earl Ray was a petty criminal, a ninth-grade dropout who was discharged from the US Army for ineptness. He was a four-time criminal before he ever visited Memphis. He escaped prison in Missouri and had been on the run for almost a year at the time of King's death. We have been assured by the government—and by a series of authors who align themselves with the government's official narrative—that Ray stalked King and murdered him as the ultimate act of racial hatred—end of story.

It's a simple explanation that has a certain degree of plausibility. After all, Reverend King, a Southern black minister, was the embodiment of the modern civil rights movement. To say that King was not a popular figure among many white people in the South and elsewhere in the 1960s is to state the obvious. He incurred a lot of hatred.

Ray was a white felon, a small-town Illinois kid—not a Southerner—with an alleged hatred of blacks (which somehow was never documented in any of his military or prison records). So we're told, an uneducated, unskilled, low-class white man who was in trouble with the law his whole life killed Reverend King. It fits a predictable storyline rather neatly.

The truth about James Earl Ray is that he was incapable of completing the series of sophisticated, complex, well-coordinated, and adequately financed tasks that the government claims. Even though he most likely took certain secrets with him to the grave, Ray did not have the motivation, skills, or personal discipline to stalk, locate, and shoot King. Throughout his life of crime, Ray was easy to catch and easily fell into the hands of the police. Yet, for two months following the assassination, Ray—a man who had never before flown on a commercial airline—eluded the largest manhunt in the history of the United States and escaped to various places in Canada, England, and Europe. This course of action was starkly beyond Ray's individual ability. More importantly, on his own, Ray didn't have the money to stalk King or to escape to Europe. Yet, Ray *did* have money the eleven months prior to King's assassination and to get to Europe. Point of fact, it was the best financial year of Ray's entire life.

THE CRIMINAL COURT'S "SHOT CLOCK" IN MEMPHIS

It took only three minutes and forty-three seconds for the criminal court of Shelby County, Tennessee, to ponder James Earl Ray's guilty plea. It was almost as if the court were operating under a shot clock. This is the amount of elapsed time during the judge's questioning of Ray on the audio recording of the hearing from the archives of Shelby County, Tennessee.[1]

This brisk pace of "justice" is not surprising when one considers that the questions asked of Ray by criminal court judge W. Preston Battle Jr. and the answers Ray was supposed to give were rehearsed the day before. Ray had his lines (as did Judge Battle), but Ray was not cooperative in playing along once he was in open court.

Judge Battle satisfied himself—seemingly—before accepting Ray's guilty plea that the court learned in those fleeting moments all it would ever need to know about whether Ray truly committed this crime. It took three minutes and forty-three seconds to close the door forever on the full proof in open court of the evidence on who killed King. Topping off the charade, Battle's rote questioning of Ray that day was terribly flawed. What we do not know about Battle's flaws is whether they were deliberate or inadvertent.

Ray wasn't asked if he received help in carrying out the assassination. Ray wasn't asked where he got the money he traveled on for the eleven months prior to the crime or for the two months he was in Canada and Europe after the crime. Ray wasn't asked how long he had been following King, where he practiced his marksmanship, why he chose the rifle he did, where and when he sighted in the rifle scope, or for how long he had been planning the assassination. Ray wasn't asked how he found out where King was located in Memphis, how he escaped the US for Canada, or how he got a Canadian passport. Ray wasn't even asked why he did it. In fact, Ray wasn't asked much of anything. None of these questions were addressed in the six-page guilty plea that Ray signed.

Nevertheless, it wasn't long before Battle, as well as Ray, had second thoughts about the guilty plea. Perhaps Battle's change of heart was a matter of conscience, if his error was deliberate. If it was inadvertent, perhaps he reviewed the audiotape or the transcript, discovered his errors, and pondered how or if he should correct them. A week after accepting Ray's plea, Battle expressed the questions that remained in his mind, unanswered by Ray's brief appearance in his court.

To Associated Press reporters, Battle said, "Like others, I would truly like to know how Ray actually found the spot from which to fire." His comments were reported in newspapers across the country. If this was a question in Battle's mind, why didn't he put this question to James Earl Ray at the sentencing hearing and require him to answer it? Was it because he was afraid Ray didn't have the answer or that he could not have made up a convincing one? Yet, it was Battle's duty to establish a factual basis for the guilty plea before accepting it. If Ray couldn't explain how he found the place from which to fire at King, this would raise a serious doubt—certainly a reasonable doubt—as to whether Ray did it.

The Memphis police didn't even know that King was going to be at the Lorraine Motel until he arrived there. But the FBI knew because their informant, who was an insider in the King entourage, was feeding Hoover's men with unbelievable detail about King's daily plans, movements, and even what was on his mind. One of those details was King's room number, 306.

Battle also wondered how Ray selected the rifle. Why didn't he ask Ray about it? Why didn't Battle require Ray to explain why he bought one rifle one day and took it back the next to exchange it for another one? Did Ray's actions demonstrate expertise or ignorance about high-powered rifles?

Battle also expressed questions as to whether Ray was alone in surveilling King's movements at the Lorraine Motel. Again, why didn't Battle ask Ray if he did this alone or had help watching King? But the most puzzling aspect was Ray's escape from Memphis, which Battle described as miraculous. "To me, it seems miraculous that he was able to flee to Atlanta despite the all-points bulletins without his white Mustang being spotted on a highway." Yet Battle gave lip service to the criminal justice process by commenting that he'd prefer to have the "full proof" in open court.

Battle never knew that Ray's lawyer, Percy Foreman, had suborned perjury of Ray's testimony. Ray lied to every question about his guilty plea that Battle put to him in court on March 10, 1969, except for the key question on pressure, which Ray never answered. He told precisely the lies Foreman demanded of him. Battle died twenty-one days later without ever knowing.

Doubts did not extend to the Tennessee Supreme Court. In a matter of just a few months, it finally, permanently, and irrevocably disposed of Ray's appeal without reviewing Battle's flawed questioning, without any independent determination of guilt or innocence, and without granting him a trial. The Tennessee court system closed its eyes and heart to the fact that there was never any determination whether impermissible pressure was used on Ray and his family to get him to plead guilty.

The Tennessee Supreme Court emphatically opined: "We are not deciding on the defendant's guilt or innocence."[2] What greater duty or priority does the judicial branch of government have in a free society than determining the guilt or innocence of the accused? This becomes an even heavier burden when society needs answers. In the late 1960s, society needed answers about a violent crime against society as well as to the victim and his family.

THE KING ASSASSINATION MYSTERY TAKES A LIFE OF ITS OWN

Since the late 1960s, the US Justice Department, the FBI, Tennessee prosecutors, news media, New York publishing houses, and even one of James Earl Ray's attorneys have assured us that he is not merely guilty but that he is the *only* one who is guilty because he acted alone and unassisted.

The storyline of Ray's supposed (lone) act of violent racism was set in stone within hours of King's death—before the dew had dried on the next morning's newspapers thrown onto Memphis lawns. By noon the day after the murder, US attorney general Ramsey Clark announced in Memphis that King's murder was the act of one man. This was the initiation of the official narrative that Ray was the lone gunman, a narrative repeated by the mainstream media for thirty years. FBI director J. Edgar Hoover backed up Clark, telling the Associated Press that the evidence indicates that "a single individual" was responsible for King's death. Clark, in inexplicable double-talk, added: "There is no evidence of a widespread plot."

Neither was there evidence of a widespread crime, just a local, precise, effective one, considering that the victim was dead with one shot and the triggerman escaped the scene. The word "professional" comes to mind, does it not?

Clark didn't need to say a word about motive because the police were looking for a white man whom they said killed King. The racial implications were obvious.

Not only were Clark and Hoover in agreement on the storyline, but so was everyone else who mattered. This included the local prosecuting team in Memphis headed by the Shelby County district attorney general, Philip Canale; Memphis fire and police director, Frank Holloman, who spent years in the FBI as a top aide to Hoover; Governor Ellington; the *New York Times;* and eventually even Ray's trial attorney, Percy Foreman— they all agreed that Ray plotted and planned the assassination alone, stalked King alone, and pulled the trigger and fled—alone. Attorney and author Gerald Posner has guaranteed that Ray did it. Among all of the contemporary officials whose duties touched on this case, only Tennessee Commissioner of Correction Harry S. Avery had the courage to express publically that a conspiracy was at work. Ellington quickly dismissed him from office.

More recently, author Hampton Sides, who grew up in Memphis, has made the case that white Southerners in the 1960s wanted King dead, and almost any one of them could have done it, especially anyone who supported George Wallace's third-party candidacy for president. Sides opined that the plain truth is that Ray was an enthusiastic Wallace supporter and occasional campaign worker. He connects the dots: Ray was white (strike one); Ray was a Southerner, almost (strike two); Ray supported George Wallace (strike three). How much more of a motive do you want? After all, Sides seems to believe that almost every white Southerner wanted King dead, inadvertently assigning motive to untold thousands, not just James Earl Ray. It should be noted that Ray never registered to vote at any time in his life.

I MET JAMES EARL RAY

I remember the first time I met James Earl Ray. It was April 23, 1990, and I was a reporter at the *Tennessee Oak Ridger,* an award-winning daily newspaper in East Tennessee.

I had no clue how important that date on the calendar already was, and would continue to be, to James Earl Ray. On April 23, 1967, Ray escaped from the penitentiary in Missouri. It was April 23, 1998, eight years to the day from my first meeting with him, that James Earl Ray died.

I drove from Oak Ridge to the tiny village of Petros, Tennessee, home of Brushy Mountain Prison. They were expecting me at Brushy, and in the days before the September 11 attacks, the authorities were relaxed and treated me as a routine visitor. The high, thick, masonry walls of Brushy made it look like a nineteenth-century fortress. As I approached, I saw trustees walking up and down the road unsupervised and seemingly free to come and go as they pleased.

Ned Ray McWherter, a Democrat, was governor at the time and had made life in prison fairly easy for James Earl Ray. A prior governor, Ray Blanton (also a Democrat), had done likewise. Tennessee's three Republican governors during Ray's twenty-nine-year stay in state custody—Winfield Dunn, Lamar Alexander, and Don Sundquist—had been harsher on Ray, at least as Ray told me. It was Sundquist who meted out the death sentence that Ray thought he had avoided when Sundquist refused to allow the state's cooperation with a privately paid effort to obtain surgery that would have saved Ray's life in 1998.

As I entered the prison, I was told they called it a "contact" visit. A guard escorted me up a flight of steps and left me alone in a conference-type room with a big table and chairs. In a matter of minutes, the guard reappeared with James Earl Ray, the man who confessed to the murder of Martin Luther King Jr. but recanted his guilty plea within a week.

Ray walked in unfettered at hand or foot. He was in a state issue dull gray shirt and blue pants with a white stripe down the side. We exchanged greetings, shook hands, sat down, and began to talk.

He had a large envelope with him that contained papers and audiocassette tapes. Before I could even ask my first question, Ray gave me the cassettes and told me there was an interview of my late uncle, Harry S. Avery, on the tapes. Harry Smith Avery was commissioner of correction under two successive Tennessee governors in the 1960s, Frank Clement and Buford Ellington. He was the man in charge of Tennessee prisons in 1969 when Ray pleaded guilty in Memphis to murdering King.

The content of Ray's tapes pertained to Avery's contemporaneous view that there was a conspiracy to murder King and a possible intervention that destroyed the duplicates of his personal evidence files on Ray that he was attempting to turn over to Richard Sprague, the first general counsel of the HSCA. Those files contained copies of Avery's interview notes with Ray as well as Ray's early prison correspondence. Avery believed that Ray's correspondence indicated a conspiracy.

I interviewed Ray four times from 1990 to 1992, three times in person and once on the phone. The next time I saw Ray, he was in solitary

Audiotapes given to the author by James Earl Ray in 1990 (Courtesy author's collection)

confinement at Brushy Mountain. It still was not complicated to enter Brushy as a visitor, even to the solitary building, a low-slung concrete bunker of much more recent construction than the main prison building.

Ray had been implicated when contraband was discovered in his cell and connected to a plot to escape. The authorities took this seriously because Ray had escaped from both Jeff City in 1967 and Brushy in 1977. Ray was loose from Brushy for three days but never got more than a few miles from the prison, which is located in rough terrain covered with poison oak and filled with rattlesnakes and copperheads. Ray complained at that second visit that it was unnecessary to keep him in solitary. He wryly joked that at age sixty-two, he was more of a candidate for a rocking chair than the electric chair.

The last time I saw Ray in person was in 1991 at Riverbend Maximum Security Institution in Nashville. This time, every detail was inspected: every delivery load, every person, every vehicle. There were constant patrols just outside the wire. Brushy's massive masonry walls seemed antiquated compared with the hurricane fencing wrapped with razor wire at the modern Riverbend. You could see from the patrol road all the way to the buildings—there was no place to hide.

My final contact with James Earl Ray was a phone interview in 1992 while Ray was incarcerated at Riverbend. Ray's friends from Memphis, Earl and Thelma Potts, called me to let me know that Ray had something to say about the divorce recently granted to his jailhouse wife, Anna Sandhu Ray.

FAMILY CONNECTIONS

Harry Smith Avery was my mother's uncle, making him my great uncle. A Vanderbilt-educated attorney, he served a term as a House member in the Tennessee General Assembly and was commissioner of correction for the state of Tennessee when Ray was sentenced to ninety-nine years and transferred to the state penal system. He was also elected to the Tennessee Constitutional Convention that met in 1953.

Avery strongly believed there was a conspiracy to kill King, and he began his own investigation to find out about co-conspirators the moment that Ray was in his custody. He ran afoul of Governor Ellington as soon as word reached him that Avery was investigating Ray. Yet Ray never trusted Avery, and both Harold Weisberg and Mark Lane questioned his

Harry Smith Avery, former member of the Tennessee General Assembly and commissioner of correction from 1963 to 1969 (Courtesy author's collection)

motives in interviewing Ray. Ellington warned Avery to stop his investigation, but Avery kept at it anyway. When Ellington discovered that Avery had spurned his demand to drop the investigation, the governor's staff unleashed a torrent of newspaper criticism against him, had him investigated by the Tennessee Bureau of Investigation (TBI) and leaked part of the report, and then fired him on May 29, 1969.

The day after Harry Avery was fired, he revealed at a Nashville press conference that his nephew, Alamo, Tennessee, attorney John Buchanan Avery Jr. (known to his friends as "Buck"), had been contacted by the *Nashville Tennessean* newspaper, which offered to pay his legal fees to represent Ray as a means of obtaining exclusive news stories.[3]

Buck Avery was my mother's brother and nephew of Harry Avery. He was a well-established attorney and was well known in statewide political circles and among lawyers. He was a former state senator who had served in both houses of the Tennessee General Assembly. But he knew that Ray had a valid literary contract with author William Bradford Huie, and he would have nothing to do with the scheme to purchase access to Ray's exclusive stories by trading on his relationship with his uncle Harry Avery, the commissioner.

Around 1980, Ray wrote my brother, Jim Emison, who practiced law in our little cotton-farming hometown of Alamo and requested he represent him. Jim turned him down.

I spoke and discussed at length with Harry S. Avery about his investigation of and conversations with James Earl Ray. He told me that Tennessee governor Buford Ellington knew, likely from Ray's attorney Percy Foreman, that Ray was going to plead guilty before the criminal court in Shelby County, Tennessee, and this information was shared with the US Department of Justice in Washington.

The audiotapes Ray gave to me were from interviews with Avery in 1978. There were two hours of interviews, conducted by Ray's jailhouse wife, Anna Sandhu Ray. There is also a phone conversation on this tape between Ray's brother, Jerry, and Maria Martin, an associate of Ray's in southern California. Ray kept these tapes in his cell for twelve years prior to giving them to me on April 23, 1990. Jerry Ray has confirmed his voice on the tape. My cousin, Dr. Robert Bruce Avery, has confirmed his father's voice on the tapes, as have others who knew Harry Avery.

The audiotapes tell the untold story about the surreptitious stealing of the only copies of Ray's incoming and outgoing correspondence that was compiled from the early days of his incarceration in the Tennessee penitentiary system. Harry Avery believed that this correspondence contained leads that should be thoroughly investigated in order to uncover assassination co-conspirators. His experience as a former arson investigator and commissioner of correction placed him in a position to make such a judgment.

What's more, these files were taken—and presumably destroyed— sometime before investigators from the HSCA came to my uncle Harry Avery's home on Center Hill Lake in December 1976 to interview him. A second, duplicate file was also mysteriously missing from the office of his attorney, Thomas Wardlaw Steele, in downtown Nashville. No official investigators anywhere had shown any interest in his file until Harry Avery contacted the HSCA staff in 1976.

JAMES EARL RAY—OR JAMES EARL RACIST?

The government bolstered its story by claiming that King's assassination was a crime of racial hatred by one fanatic racist. If we swallow that account, it would lead to a very crowded crime scene. The FBI was watching King. The FBI's paid black informant in King's inner circle, photographer Ernest Withers, was also watching and reporting on him. The Memphis police were watching King—at least a dozen uniformed officers but perhaps up to three dozen.[4] News reporters were watching King, and at least one reporter, Joe Sweat of the *Memphis Commercial Appeal,* was present at the Lorraine Motel when the assassination occurred.[5] Even the Department of Defense was watching King that day with two separate Army squads. All of these organizations were in Memphis, observing King's movements, activities, and associates the day he was murdered. All of these organizations converged on the Lorraine Motel, where King had spent much of the day. James Earl Ray would have practically had to elbow his way through this crowd of state and federal lawmen, paid informers, reporters, and military spies to take a shot.

No, this was not a crime of passion or racial hatred. It was a professional assassination—a political crime that was carefully weighed, carefully planned, professionally carried out, and then craftily covered up by pinning the crime on an unlucky criminal.

Ray was not a careful man; if he was, he would not have spent most of his life in jail. He was not one who developed and carried out disciplined, patient, detailed plans. Ray wasn't professional about anything—even stealing—and he was far from crafty. Harry Avery described Ray as "a nitwit, two-bit, felon; that's all."[6] *JET* magazine described Ray as a "stumblebum hood."[7] The Army discharged him for "ineptness." All three descriptions are apt—and raise questions as to how he could have possibly assassinated a man receiving extraordinary public and government attention.

CHAPTER 2
Reasonable Doubt, Unreasonable Accusations

The evidence in every criminal case, including murder, falls into certain categories: eyewitness evidence; physical evidence, such as fingerprints or ballistics; circumstantial evidence; and statements to the police by the defendant—including confession—or his testimony in court. In some situations, a skilled professional can offer expert testimony as evidence. Motive and opportunity are also considered. Very few murders take place without a reason that can be rationally explained, even if the reason is hatred or an extreme spike of anger.

In American law, the accused in every criminal proceeding is presumed to be innocent until a jury of peers is convinced beyond reasonable doubt that the prosecutors have proven their accusations against him or her. Only then can liberty or life be taken. The US Constitution specifies nothing about the presumption of innocence or reasonable doubt because these principles were already settled in the courts of the original thirteen colonies. Prior to the ratification of the Constitution, there were no national courts, so the state courts were all that existed.

"Reasonable doubt" constitutes the highest of all burdens of proof, and American law almost always reserves it to criminal cases. The issue of property is settled with a lower burden of proof. A criminal defendant has a right to legal counsel, to confront witnesses against him, to compel the testimony of witnesses on his behalf, to remain silent to questions directed to him by law officers, to refuse to testify against himself, and to a speedy trial by jury of his peers before an impartial tribunal. A criminal also has the right to not be tried twice for the same offense. Even upon conviction of a crime, cruel and unusual punishment is constitutionally prohibited.

James Earl Ray's hearing was too speedy and not impartial, and as a result, many facts have been ignored or disregarded. The evidence against

James Earl Ray, in light of the accusations against him, primarily deals with the .30-06 caliber rifle and ammunition. A good understanding of a high-powered rifle with a scope on it and the .30-06 caliber round will help in understanding the firearms evidence. It is also crucial to look specifically at the Remington Model 760 GameMaster rifle .30-06 caliber with a Redfield 2x7 telescopic sight mounted on it.[1] This is the combination of rifle and scope Ray purchased under the assumed name of Harvey Lowmeyer at Aeromarine Supply Co. in Birmingham, Alabama, five days before Reverend King was assassinated.

.30-06 SPRINGFIELD RIFLE CARTRIDGE, THE REMINGTON MODEL 760 GAMEMASTER RIFLE, AND THE REDFIELD SCOPE

The caliber of all pistol and rifle ammunition is identified by the diameter of the bullet expressed in either metric units in millimeters (9 mm) or English units in hundredths of an inch (such as .308).[2] Thus, any cartridge that begins with a ".30" means that the bullet has a diameter of 30/100 of an inch, commonly spoken as "30 caliber." For example, the cartridge for the 50-caliber machine gun has a bullet diameter of one-half inch.

There are several different types of 30-caliber rifle cartridges. Each has the same diameter bullet but a different length, diameter, and overall size of the shell casing. The different size of the shell casing is needed for a different size gunpowder charge, which produces a unique muzzle velocity for each type of cartridge.

The .30-06 Springfield rifle cartridge was developed more than one hundred years ago for the purpose of killing humans. It is a powerful, high-velocity, highly accurate rifle round. When fired by an expert marksman using a high-quality weapon, it can kill a man at 1,100 yards (1 kilometer). A few, truly exceptional marksmen can hit a man-sized target at this distance without a scope.

All center-fire ammunition has four components: a brass shell casing; gunpowder, located inside the brass case; a primer, centered at the rear of the brass case ("center-fire"), which is struck by the firing pin to ignite the gunpowder; and a bullet, which is seated at the other end of the case. When fired, the expanding gas of the ignited gunpowder accelerates the bullet down the barrel.

Sport or commercial rounds typically have a lead bullet with a partial

The .30-06 high-velocity rifle cartridge, developed in advance of World War I with human lethality in mind (Courtesy author's collection)

jacket of copper that leaves only the tip of the lead bullet exposed. This is important for hunting because it allows the lead bullet to deform ("mushroom") more quickly upon impact and inflict a much larger diameter wound on the game animal than the actual diameter of the bullet. Military rounds are similar, except the lead bullet is entirely jacketed in copper right down to the tip. This is where the term "full metal jacket" comes from. It too mushrooms upon impact, but not as dramatically as the sport round. This gives the full metal jacket greater penetrating power.

The .30-06 Springfield cartridge was developed for the existing 1903 Springfield Armory rifle (designated the M1903 Springfield) that was originally manufactured for a slightly smaller and less powerful brass case. This rifle was adapted to accept the .30-06 Springfield cartridge in 1906, hence both the "06" as well as the "Springfield" designation for the cartridge.

The .30-06 Springfield rifle round was developed as military authorities in Europe moved away from round-nose bullets and began adopting the pointed-nose rifle round as standard issue. The pointed rifle bullet, or so-called spitzer bullet (derived from the German word *Spitzgeschoss,* which means "pointed bullet"), is more aerodynamic and therefore more accurate.

The ballistic performance of the .30-06 Springfield rifle round is impressive. The military-type round has a muzzle velocity of approximately 2,900 feet per second, which is slightly less than 2,000 miles per hour. Each round has an approximate energy of 2,800 foot pounds (equivalent to the energy needed to lift a 2,800-pound weight one foot). Sport rounds have slightly less velocity and energy. It is sufficiently lethal that this rifle cartridge is used by many deer hunters today in North America, especially in the open country of the plains states, where longer shots on game are typical. It is also a popular caliber for bear hunters. There are several common big-game rifles with much greater stopping power, but the .30-06 is extraordinarily lethal against a human target.

The bolt-action M1903 Springfield was the standard assault rifle of the US Army from 1905 to 1936. This rifle was replaced with the M1 Garand, a gas-operated, semi-automatic rifle that holds eight rounds in an off-set pattern magazine loaded from the top of the weapon.

The rifle bullet that killed King was a .30-06 Springfield 150-grain soft-point sporting-type round manufactured by Remington Peters.[3] This is the type of ammunition James Earl Ray purchased in Birmingham in a 20-round box when he bought the Remington GameMaster model 760.[4] Remington Peters still manufacturers this same round.

In 1952, Remington introduced the Model 760 GameMaster, which was a pump- or slide-action, high-powered hunting rifle manufactured in several calibers, including .30-06. The rifle had a box-type,

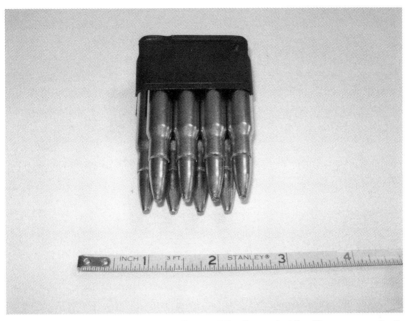

A loaded, eight-round magazine for an M1 Garand rifle (Courtesy author's collection)

removable magazine that held four rounds in the .30-06 model. The Model 760 GameMaster was a huge success for Remington. It remained in production through 1981, and the company produced more than a million.

When Ray purchased the rifle in Birmingham, he had the store mount a Redfield 2x7 scope on it. The "2x7" indicates that the power of magnification of this scope varies from two to seven times. When the Redfield scope was set on "two power," any object in the scope would appear twice as close as with the unaided eye. This could be increased up to seven times magnification.

Ray claims that he bought the rifle and took it to Memphis under the instruction of a shadowy figure he knew only as "Raoul." He says that he met Raoul in Canada during his trip to Ontario in the summer of 1967. Raoul reportedly gave him money to purchase his car, a one-year-old white Mustang, and to travel to meet people as instructed by Raoul. Ray also said that Raoul gave him the money to purchase the rifle, which he turned over to Raoul the night before King was shot.

A view of the Lorraine Motel from the bathroom from which the government claims James Earl Ray fired the shot (Courtesy author's collection)

WITNESSES TO THE ASSASSINATION OF MARTIN LUTHER KING

The numerous writers who contend that Ray acted alone and killed King because he was a racist ignore the weak and almost non-existent evidence and overlook the fact that there were no eyewitnesses who saw the murderer do his deed.

The single, fatal shot came from a distant, concealed location somewhere in front of King as he stood on the balcony of the Lorraine Motel. Obviously, the murderer intended to get away and remain unknown.

No one saw a rifle. No one saw a muzzle flash. No one saw the shooter. Incredibly, only one of numerous witnesses actually heard and recognized the shot as a rifle report. Some reported hearing what they thought was an automobile backfire. Others, including Rev. Ralph David Abernathy, who was in the motel room only a few feet behind King, as well as Andrew Young, who was in the courtyard approximately twelve feet below King, thought they heard a firecracker.[5]

The FBI and the Memphis police say that the shot came from the community bathroom on the second floor of Bessie Brewer's rooming house at 422½ South Main Street, where James Earl Ray had checked in that afternoon under the name John Willard.

They say that Ray stood in the bathtub and looked out the rear window of the rooming house, where he could see across Mulberry Street and observe King's room and balcony. There was no such view from the room Ray rented. They say after a few minutes' observation while standing in the bathtub, a serendipitous moment occurred. King appeared on the balcony conversing with several men in his traveling party. They say that Ray rested the rifle on the windowsill, took aim, waited until the other men walked away, and then fired the single fatal shot that struck Martin Luther King Jr. in the neck, severing his spinal cord. The police originally insisted that the rifle made a notch in the windowsill until FBI forensics proved this wasn't so.

Ray wrapped his rifle in newspaper to conceal it, authorities say, exited the bathroom, and walked back to the room he had rented down the hall. Two witnesses on that floor of the rooming house did see someone walk from the vicinity of the bathroom, but neither Willie Anschutz nor Charles Stephens (a raging alcoholic and reportedly drunk at the time) saw enough of the man, whomever he was, to identify him. Ten years later, HSCA Chief Counsel Blakey relied on the word of a drunk to conclude that it was Ray he had seen.

The problem with this story is that is not what Stephens told Memphis police the evening of the assassination. When asked by police if he could recognize the man who left the community bathroom with something wrapped in newspaper, Stephens's signed statement says, "I couldn't because I didn't get that good a look at him." Police asked if Stephens saw the man's eyes: "No, sir, I couldn't." Blakey says that Stephens told the FBI a different story in 1978 than he told Memphis police ten years earlier. Blakey repeatedly relied upon the tactic of changing witnesses' recollections a decade later in order to implicate Ray.[6]

When Ray re-entered his room, they say he put the rifle back in its original box from the Birmingham gun shop, threw it down on the bed with his shaving kit, a partial box of live ammunition, his transistor radio with his Missouri penitentiary inmate number scratched on it, and other personal items inside a zippered travel bag, and bundled the whole thing in the old green blanket from his bed.

He walked down the hallway toward the front of the building with

A modern-day view of South Main Street in Memphis, with Canipe's storefront and the small alcove to the right of the street pole (Courtesy author's collection)

the bundle in his arms, went down the stairs, and turned out onto South Main Street, where he took just a few steps to his left and placed the bundle in the alcove entrance to the business next door at 424 South Main, Canipe Amusement Company.

No one saw James Earl Ray with a rifle. No one saw James Earl Ray go into the bathroom or leave the bathroom. No one saw James Earl Ray pull the trigger. No one saw Ray with the green bundle in the rooming house, and no one saw him drop the bundle at Canipe's store. As a matter of fact, no one can identify having seen James Earl Ray—period.

However, there is one eyewitness—or possibly two—who saw someone other than Ray in the hallway right after the shot was fired.

Arthur Hanes Jr. told me that a male witness "unknown to the prosecution" saw a "diminutive man in an army jacket" walk from the area of the bathroom carrying what appeared to the witness as a broomstick. "Among us [Hanes Jr. and his father], we interviewed, I guess, every wino in Memphis—some a little better than others, all in all, no help," Hanes said. Unfortunately, he could not recall the name of the witness.[7]

Grace Walden, the common-law wife of Charles Stephens was in the corner room of the second floor of the rooming house. The evening of the King assassination, she told *Memphis Press-Scimitar* reporter Wayne Chastain that she saw a man in the hallway, described as "short and wiry, with salt-and-pepper hair, wearing a colored plaid shirt and army jacket." Nothing about the army jacket was immediately reported in either of the two Memphis daily newspapers.[8] Stephens described in his statement that night to Memphis police that the man in the hallway had "sandy" hair. James Earl Ray had neither salt-and-pepper nor sandy hair but dark brown hair.[9]

Hanes told me he was aware of Walden's testimony but insisted his witness was someone else, a man whose name may now be lost to history but whose existence is not lost to Hanes's memory. He said that they noted the man's comments but didn't pay a lot of attention until weeks later when they got access to the contents of Ray's white Mustang.

"Sometime maybe three, four, five, six weeks later we got the contents of the Mustang," Hanes said. The army jacket was in the trunk of the Mustang—a very small jacket, according to Hanes. It was an "electrifying" piece of evidence, Hanes said. "If Foreman hadn't come barging in, I guess I could have invented the idea 'if the glove don't [sic] fit you must acquit' because, that army jacket—James Earl Ray couldn't get his little finger in it. It was diminutive."[10]

Hanes clearly saw this as physical evidence of the presence of someone else at the scene of the crime at the time the crime occurred: "The implication to me was, that was Raoul." Hanes said that Ray left the rooming house in the afternoon, leaving Raoul in his room with the rifle. "The implication to me was that Raoul was the one wearing the army jacket"—the man the FBI said never existed.

Another key witness in Ray's defense was Guy Canipe Jr., who Hanes said was prepared to testify that the bundle, including the rifle, was dropped at his storefront a few minutes before the shot was fired. Obviously, if the government claimed this was the murder weapon, and someone's testimony challenged who possessed it at the time the shot was fired, this was going to be highly favorable for Ray. Hanes told me, "The state was bound and attached in November of [19]68 to the theory that James Earl Ray, acting alone, killed King. The evidence going to trial, we felt 100 percent confidant, that that theory could not stand— that the evidence belied it."[11]

In short, Hanes expected an acquittal.

PHYSICAL EVIDENCE: FBI's 1968 ANALYSIS OF THE RIFLE AND BULLETS

The autopsy conducted by the Shelby County, Tennessee, medical examiner, Dr. Jerry T. Francisco, indicates that King was killed by a shot to the neck that severed his spine. The rifle slug that caused his death was identified as a ".30 caliber metal-jacketed 'soft-point' sporting type bullet of Remington-Peters manufacture."[12] The bullet recovered during the autopsy has been subjected to numerous tests.

Memphis police discovered the green bundle in front of Canipe's business almost immediately. There are three separate versions of precisely who discovered the bundle and when, which raises questions about this critical evidence. It included the GameMaster rifle (serial

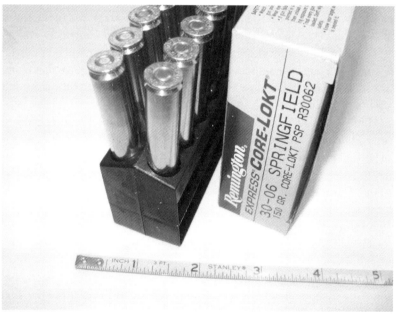

Remington Peters .30-06 150-grain soft-point ammunition, still extremely popular today (Courtesy author's collection)

number 461476) with the mounted scope, one spent shell casing still in the chamber and no rounds in the magazine, nine live rounds of .30-06 ammunition in a Remington-Peters ammunition box (five sport rounds and four military-type "full metal jacket" rounds), the front section of the April 4 morning newspaper the *Memphis Commercial Appeal,* a pair of binoculars, two cans of beer, maps, toilet paper, and numerous toiletry items such as shaving cream, after shave, deodorant, and toothpaste.[13]

Little or no analysis of the physical evidence was conducted in Memphis because the items identified above as part of the green bundle were in the hands of the FBI the same day as the shooting. By early the next morning, an FBI agent delivered the items to the FBI laboratory in Washington, DC, including the death slug removed from King's body at his autopsy the night of April 4.[14]

The original FBI ballistics report, issued April 29, 1968, noted the following about evidence recovered in the green bundle outside of Canipe's store:

- The spent cartridge found in the chamber of the GameMaster rifle had been fired from that rifle and was a sport-type round. There were no rounds loaded in the magazine.
- Nine rounds of live .30-06 cartridges were recovered in the cartridge box marked as 150-grain, soft point Remington-Peters sport rounds, the same type purchased by Ray at Aeromarine Supply Co. in Birmingham. Five of the nine live .30-06 rounds were the same as the 150-grain, soft point Remington-Peters sport rounds purchased by Ray in Birmingham. Four of the nine live .30-06 rounds were military-type full metal jacket rounds manufactured by Remington Arms Co. but different from the rounds purchased by Ray.
- The cartridge box similar to the one recovered "normally contain Remington-Peters ammunition identical to the five commercial-type cartridges."
- The death slug removed from King's body was "the same type" as the 150-grain sport rounds "found in the [Remington] Peters cartridge box."
- The death slug "could have been fired from the rifle, but its deformation and the absence of clear-cut marks precluded a positive identification."
- The death slug could not be metallurgically matched to the other Remington-Peters rounds.[15]

In other words, the FBI can't say that the gun purchased by Ray is the gun that killed King. It could have been another .30-06 rifle. Millions of .30-06 rifles are floating around in private hands, including the one million identical GameMaster rifles manufactured by Remington. Without definitive ballistics evidence, it is impossible to say whether Ray pulled the trigger or was in any way knowingly associated with the crime. The case remains nothing more than an allegation. Apparently unaware of the implications to the administration of criminal justice in America, Blakey told me, "contrary to popular misconception, often guns cannot be matched to bullets; in fact, the Committee's own experts fired Ray's rifle multiple times, and it was not always possible to match each round with Ray's rifle!"[16]

Furthermore, they can't explain why the bundle they say Ray placed in front of Canipe's store included rifle rounds that he didn't purchase in Birmingham. Clearly, those rifle rounds came from somewhere else, or someone else. But from whom?

PHYSICAL EVIDENCE: THE US HOUSE'S REVIEW OF THE RIFLE AND BULLETS,
1977-79

The results of the original 1968 FBI analyses were reevaluated when the US House of Representatives began its investigation in the mid-1970s under the House Select Committee on Assassinations (HSCA). Additionally, much of the physical evidence was re-analyzed by independent panels of experts outside the FBI as part of the investigation. The HSCA explained why it took this step in 1977: "In light of the criticism of the FBI's treatment of the firearms evidence, and as part of [the HSCA's] obligation to investigate fully the events surrounding King's assassination, the committee decided to convene a panel of experts to reexamine the firearms evidence."[17]

The panel of five experts was drawn from state and local police forces and laboratories around the country. The panel consisted of two senior firearms examiners from New York and Washington, DC, and three firearms and tool-mark examiners from Florida, Wisconsin, and Iowa. The experts were to work collaboratively or independently of each other as circumstances dictated, draw their conclusions separately, and then share their results with each other and resolve any discrepancies.

The panel conducted a dozen test firings of Ray's rifle into a water tank, but this resulted in excessive nose deformation on the test bullets. Other test shots were fired into a horizontal cotton waste recovery box that left the bullets more intact. They used bullets from both firings for comparison. Additional .30-06 Springfield caliber cartridges were used to load and unload the rifle in order to obtain unique marks made on the relatively soft brass cartridges by rifle components.

The panel was given nine questions to answer for the committee.

FBI and HSCA Evidence Numbering System

Q1	Rifle box recovered in the bundle at Canipe's storefront
Q2	Remington .30-06 GameMaster rifle and Redfield scope
Q3	Spent cartridge case, recovered in the chamber of the Q2 rifle
Q4-Q8	Five sport-type rounds, found in the bundle
Q9-Q12	Four military-type rounds, from the bundle
Q14	Binoculars purchased by Ray in Memphis, from the bundle
Q19	*Memphis Commercial Appeal* from April 4, 1968, recovered in the bundle
Q24	After-shave bottle, from the zippered plastic bag in the bundle
Q53	Schlitz beer can, from the zippered plastic bag in the bundle
Q64	Death slug removed from King's body at the autopsy
Q71	Windowsill from the shared bathroom at the rooming house
Q76	Shirt worn by King, removed at the autopsy
Q77	Necktie worn by King, removed at the autopsy
Q78	Suit jacket worn by King, removed at the autopsy

1. Was the Q64 death slug fired from Ray's Q2 rifle?

This question is the crux of the entire investigation. The FBI was unable to establish in 1968 that the death slug was fired from the rifle. If the

HSCA's panel of experts could answer the question in the affirmative, then this would be a strong indication that James Earl Ray was the triggerman.

The panel noted that when they prepared to test fire the rifle, the Redfield scope crosshair was set at "3X." The FBI noted that the scope was set at "6½" when it test fired the rifle on April 5, 1968, a discrepancy that would have drastically altered the success of the shot. This setting made the center of the bullet group three inches off to the right and slightly below the line of aim at a distance of 207 feet, the distance the FBI estimated as being between Ray and King. The FBI report says that the misalignment of the scope could have resulted from being tossed into Canipe's entrance way or subsequent handling by law enforcement. The panel decided not to test fire the rifle for accuracy.[18]

So what did the panel conclude about the bullet removed from King and its relationship to Ray's gun? After eighty-one comparisons between the Q64 death slug, the four bullets test fired by the FBI in 1968, and the twelve bullets test fired by the panel, "The panel was unable positively to identify or eliminate the Q64 bullet as having been fired from the Q2 rifle."[19] For a second time, firearms experts working for the federal government were unable to connect Ray's rifle to the crime.

The HSCA reported that all five members of the panel found similarities ("correspondence") among the test-fired bullets and the death slug. "On the other hand," the report states, "with respect to individual identifying characteristics, no significant correspondence was found between the Q64 bullet and the test bullets; conversely, no gross differences were found."

The FBI tried to match the rifle and death slug in 1968 and couldn't do it. The HSCA tried in 1977 and couldn't do it. The rifle was tested again in 1997 with the same results. So, the HSCA ignored this proof, or lack thereof, as inconvenient. Rather than acknowledging that the case against Ray was weak, that the physical evidence proves nothing, Blakey fell back to the time-honored tradition of assuring Ray's motive. According to Blakey, Ray killed King "not solely" as a matter of racism, as the FBI "and some early authors thought, but also for ego gratification."[20]

Blakey's assertions are laughable. He wants the public to believe that a man who fired a shot from a concealed, remote location, who escaped the scene and fled to England and Europe with elaborate false identities, murdered King so that he could stroke his public ego and revel in his notoriety.

2. Was the Q3 spent cartridge found in Ray's rifle fired in that rifle?

The short answer to this question is yes. The panel concluded that the imprint markings on the cartridge primer made by the firing pin in Ray's rifle was consistent among the spent Q3 cartridge case recovered in the rifle and the cartridges test-fired by the panel and the FBI.

There is nothing surprising or particularly meaningful about the fact that the Q3 cartridge case found in the rifle was fired in the rifle.[21] There was no determination, nor could there have been, as to the time that cartridge was fired in the rifle. It could have been fired at any time from the time Ray bought it on March 30 and left it with Raoul the evening of April 3.

3. Had the Q3 expended cartridge case been loaded into the rifle through the magazine or directly into the chamber?

The panel identified bolt "drag marks" (longitudinal striations) on the Q3 cartridge case made by the rifle. These marks were present on the test-fired cartridge cases as well as unfired cartridges, and all were consistent with the spent Q3 cartridge.

This indicates that when the Q3 cartridge was loaded into the .30-06 GameMaster, it was first placed into the magazine, the magazine then placed into the rifle, and the slide (or pump) was operated to move the cartridge from the magazine into firing position in the chamber.[22]

It would have been just as easy for Ray, or whoever loaded the GameMaster, to put up to three more rounds in the magazine just in case the first shot missed. If we are to believe that the Q2 rifle is the murder weapon (which the FBI cannot prove), loading only a single round into it to shoot at King was an act of supreme confidence in precision marksmanship and an equally supreme confidence that the weapon would not be needed to effect a get-away.

4. Is the Q3 expended cartridge case the same type and brand as the five sporting-type cartridges (Q4-Q8) or the four military-type cartridges (Q9-Q12)?

The panel found that the Q3 cartridge was identical to the five Q4-Q8 sporting-type rounds.[23]

5. Is the Q64 death slug the same as the Q4-Q8 sport-type cartridges or the Q9-Q12 military-type cartridges?

The panel found the Q64 death slug and the Q4-Q8 sport-type cartridges to be the same type. The Q64 death slug "is not the same type of bullet as those in the Q9-Q12 (full metal jacket) cartridges."[24]

6. Are the Q64 death slug and the Q3 spent cartridge found in the rifle components of the same cartridge?

If this could be proven, it would be a major step in tying the rifle to the actual shooting of King. The panel noted in the immediately preceding question that the Q64 death slug was the same type as the Q3 spent cartridge and the other Q4-Q8 sporting-type cartridges, but that is as much as the panel could say about the Q64 death slug and the Q3 spent cartridge. Unfortunately, "there is no scientific test that can determine whether a given slug has been fired from a given cartridge case."[25]

7. Were any of the live rounds (Q4-Q12) recovered in the box from the green bundle ever loaded into the chamber or magazine of Ray's Q2 rifle or any other firearm?

This is a doozy of a question because the answer points directly to the involvement of another person or persons—*conspirators,* if you will. Apparently, the FBI did not attempt to address this question in 1968—or at least they did not document the answer if they knew it.

The panel examined the cartridges visually and microscopically and found that there were no "marks to indicate that they were ever loaded in the magazine or chamber of the Q2 rifle or any other firearm."[26]

Let's assume for a moment this crime *was* perpetrated by James Earl Ray, alone and unassisted. The scientific evidence that the Q4-Q12 recovered live rifle rounds were never loaded into any other weapon means that the only round the authorities ever held that Ray loaded into a rifle was the Q3 spent cartridge found in the Q2 rifle after it was abandoned. However, this cannot be proven because the firing of a high-powered rifle round obliterates any fingerprints that were on the cartridge so it is impossible to know who loaded and/or fired the Q3 spent cartridge.

One of the original books about Ray claims that Ray admitted to firing the rifle on the way to Memphis after buying it in Birmingham with the twenty-round box of ammunition. In *He Slew the Dreamer*, William Bradford Huie claims that Ray told him he used several rounds from the box of sport cartridges along with several "army" cartridges and fired the rifle on a "side road near Corinth [Mississippi]."[27]

Actually, Ray told his attorneys Arthur Hanes Sr. and Arthur Hanes Jr.—not Huie—that he fired the rifle. Huie never gained admittance to see Ray at the Shelby County jail. Arthur Hanes Jr. said in an email message that Ray admitted to firing the rifle and told this story "to both my father and separately to me."[28] Huie made no attempt to describe any of Ray's actions in terms of sighting in the rifle scope. In fact, there is no story described by anyone as to Ray attempting to sight in the rifle scope, only that he test fired it. Sighting in the scope is vital for an accurate shot.

Furthermore, using two completely different types of ammunition (sport and military) to attempt to sight in a scope is not the right way of going about it. The accuracy of a scope could vary by using different rounds in the sighting process. Even Huie acknowledges that Ray was ignorant about rifles.[29]

Donald Wood Jr. waited on James Earl Ray in Aeromarine Supply Company and sold him the .30-06 GameMaster. He said that Ray didn't even handle the rifle in the store. When interviewed by HSCA investigators, Wood told them, "He [Ray] did not seem to know anything at all about firearms, I mean nothing."[30] The FBI must think that Ray is a fast learner because according to their calculations, five days later he loaded one round into the rifle and severed King's spinal cord from 207 feet away.

Aeromarine Supply Company in Birmingham, Alabama (Courtesy Shelby County Archives)

Wood also said that when he mounted the Redfield scope on the GameMaster, he used a device known as a bore sight. He told HSCA, "Sometimes it will be right on within an inch, another time it may be three or four inches off."[31] As indicated above, the Redfield scope was off three inches to the right when tested by the FBI the day after King was murdered.

If Ray didn't seem to know anything about firearms, he was even more unfamiliar with sighting in a scope. It is a rather tedious and methodical process. The only truly accurate way of sighting a scope is to shoot it from a bench or other fixed object. Resting the gun over the hood of a car will not generate accurate results.

In 1976, George McMillan rehashed the story of Ray test firing the rifle near Corinth in *The Making of an Assassin*. He mentions nothing about the methodical process of sighting in a scope, just that Ray casually "test-fired" the rifle.[32]

Huie's and McMillan's early descriptions of Ray firing the rifle became integral parts of Gerald Posner's and Hampton Sides's more recent accounts of Ray as the lone assassin. Certainly, Ray never disclosed any details about test-firing the rifle, nor was he asked about this by investigators. Furthermore, there is no evidence that he even intended to sight in the scope.

Posner reported that Ray qualified as a "marksman" in the Army on his first try at the firing range. Marksman is the lowest of three military rankings. Strangely, Poser noted that Ray's marksmanship ranking in the Army "doesn't necessarily indicate" he could make an easy assassination shot twenty years later.[33] Yet he has assured the public that Ray did it.

What were the findings of the HSCA's expert panel regarding the military-type Q9-Q12 cartridges? The panel found "a series of marks and striations in the extractor grooves, on the sides, and across the bases of the Q9-Q12 cartridges that differed significantly from the marks and striations that the Q2 rifle leaves." And what is indicated by these "marks and striations"? A bombshell: "The panel concluded that these cartridges once were part of a disintegrating machinegun link belt or were contained in an eight-round clip of the type used with the Garand M1 rifle."[34]

What M1 rifle? What clip? According to the government's evidence against Ray, he never bought or even used an M1 except when he was in the US Army. Who furnished Ray with such a rifle? More importantly, who sold or perhaps gave James Earl Ray the military-type rounds that he supposedly had in his possession in Memphis? Ray claimed in his HSCA testimony that he purchased the military rounds from Aeromarine Supply Company, but Aeromarine personnel said they never sold him any military ammunition.

Three of the four writers who support the government's theory— Huie, McMillan, and Sides—fail to say a word about the military-type ammunition or its mysterious source. The fourth, Posner, writes glibly that Ray bought the military rounds at an "unidentified store" and attaches no significance to it.[35]

There is no substantiation anywhere in the record for Posner's suggestion that Ray simply stopped by another gun store and bought military-surplus ammunition. With upwards of three thousand agents from more than fifty offices working on the assassination case, it is inconceivable to assume that the FBI would not have found such a store. The truth about the acquisition of the military rounds may never be revealed.

8. Did the Q2 rifle cause an indentation in the Q71 windowsill?

The panel tested for lead and nitrites to learn if the windowsill had been contaminated with gunshot residue from the rifle. The test for lead was positive due to lead in the paint. The test for nitrites was negative. The panel concluded that the evidence was insufficient to say whether the Q2 rifle had caused an indentation in the Q71 windowsill.[36]

9. Was the damage to King's clothes produced by a bullet, bullet fragments, or something else?

The panel tested for nitrites and lead residue in the Q76 shirt, Q77 necktie, and Q78 suit jacket worn by King when he was shot. There was no gunpowder residue on any of the items of clothing, indicating the gunshot was fired from a distance. There was lead residue and bullet fragments in all three items. They concluded "that all damage to the Q76 shirt, Q77 necktie, and Q78 jacket was consistent with the damage that would be caused by a high-velocity bullet which fragmented on impact, and by the resultant secondary missiles such as bone and teeth fragments."[37]

Summary of the Ballistics Findings of the HSCA Firearms Panel

First, it cannot be proven that the Q64 death slug was fired from the Q2 rifle that the authorities claim was the murder weapon. Therefore, the rifle purchased by James Earl Ray cannot be tied definitively to the crime of the murder of Rev. Martin Luther King Jr.

Second, there is no evidence that the scope was ever sighted, as it was off by the same three inches when the FBI test fired it as it was when Donald Wood Jr. bore-sighted the scope in the Aeromarine Supply Company when he sold it to Ray. Ray had no expertise of sighting in the riflescope, nor is there a shred of evidence he was an accomplished, much less practiced, marksman.

Third, the Q2 rifle was loaded with only one round of ammunition, indicating great confidence in how accurate the weapon's scope was sighted as well as the shooter's ability to hit a target. Both of these things are inconsistent with everything we know about James Earl Ray's experience and expertise.

Fourth, the Q64 death slug cannot be metallurgically matched to the Q4-Q8 Remington-Peters sport-type cartridges found in the bundle recovered in front of Canipe's store. Therefore, it cannot be known if the Q64 round was in the box of cartridges purchased by Ray or came from another source.

Fifth, there is no accounting for the origins of the full metal jacket, military-type cartridges Ray had in his possession. Ray's inconsistent, unconvincing explanations about purchasing them do not add up, and it is impossible to know whether Ray is deliberately covering for someone or he just has a faulty memory. There is also no explanation as to why, how, or by whom those military cartridges had been loaded into a .30-06 rifle and/or magazine distinct from the one in Ray's possession.

PHYSICAL EVIDENCE: THE FINGERPRINTS

If the ballistics evidence fails to prove Ray's guilt, the fingerprint evidence is equally weak and contradictory. The Memphis police and the FBI lifted and examined hundreds of fingerprints in the course of the investigation. There were five main source locations of fingerprint evidence: the 422½ South Main Street rooming house in Memphis; the green bundle dropped in front of Canipe's store; the New Rebel Motel in which Ray stayed on the evening of April 3; Ray's white Mustang, dropped off near an Atlanta public housing project; and the rooming house in Atlanta where Ray stayed. Fingerprint evidence was also found on various documents, letters, and money orders thought to have been in Ray's possession, including a hold-up note written on a paper bag left at the scene of a London bank robbery on June 4, 1968, before Ray briefly escaped to Portugal. (Ray denied ever robbing the bank.)[38]

The evening of King's murder, April 4, 1968, Capt. Nick J. Carimi of the Memphis police department lifted several prints from the second-floor community bathroom at the rear of the rooming house. The government's story is the shot that killed King came from this bathroom.

The following day, "several more prints" were lifted in room 5B of the rooming house, the room Ray rented under the name of John Willard. These prints—ten in all—were turned over to the FBI on April 6 and personally delivered the same day to the FBI

Laboratory in Washington by special agent Robert Fitzpatrick.

The FBI found only two of the ten fingerprints of value for comparison. One fingerprint, taken from the dresser in room 5B, was the print of a Memphis police officer. The other fingerprint, taken from the fireplace in the same room, was not identified. The presence of this fingerprint corroborates Ray's story that another person was in the room. Ray said the person was Raoul, whom the government claimed did not exist.

One additional print was found on the bathroom windowsill. This fingerprint belonged to FBI special agent Frank Johnson.[39]

There was no fingerprint evidence that Ray was ever in the bathroom. His fingerprints were not on the door, the doorknob, or the bathtub in which the government says Ray stood to make the shot. Nor were Ray's fingerprints found on the windowsill, where the government says he rested his GameMaster rifle loaded with a single round of ammunition. Not only does the fingerprint evidence fail to place Ray in the bathroom at the time of the shot, the government cannot prove Ray was ever in that bathroom at all.

Several fingerprints were found on items recovered from the green bundle that Ray supposedly dropped in the alcove of Canipe's storefront at 424 South Main Street. The big surprise from the green bundle is not the fingerprints identified on various items of evidence but the absence of fingerprints on several key items.

The FBI identified fingerprints on the Q1 rifle box used by Aeromarine Supply to package the Q2 GameMaster rifle for Ray. It also identified one fingerprint on the Q2 riflescope and the rifle itself.[40]

However, the final report of the HSCA along with its Appendix Volumes blur our ability to determine just what fingerprints were identified. The HSCA says in Appendix Volume II that the FBI found a fingerprint of Ray's on the rifle. In Volume XIII, the report notes that its fingerprint expert, Vincent J. Scalice, "was unable to compare a lift from the telescopic sight (Q2), however, because the photography of the original lift was poor."[41] Later, in the same volume, it lists the results of the comparisons of all the fingerprint photographs (by number) taken in 1968 and reexamined by HSCA experts in its investigation: "The panel concluded that James Earl Ray made the latent impressions from the telescopic sight (photograph 3), the aftershave bottle (photograph 6), the Mexican map (photographs 57 and 59); the London robbery note (photograph 165); . . . the check from the Indian Trails Restaurant (photograph 173); [and] a coupon from Eric S. Galt to Modern Photo Bookstore (photograph 115). These results agree with the earlier findings of the FBI."[42]

Except, the results don't agree with the "earlier findings of the FBI" because the report mentions only the Q2 scope fingerprint and nothing about a fingerprint on the rifle itself. Nor does the fingerprint panel offer a single word of explanation as to this discrepancy. Perhaps Scalice verified the print on the rifle but none of the others.

Furthermore, Scalice clouds the fingerprint on the scope as well. He stated in a signed report to the committee that the photograph of the fingerprint on the scope "is of too poor quality for comparison purposes." He said the original fingerprint must be submitted for examination, but there is not one word in the report indicating that this was ever done.[43] Scalice never saw the original fingerprint evidence because he left the HSCA's service shortly thereafter. Whether the subsequent panel of fingerprint experts ever saw the original evidence is a matter of conjecture; it is not elsewhere addressed.

The day after the assassination, US attorney general Ramsey Clark called a press conference in Memphis and announced that a palm print was found on the GameMaster rifle.[44] The rifle had been in the hands of the FBI crime lab by this time. No subsequent investigation mentioned this palm print or whether the print was ever identified. If it wasn't Ray's palm print—and apparently it was not or it would have been confirmed by the FBI and the HSCA—to whom did it belong?

Ray's fingerprints were also identified on the Q14 binoculars, the Q19 newspaper, and the Q53 Schlitz, which was one of two cans of beer inside the closed, zippered plastic travel bag. The other can of Schlitz had no recoverable fingerprints.

A palm print on the Q1 rifle box was identified as that of Donald Wood Jr., the man who sold Ray the rifle in Birmingham, mounted the telescopic sight, and placed it in the box. Wood handled the rifle when he was showing it to Ray. In fact, Wood told the FBI that he alone handled the rifle in the store and that Ray didn't even touch it in his presence. Wood's palm print was on the cardboard gun box with which Ray left the store, but none of his prints were on the rifle or the scope. In showing Ray the rifle, he must have touched it in multiple places with both hands, as with the scope that he mounted and bore-sighted. Every gun that Mr. Wood sold left the store with his fingerprints all over it, especially the ones where he personally mounted a scope. There was nothing different about this sale to James Earl Ray. Obviously, the rifle and scope were wiped down between the time Ray bought the rifle in Birmingham and the bundle was dropped in front of Canipe's store five days later. The box was not wiped down because it still had Wood's palm print on it.

Equally intriguing is the lack of fingerprints on the live rounds that were recovered in the green bundle, especially the Q9–Q12 military-type full metal jacket rounds that the firearms panel said had been previously loaded into a M1 Garand clip (magazine) or a machine gun belt.

The loading of an eight-round M1 clip is a highly manual exercise, requiring more than a little dexterity. It requires both hands, as the index and middle fingers, opposed by the thumb, force each round into the clip. The steel sides of the M1 Garand clip are manufactured to crimp slightly, thus acting as tension to hold the rounds firmly in place. Whether loading or unloading this particular clip, fingerprints on every round cannot be avoided. Because no fingerprints were found on these rounds, it is clear that they were carefully wiped down. Who wiped down these rounds? Why were they wiped down, if not for the purpose of concealing the identity of the person or persons who possessed and handled them before supplying them to Ray?

Manual manipulation of a .30-06 round required to load a M1 Garand, impossible to achieve without leaving fingerprints (Courtesy author's collection)

It makes no sense that James Earl Ray would handle multiple items in the green bundle with his bare hands yet carefully wipe down the individual live rounds. No one knows where those rounds came from. Ray himself had inadequate and contradictory answers to this. All we know for certain is that he did not buy them at Aeromarine Supply Company in Birmingham when the bought the rifle and scope. They came from an undisclosed source. As far as the FBI could ever determine, he never purchased or used an M1 Garand or the eight-round magazine necessary to make it work during the eleven months he was on the lam prior to the assassination.

It makes no sense that Ray handled several items with his bare hands and placed those items inside the plastic zippered bag that was part of the bundle. How did a man who was in a hurry to escape not deposit fingerprints on the plastic bag when his fingerprints were found on items inside the closed zippered bag?

How would Ray get only one thumbprint on the Q2 rifle if he stood in the bathtub in the hall bathroom for fifteen minutes as law enforcement agencies said he did waiting for King to walk into his field of fire? If the assassination happened the way the government says it happened, Ray would have had no time to wipe down the rifle. However, no gloves were found that might have been used to avoid leaving fingerprints.

The ballistics and fingerprint data point to a set-up. Ray didn't have an M1 Garand or the magazine to go with it, but whoever supplied him with the full metal jacket military ammunition likely did. Whoever this person was, he was a co-conspirator and perhaps James Earl Ray's handler. He told Ray where to go, what to buy, and when to buy it. Someone gave James Earl Ray money to buy the white Mustang. Someone gave him money to buy the gun. Someone other than Ray obtained the full metal jacket ammunition, and someone wiped down the gun and the ammunition.

Who Discovered the Green Bundle?

There are three official versions of the story about who discovered the green bundle in front of Guy Canipe's store at 424 South Main Street. This is an important question because it pertains to the chain of custody for the evidence that was recovered in the bundle, including the rifle purchased by Ray in Birmingham and subsequently brought to

Memphis. It could have given Ray's attorneys an opening to challenge its admissibility. If the bundle could not be introduced as evidence, there would have been no rifle, no fingerprints, and no case against Ray. Ray would have been extradited to Missouri to serve his long sentence there. He would have been an ignominious, unknown state prisoner who would have been an old man by the time he was released, if ever.

The official homicide report by the Memphis police department says that a Lt. Judson Ghormley of the Shelby County sheriff's office "notified the police headquarters of finding [the green bundle], then guarded the evidence until the investigating officers arrived."[45] Ten years later, Ghormley claimed in a sworn affidavit to the HSCA that he discovered the green bundle "lying in the doorway with the barrel of a rifle protruding."[46]

Guy Canipe gave a signed statement to police just a couple of hours after King was assassinated, saying that he and a Shelby County deputy sheriff discovered the bundle. Canipe did not name the deputy. Whether that deputy was Lt. Ghormley is speculative. His statement says that he heard someone drop the bundle in front of his store. "I'm not sure what time it was, it was between 5:00 and 6:00 [p.m.], I know that." The precise time is extremely important because the HSCA final report says that King was shot "shortly *after* 6 p.m." (author's emphasis).[47]

Canipe's statement continued:

> I walked out to the street, to see who had laid the stuff there, and no one was in sight. Immediately after, this white Mustang car pulled away from there. Before the car pulled away, I heard a package drop in my front door, and looked to see and saw a man walking away . . . I didn't observe the license or nothing on the car, and immediately after that, a Deputy walked by with his gun drawn, I know he was a Deputy cause [sic] I saw his badge on his arm. He couldn't have been two minutes behind. The place then was suddenly covered up with police. There were people there with guns, rifles and I guess shotguns, I don't know . . . I did not touch none of the contents that were dropped in front of my building.[48]

The sequence of events in Canipe's statement indicates that chaos ensued shortly after someone dropped the bundle, implying that the bundle was there *before* the shot was fired. No doubt the FBI asked questions about the timing of the bundle and the shot when they interviewed Canipe on April 10, 1968. The HSCA investigators also interviewed Canipe in 1977. When the HSCA issued its final report, it downplayed the possibility of the bundle being planted evidence by stating that Canipe told its investigators he had no recollection of hearing the shot, and thus could not say it was before or after the bundle was dropped.[49] What the HSCA did not say in its report is that the FBI interviewed every Memphis fireman and policeman on duty near the location of King's assassination, along with every member of the Shelby County sheriff's office. Its April 13, 1968, report to the FBI director stated: "Interviews with these officers reveal that *no one actually heard the shot fired,* although some admit hearing 'something'" (author's emphasis).[50] This raises an important question as to whether a silencer was used on the rifle that actually fired the fatal shot. The use of a silencer would also indicate a professional hit. Ray did not have a silencer, nor was the Remington GameMaster fitted to accept one.

To make certain no one can analyze Canipe's statement to the FBI or the HSCA on their own, the HSCA incorporated the FBI interview into its own evidence chain and sealed them both for fifty years. Neither interview will be available until the year 2029.[51]

Police inspector N. E. Zachary, who was in charge of the Homicide Bureau, provided yet a third version of how the bundle was found. At James Earl Ray's sentencing hearing, he told the court it was he who discovered the bundle. The prosecution created a model mock up of the buildings in the area, and this is referred to during Zachary's direct examination by Robert Dwyer of the district attorney's office at Ray's sentencing hearing on March 10, 1969:

ROBERT DWYER: In regards to Main Street on the mock-up, Inspector, did you find anything up there, and in particular, in front of Canipe Amusement Company?

N. E. ZACHARY: I did.

. . .

DWYER: Alright, Inspector, what, if anything, did you find there, please, sir?

ZACHARY: I found a package rolled up in a bedspread which consisted of a blue briefcase and a Browning pasteboard box containing a rifle. It was in this doorway at about this location right here [*indicates to the mock-up*].

. . .

DWYER: What, if anything, did you have caused or done to the package, please, sir?

ZACHARY: At that particular time, I put a guard on it with instructions to let no one touch it or move it until we could take photographs of it.[52]

J. Tony Serra is a nationally known criminal defense attorney who successfully defended Black Panther leader Huey Newton against a murder charge.[53] Through a criminal defense attorney and personal friend, I contacted Serra to comment on the legal relevance of these various stories about the discovery of the green bundle. I provided only the facts of the case to Serra as a hypothetical situation. He did not know that these facts pertained to the assassination of Martin Luther King.

Serra wrote to me that the muddled story of the discovery of the green bundle "will probably not be sufficient to grant a defense motion to exclude evidence for lack of proper foundation." However, he offered his opinion that the bundle "sounds like a 'plant' to incriminate the defendant by another." Serra indicated he does not believe a defendant would have purposely dropped the bag with all that evidence in it.[54]

Serra's gut feeling about the bundle being "planted" by someone to incriminate Ray is consistent with Canipe's timing that nothing was happening in the street at the moment the bundle was dropped. It was about two minutes later that Canipe saw a deputy with his weapon drawn, followed by the street being "covered up" with police.

The government claims that Ray discarded the bundle of evidence in order to avoid the police, who heard the shot and were swarming the area. However, Canipe says that the swarm of police did not occur until a couple of minutes after someone threw the bundle at his front door. If it happened the way Canipe recalled, Ray would have already gotten away before the police swarmed the street, thus there would have been no reason to discard the bundle. Ray could have easily walked into a deserted street to his car with the murder weapon bundled up and have gotten away undetected. He would have had no reason to throw away the rifle.

Memphis policeman W. B. Richmond corroborated the timing of Canipe's story and reinforces the question as to whether the shooter had used a silencer. Richmond was on duty at the time of the assassination and was stationed in between the Lorraine Motel and the row of buildings from which the shot came. Richmond said in his written statement of April 9, 1968, "I heard a loud sound as if it were a shot, and saw Dr. Martin Luther King fall back from the handrail and put his hand up to his head." He called in the shooting to police headquarters as he ran over to the fire station to yell to officers of the TACT squad that there was a shooting. Richmond said he "ran to the front of the fire station," which faced South Main Street, "and didn't see no one running or walking except the TACT force men who had left the fire station in different directions. That's about it."

Whoever dropped the green bundle had already done so or else would have been spotted by police officers who "suddenly covered up" the street with guns drawn (according to Canipe) and scattered in all directions (according to Richmond). The bundle must have already been there on the street a couple of minutes before the shot was fired, according to both Canipe and Richmond.

WHERE DID THE SHOT COME FROM?

From the outset of the investigation by the Memphis police department and the FBI, both attempted to fix the location of the discharge of the fatal rifle shot from the second floor the rooming house where James Earl Ray had rented a room for the week. There were problems in doing so because, among other reasons, eyewitnesses down on the street and in the vicinity of the facing side of the Lorraine Motel disagreed as to the point of origin of the shot.

One of many nagging facts about this case is that James Earl Ray checked into a second-floor room that had no vantage point from which to fire toward the Lorraine Motel. If he took the room as a location from which to shoot King, and he knew he was staying in the Lorraine Motel, it was a failure from the start.

In the hope of settling questions about the location of the rifle shot, Memphis police director Frank Holloman requested the Memphis Division of Public Works to conduct an engineering survey of the site. On April 23, 1968, Arthur C. Holbrook (the Memphis city engineer) and a crew of six set up an engineer's transit, an essential surveying instrument, over the spot that King was standing when the fatal shot struck him in the neck. The transit was placed at fifty-nine inches above the catwalk in front of room 306 as close to the location where the bullet entered King's body as possible. Medical examiner Dr. Jerry T. Francisco's autopsy noted that the bullet was on a slightly downward trajectory when it struck King.[55]

Holbrook's survey indicated the fatal shot may have been fired from a rifle resting on the windowsill of the second floor bathroom across the street at 422½ South Main Street, 207.02 feet away, but it did not eliminate other possible locations.[56]

The HSCA commissioned the Albuquerque, New Mexico, civil-engineering firm of Koogle & Pouls to resurvey the scene in June 1978; the firm had no previous involvement with either the JFK or MLK assassinations. HSCA asked Koogle & Pouls "to survey the scene and report on the probable location of the assassin, specifically requesting determination of the horizontal and vertical angles, distances, and physics involved in possible trajectories to the point of impact."[57]

Herbert G. Koogle, president of the firm, brought his own team of surveyors and engineers to Memphis. They had more modern equipment than had been used ten years earlier.

Koogle met with the HSCA forensic pathology panel of three top medical examiners at the scene on June 9 and 10, 1978, and took numerous measurements. "After considerable discussion with the three medical examiners, it became apparent that a 3-4 degree difference in angularity of the trajectory would not enable them to reach a definite conclusion about the possible location of the shot. With the lack of photographic or specific eyewitness evidence concerning Dr. King's posture when he was hit, it is not possible to establish with certainty the vertical angularity of the trajectory."[58]

They cannot prove where the shot came from. It could have come from the bathroom window, but it also could have come from the roof or the ground. Without verified fingerprints in the bathroom, the case for Ray's guilt is a slim margin at best.

IN DEFENSE OF RAY

The victim was the most prominent, black, civil rights leader in the nation. The accused was a white man said to be a racist, a white man with a criminal record and a prison escapee, a white man who carried a .30-06 rifle with him to Memphis, a white man who fled Memphis at the first sign of trouble.

The evidence does not support the allegations against Ray. Because Ray pleaded guilty, however, Tennessee prosecutors never had to put on any proof about the flimsy ballistics evidence or the source of Ray's funds for his various purchases.

But his skills were at the basest level, not what would have been needed to carry out such a plot as the one constructed by the government. Either Ray suddenly became an extremely efficient thief and murderer, or someone fed him the details. The less likely of those two scenarios is the former.

CHAPTER 3
Was There a Motive?

The reality during the 1960s civil rights movement in the United States was that Rev. Martin Luther King Jr. was revered and loved as well as hated. Many simply wished that King and the civil rights movement would go away. These factions split primarily along racial lines in the South and perhaps only a little less so in the North. King was a polarizing personality who drew affection and enmity from every action, statement, and appearance.

The physical evidence that would prove whether James Earl Ray assassinated King simply does not exist. In that case, why did the government pin it on Ray? Did he have an easily digestible motive to murder King?

The Writers Who Railroaded Ray

Authors Huie, McMillan, Posner, and Sides all ascribe the motive of James Earl Ray in one way or another to a single, solitary act of racial hatred. James Earl Ray and his brothers referred to Huie and McMillan as the "Scribblers" rather than writers or biographers, according to Ray's brother Jerry.[1] Posner and Sides came along after the original Scribblers, but both of their books lean heavily on Huie's and McMillan's theories.

Much of the stories told by the four writers simply do not add up. In fact, virtually nothing of either Huie's or McMillan's incriminating and incendiary allegations about James Earl Ray was ever verified or corroborated by FBI or HSCA investigators. Virtually all has been disproven and debunked in specific detail. This did not stop Posner and Sides from re-telling these discredited allegations in their own books. Most importantly, however, none of the four writers ever met or interviewed James Earl Ray. Both Huie and McMillan openly acknowledged that they paid cash money to the Ray family and other sources quoted in their books.

William Bradford Huie (Courtesy the Southern Literary Trail with permission of the William Bradford Huie estate)

To understand the murder of King as a symbol of the era's racist tendencies, including the development of the non-existent case against Ray and the symbol into which he was fashioned, it is crucial to understand the historiography of what else has been written on these issues. A careful and critical study of the publications of the four writers provides a progression of the changing allegations against Ray and their influence on the public views. Through their books, they have guided public opinion to the pre-determined storyline that a lone nut with a gun—a racist nut—murdered Dr. Martin Luther King Jr.

Long before King was murdered, Huie and McMillan were well-known journalists writing favorably about the civil rights movement in the South. Due to their location and presence, they had the most access to Ray's family. Posner and Sides never met Ray or any of his brothers.

Huie was Ray's original literary agent in 1968. By this date, Huie was a wealthy novelist, television interviewer, and screenwriter. His work focused on the fact that Ray pleaded guilty to the charge of murdering King, so the obvious motive was a stand against the civil rights crusade. While Huie addressed the issue of motive, he contributed far less to the theories about why Ray did it than McMillan, who saw deep-seated, seething racial hatred everywhere he looked into James Earl Ray's life whether it was present or not.

Huie, and especially McMillan, quoted Ray's relatives extensively. Most notable were McMillan's transcribed interviews with Jerry Ray, not a word of which was captured on audio tape. When the HSCA delved into these men's allegations and these men's accounts from Ray's relatives, the committee did not find it worthy to ask either to testify under oath. The veracity of their stories was assumed by the HSCA, even when the committee's own investigators discredited or disproved those stories.

So, Did James Earl Ray Have a Motive?

McMillan asserted that shortly after escaping from the Missouri State Penitentiary (MSP) on April 23, 1967, Ray attempted to recruit his brothers into the plot to murder King. McMillan claims to have spoken to Ray's brothers "hundreds of times" (which might be true).[2]

McMillan wrote that Ray was unsuccessful in securing his brothers' involvement to murder King. Ray's brothers would have nothing to do with it, but not because of any moral qualms; rather, it was "too big a job" for them. As McMillan related, James Earl Ray thought it was his duty to murder King and that he and his brothers hated just about anyone other than white people—blacks, Jews, Vietnamese, Mexicans, you name it.[3] Anyone who has actually known James Earl Ray would likely laugh at the idea that he ever considered anything in his life to be a "duty." Ray's brothers have denied telling McMillan virtually everything that he attributed to them in *The Making of an Assassin.*

McMillan's strong implication is that Ray's plot was so crazy and so dangerous that once his brothers turned him down, there was no hope of getting anyone else involved. So, James Earl Ray decided in the early summer of 1967—nine or ten months in advance—to murder King all by himself. However, his explanation is silent as to the source of money for living expenses during the period Ray traveled around the country and to Mexico and Canada without a job or apparent means of support.

Sides suggested that Ray must have known about a big pot of money put up by segregationist Southern businessmen as a bounty on King's life. According to him, Ray's plan was to stalk and murder King, then contact these unknown businessmen and claim the cash. This doesn't make sense for at least three reasons. First, it fails to explain where Ray got the money to live for almost a year. He wasn't working. He was an escaped felon with twenty years hanging over him. And yet, it was financially the best year of his life. Second, Ray would have found himself in a long line of phonies attempting to claim the same bounty once King was dead. Third, how would Ray have identified these "rich Southern segregationist" businessmen, whose existence (if they ever existed) and identities were not even known to the FBI at the time?

Posner asked us just to trust him—he guarantees Ray is guilty. This is a tall order, as Posner reported many arguable things in his book. For example, Posner said that Ray knew where to find King from television or radio on April 3 or from the front page of the April 4 issue of the *Memphis Commercial Appeal.*[4] The electronic media explanation is unsupported by fact, and newspaper explanation is woefully inadequate. The newspaper story on April 4 only mentioned that King had been at Lorraine Motel at lunch the previous day.

Furthermore, Posner noted that King's room number at the Lorraine, 306, had been "mentioned in the local press coverage."[5] This is an inaccurate statement without which there was no basis at all to explain how Ray knew King's location. Out of every news story in the April 3-4, 1968, Memphis newspapers, only the *Memphis Commercial Appeal* on April 4 said that King was found "eating lunch at the Lorraine Motel."[6] However, no room number was specified. Prior to the assassination, there was no mention in any paper where King was staying. It was not until the late afternoon of April 4 that the *Memphis Press-Scimitar*, the afternoon daily newspaper, mentioned that King had spent the night before at the Lorraine.[7] Even then, there was no mention of a room number. By its publication a little after 3 p.m., Ray had already checked into Bessie Brewer's rooming house. With a little investigation, Posner's assertions are baseless.

No one has been able to pin a plausible motive on James Earl Ray. McMillan could not make his racism motive stick with any credibility. He repeatedly attributed extremely incriminating statements from Ray's brothers, who claimed they were lies. They had no reason to tell implicating stories to McMillan, as they did not want to see their brother remain in prison the rest of his life.

The FBI was also unsuccessful in making the racism motive stick on Ray. The FBI interviewed dozens of inmates or former inmates who served time with Ray at the Missouri penitentiary. The FBI even interviewed the former warden and could not find evidence that Ray was involved in any race-related disturbances at the prison.

Money was the one and only possible motive Ray could have had. But asserting that Ray got paid to kill King is to assert that there *was* a conspiracy—and none of the four writers or anyone in government was going to suggest that as a motive.

Ray's three minute and forty-three second sentencing hearing in Shelby County, Tennessee, criminal court did not address the issue of motive. There was no need for Judge Battle's court to address motive because, by entering the guilty plea, Ray assumed responsibility for the crime of murdering King. This was not the case once the HSCA began its investigation because part of its mandate was to solve the crime and provide answers to questions that had not been answered fully.

Huie and McMillan raised numerous possibilities for Ray's motive. The HSCA looked at most of these allegations, and, try as they might, were unable to definitively corroborate any of them. Some of the stories were directly contradicted and discredited as baseless.

McMillan and Huie claimed that Ray befriended an older co-worker at the International Shoe Company tannery in East Hartford, Illinois, in 1944. Henry Strumm had emigrated from Germany in 1928 and became a US citizen in 1936. McMillan claimed that Strumm was pro-Nazi and pro-Hitler. Ray, a teenager at the time, is said to have absorbed pro-Nazi racial hatred of blacks and Jews and viewed Hitler favorably and President Roosevelt unfavorably, thus becoming unpatriotic and un-American.

McMillan also said that Strumm carried a picture of Hitler in his wallet and would show it off to people. This claim seems more than outlandish, as a German immigrant who spoke with a heavy accent would not have been likely to show off Hitler's picture to people during a war in which tens of thousands of American families were receiving telegrams from the War Department advising them of a son's death.

McMillan also reported that Ray and Strumm would ride the streetcar together and go to a favorite café to talk pro-Nazi politics. This is an interesting allegation, because if it is true, it is the only time in Ray's life he seemed interested in any political events or ideas. Ray and Strumm would wait for the two most remote stools near the back of the café and talk for hours about "Hitler politics." The deep, resonant relationship between Ray and Strumm "was at the center of both men's lives," according to McMillan.[8]

However, there are several problems with the attempted Nazification of James Earl Ray.[9]

McMillan never met or spoke to Henry Strumm. Strumm was interviewed by the FBI in early 1969 but died before HSCA investigators could speak to him. He told the FBI that he could not recall ever having met James Earl Ray. Strumm denied ever spending time with Ray in the nearby café, being pro-Nazi, or giving Ray a copy of *Mein Kampf.* Furthermore, Strumm gave the names of two Alton, Illinois, co-workers whom he said "would verify that he had driven to and from work with them every day during that time" when he was supposedly riding the streetcar with Ray.

HSCA investigators were convinced: "In the absence of evidence of more recent contact by Ray with members or sympathizers of the Nazi Party, there is an insufficient basis for concluding that the ideologies of

Adolph Hitler or the American Nazi Party had a discernible effect on his participation in the assassination."[10]

In the closing days of the HSCA investigation, chief counsel G. Robert Blakey was a bit more direct: "the committee's investigation has not been able to establish a firm factual basis for [McMillan's] story."[11] Ray's indoctrination into Nazism may make a spectacular allegation, but it isn't true. It was just part of an effort to marginalize and stigmatize Ray as a disloyal, un-American racist.

ALLEGATION: RAY WAS AN EGOMANIAC WHO WANTED TO DO SOMETHING BIG IN HIS LIFE

William Bradford Huie claimed that Ray didn't want to remain a "nobody." He had an urge to see his face on television, and public attention and acclaim would relieve his feelings of inadequacy.[12] Both Blakey and Ray's attorney Percy Foreman stated that Ray was motivated by ego. Foreman assured the world that Ray reveled in the attention. Blakey told me that Ray's motive was "ego gratification," which he qualified with the caveat that Ray "did not plan to get caught."[13]

It may very well be true that Ray had feelings of inadequacy. Clearly, he was inadequate as a thief, as he was caught and jailed many times. He was inept by Army draftee standards, where he spent time in the stockade. He was never out of trouble for very long and spent more than 80 percent of his adult life behind bars in Illinois, California, Kansas, Missouri, and Tennessee.

But if Huie was correct in his psychoanalysis of James Earl Ray— that his motivation to murder King was to be known worldwide—why would Ray shoot at a distance from a concealed sniper's nest and then run from the law? Not only did Ray run, he did it successfully for more than two months, changing his alias twice to elude the police forces that were looking for him.

Huie's reasoning about ego doesn't make sense. It was even suggested that Ray dropped the bundle of evidence in front of Mr. Canipe's store in order to be identified. Why drop the bundle and run if all you want is to be caught? Ray could have been on the CBS Evening News that night if he had stuck around Memphis and let the police catch him. Because he ran, it was two weeks before anyone even knew Ray's true identity.

The HSCA *Final Report* rejected this whole line of reasoning regarding ego and recognition, disputing even Blakey's personal assessment: "Taken as a whole, however, the evidence that Ray was motivated in the assassination by a pressing need for recognition was not substantial. . . . To argue that Ray killed Dr. King to become somebody, however, necessarily must assume that Ray expected to be identified. The credible evidence did not support that possibility."[14]

ALLEGATION: RAY WAS A RACIST

Across the board, outsiders have "discovered" incidents in James Earl Ray's life that developed the public mentality that he was a significantly racist white male. Without these distorted stories, this image could not have been constructed and Ray as the perpetrator of King's assassination would not have been as believable.

In 1955, Ray was sentenced to forty-five months at Leavenworth prison for his role in stealing a batch of US Postal Service money orders and going on a two-week, multi-state spending spree before being caught. It is telling of Ray's lack of expertise and care in committing the crime that it took only two weeks to capture him and his accomplice.

Two years later, when Ray turned down the opportunity to transfer from the main prison to a racially integrated honor farm, McMillan read the situation as racial prejudice. McMillan generally equated racial prejudice with violent tendencies. While it is true that there was plenty of racial prejudice in America in the 1950s, the ranks of those who were willing to do actual harm to others based solely on the color of a person's skin were rapidly diminishing. Public opinion had already turned against the commission of violent acts.

Ray's 1958 release report states the following: "On July 12, 1957, Ray was approved for our honor farm but was never actually transferred to such assignment due to the fact that he did not feel he could live in an honor farm dormitory because they are integrated. Due to this fact, he was never placed under such status. He was assigned to our bakery, where he remained until released on conditional release."[15]

Ray was asked about this incident in the 1977 interview for *Playboy* magazine. He said that the main reason he did not want to go to the honor farm is whenever marijuana was found in the dormitory, extra time was handed out to all prisoners in the vicinity even if they were not involved. When *Playboy* asked if Ray meant that blacks smoked dope and he was worried about getting punished for it, he answered "Maybe."[16]

HSCA investigators looked into the matter in 1978 and noted that Ray had voluntarily worked with blacks at Indian Trails golf club while he was on the lam in 1967.

> The committee was unable to determine whether Ray's response to *Playboy* was the truth or simply an attempt to draw attention away from the documented evidence concerning this issue. Even accepting—on face value—Ray's stated reasons for resisting the transfer, they nevertheless reflected a tendency to engage in racially oriented generalization on human behavior. The incident did not, however, indicate fanatical racism on the part of the assassin. . . .The incident was viewed, therefore, as simply one more example of general lack of empathy for blacks.[17]

This was another attempt to stigmatize Ray and transform him into the image of a racist.

In June 1964, the warden of the MSP attempted to desegregate the institution. White inmates wearing pillowcases over their heads attacked four black inmates almost immediately. One black prisoner died, and three others received severe stab wounds. This attack was followed by several other beatings and stabbings through the summer and fall of 1964. All of these incidents were considered racially motivated.[18]

McMillan claimed in *The Making of an Assassin* that James Earl Ray's brother, Jerry Ray, told him that James Earl Ray was one of the white prisoners who wore a pillowcase over his head that day.[19] The HSCA reported that neither McMillan nor its own investigators found any evidence to substantiate the statement. Jerry Ray claims that he never made any such statement to McMillan.

During the course of the HSCA investigation, committee investigators interviewed thirty former inmates who served time at MSP with Ray. Five former prison officials were also interviewed. Only two of the former inmates claimed to have knowledge of the 1964 stabbing. Joe Hegwood told HSCA investigators that he knew "all those involved in the incident, and Ray was not among them." He said that the incident took place in a cellblock on the opposite side of the prison from Ray, who would not have had access to the area. Another former inmate, Jack Romprey, also claimed to have known those involved, but Ray was not among them.[20]

McMillan raised a second allegation: Ray's derogatory language about blacks in general and Martin Luther King specifically. McMillan claimed that a former cellmate, Raymond Curtis, reported that when Ray would see King on television, he would refer to him as Martin "Lucifer" King or Martin Luther "Coon."[21] James Earl Ray answered this charge directly in his book *Who Killed Martin Luther King, Jr.?* According to Ray, MSP prisoners during 1967 had no access to television.[22] Additionally, Curtis told HSCA investigators that he did not think Ray liked blacks, "but [he] could not recall any specific racial incident in which Ray was involved" and that "Ray never made any remarks to him about Dr. King."[23]

Another inmate who worked with Ray at MSP, Cecil Clayton Lillibridge, told HSCA investigators that Ray and several black inmates were placed together on a heavy work crew. Lillibridge recalled that Ray and the black inmates teased each other about their respective race, but it was viewed as a joke and did not reflect animosity between them.[24]

Again, the specific allegations by McMillan were either contradicted or unsubstantiated. McMillan said that there were 489 acts of violence at MSP between 1961 and 1963, but it is not identified how many of these were racially motivated or involved Ray. He claims that the prison was infested with bugs, that there was egregious misdiagnosis of prisoner illness, that experiments were conducted on prisoners, that prisoners had to pay other prisoners for the privilege of medical or dental treatment, that guards weren't paid enough to live on, and that homosexual activity was rampant. McMillan then blamed the whole mess at MSP on James Earl Ray. He claimed it was just what Ray was looking for in a prison. If Ray liked the squalor, vermin, abuse, and violence at MSP as much as McMillan implied, it is curious why Ray would ever break out.

The FBI attempted to link Ray with the California campaign of George Wallace during its original investigation in 1968. McMillan wrote that James Earl Ray was talking as much about having Wallace elected president as he was about "rubbing King out," when there was no credible evidence he spoke about either.[25] Posner repeated the same story and added that there is no reason to doubt McMillan because he took notes of the interview with Jerry Ray.[26] Let it be stated that notes are much easier to fake than audio recordings.

The whole idea becomes suspect when one considers that James Earl Ray never voted during his entire life. In fact, he was never registered to vote. Jerry Ray confirmed, "No, I don't think he ever was [registered to vote]."[27]

When HSCA chief counsel Blakey addressed the Wallace campaign allegations, he told HSCA committee members: "Even though Ray has consistently denied any interest in politics, there is a great deal of evidence that he was active in the 1968 Wallace campaign, and while it would be unfair to Mr. Wallace, or to his many supporters generally, to characterize his campaign as racist, it is a sad fact that his candidacy attracted voters of an anti-black persuasion. His candidacy and his party were also widely perceived as unsympathetic toward a number of issues associated with the civil rights movement."[28]

And what was the alleged contribution that James Earl Ray's "infatuation" with the Wallace campaign that "absorbed" so much of his time and talent? Supposedly he gave a ride in his Mustang to three people who wanted to register to vote.[29]

Whatever meaning, if any, this allegation about the Wallace campaign may have, it is further obscured by James Earl Ray's court objection about the stipulation in his guilty plea that had to do with the one item that acknowledged his interest and participation in the Wallace campaign. That particular sentence clause was stricken from the document.

McMillan, Huie, and Posner claimed that Ray met with his brothers John and Jerry shortly after his escape from MSP on April 23, 1967.[30] Ray asked his brothers for help in assassinating Martin Luther King Jr., according to McMillan, who recorded that this is what Jerry Ray told him in an untaped interview. He said that Jerry Ray had no real objection to murdering King, but his divorce was on his mind and he thought the job was too big for the three of them. Apparently, John Ray's objection was that there couldn't possibly be any money in "killin' a n-----."[31]

17. That in December, 1967, defendant drove to New Orleans with Charlie Stein and brought Rita Stein's children back to Los Angeles. after having taken Charles Stein, Rita Stein and Marie Martin to George Wallace headquarters in Los Angeles for purpose of registering for Wallace.

Emphasis on James Earl Ray's interest in George Wallace's presidential campaign, stricken from the stipulation of facts before being entered into court records (Courtesy Shelby County Archives)

Though McMillan described the undated meeting in his book, Posner specified the date as the day after Ray's escape, April 24, 1967. Perhaps Posner drew this date from McMillan's notes, which were supplied to HSCA investigators, but, in any case, the HSCA found discrepancies around that date. The HSCA never subpoenaed McMillan to testify under oath. When HSCA investigators interviewed Huie in 1978, he told them that Jerry and John Ray met with James Earl Ray "only a few days after the escape."[32] The location of the alleged meeting is also disputed.

Jerry Ray denied to HSCA investigators that the brothers' meeting ever took place and ever telling this story to McMillan, whom he repeatedly referred to as a liar. When Jerry Ray was interviewed by HSCA investigators in Long Grove, Illinois, in 1976 he told them that McMillan's story was "totally false."[33] Two years later, when testifying under oath before the HSCA, Jerry Ray repeated: "It definitely wasn't true. I can't remember all my conversation with Georgie McMillan, but it definitely is not true. We didn't have no meetings in Chicago meeting John or James. We never the three of us together at one time, so I can't—yeah, I can't remember what McMillan talked about because he is around me. He hung on me for years and years until he finally got his book published . . ."

Years later, Jerry Ray told me that the three brothers did, in fact, meet, and the meeting occurred within thirty-six hours of James Earl escaping from MSP. Jerry Ray admitted in 2011 to lying to the FBI and to HSCA investigators when he testified—apparently, John Ray picked up James Earl, and they headed to the Chicago area, where they joined Jerry. Jerry lied to the HSCA because he "didn't want to get John in trouble."[34] Decades removed from the investigation, Jerry revealed the truth because he was no longer concerned with being prosecuted for lying under oath. However, Jerry Ray was adamant that the three brothers never discussed killing Martin Luther King at that or any other meeting: "James never talked to me about King."[35]

It appears that McMillan's point of the story was to establish that if James Earl Ray's brothers would not help him, he had no hope of obtaining assistance from anyone else. Thus, he must have carried out the assassination alone. This is a rather monumental undertaking for a man who had never committed any major crime alone and unassisted.

According to McMillan, Ray called his brother Jerry the day before

King was killed and told him that it would be "all over" the next day. "Big n----- has had it!"[36] At the time James Earl Ray was said to have made this telephone call, the Memphis police department didn't even know where King was planning on staying.[37]

Jerry Ray repeatedly denied that the phone call ever took place or that he ever told the story to McMillan. He sued McMillan, alleging the author printed numerous untruths in his book. "I don't ever remember having no conversation with him like that," Jerry Ray testified before the HSCA, regarding McMillan's story. "I don't remember saying anything like that to him, and I know definitely James never did say anything like that to me."[38] Whereas Jerry Ray revealed the truth about the brothers' meeting years later, regarding this conversation, he told me, "It didn't happen."[39]

Blakey told committee members that Jerry and John Ray both denied there ever was a conversation with McMillan about the telephone call James Earl Ray was said to have made to Jerry the day before the assassination: "Jerry himself has denied to the committee that there ever was such a conversation. Similarly, the committee has been unable to confirm various other virulent anti-Black statements attributed [by McMillan] to James by John."[40] The HSCA's chief investigator gave no credence to McMillan's allegations.

William Bradford Huie made the allegation that Ray exhibited his hatred for blacks through racial slurs. Specifically, Huie located a Canadian woman named Claire Keating, whom he claimed repeated a racial slur she heard James Earl Ray utter while they were out to dinner in 1967 at a resort near Montreal during Ray's first trip to Canada.

According to Keating, Ray said, "You got to live near n----- to know 'em." Ray is alleged to have added, ". . . all people who live near n----- hate them."[41] Huie paid Keating $100 for her statement.[42]

Keating declined to be interviewed by or cooperate with HSCA investigators in 1977. She had already given a statement to the Royal Canadian Mounted Police (RCMP) on October 15, 1968, as part of the original King assassination investigation. She told the RCMPs that during the few days she went out with Ray, "He never mentioned the name Martin Luther King and never indicated any hatred towards Negroes."[43] The RCMP officer who conducted this interview, J. A. G. Synett, told HSCA investigators that Keating said that "the subject of race never came up during her meetings with Ray." Synett said that

Keating "seemed honest and truthful throughout the interview."[44]

A second alleged incident of a racial slur by James Earl Ray occurred in a bar in the Los Angeles area in the winter of 1967. Ray supposedly got into a heated political argument at a bar called Rabbit's Foot Club on Sunset Boulevard.

Apparently, Ray "preached" George Wallace inside the bar and started a brawl. Ray himself wrote about the incident to Huie in which he described himself as the victim of two guys who came up on him from behind, pulled his suit jacket up over his arms and stole his jacket and watch. The bartenders that night were James E. Morrison and Bo Del Monte. Morrison told the FBI on April 30, 1968, that Ray shouted to his female companion that night, "I'll drop you off in Watts [a poor, black neighborhood in Los Angeles] and we'll see if you like it there."[45]

In the late 1970s, the HSCA investigators discovered the woman was dead and they were unable to find Morrison. The only outside witness was Bo Del Monte, who denied that any altercation occurred. Del Monte disputed an earlier statement to the FBI when he told investigators that "all that happened was that a quiet discussion in which Ray questioned the safety of a white walking through Watts."[46]

Another facet of James Earl Ray's supposed racism was his interest in the country of Rhodesia, which in the late 1960s was still governed under apartheid rule.

Huie attempted to make the most of James Earl Ray's desire to get to English-speaking Africa through the information Ray wrote to him while in the Shelby County jail. Ray wrote to Huie that he had about $800 and was confident that he could get a job if he got to Rhodesia—but a round trip ticket was $820. "You can't get into one of those countries without a round trip ticket," Ray wrote.[47]

Posner reported that while Ray was still in prison in Jefferson City, he was sympathetic to the government of Rhodesia and thought of going to Australia because he thought there were no blacks there. These statements came from FBI reports filed on interviews with John Ray and Paul Bridgeman (unrelated to Paul E. Bridgeman, one of Ray's aliases), a former inmate with James Earl Ray.[48]

Sides retold the story about James Earl Ray's attempt to contact the Rhodesian government while in Puerto Vallarta, Mexico, in late 1967. Sides claimed that Ray was an "ardent believer in the cause of white rule and racial apartheid."[49] This is profound insight for someone whom

Sides never knew or met, who never made any such statement to anyone interviewed by the FBI, and who left no writings to this effect.

When the HSCA investigation studied Ray's flight to Canada, it found evidence that Ray had made inquiries or had explored the possibility of getting to Africa, including Rhodesia in particular.[50] The HSCA looked at all of these contacts with African countries and the allegations and interpretations of Ray's actions and potential motives. "In its attempt to determine whether the assassination of Dr. Martin Luther King, Jr., was motivated by racial hatred, the committee reviewed these transactions. The committee believed that Ray's fascination with segregated nations might indicate a general sympathy for these policies."[51]

However, after carefully evaluating what Huie and McMillan wrote about Ray and what the HSCA investigators could prove, the investigators noted:

> The committee undertook its review of Ray's efforts to immigrate to African countries to determine whether this behavior reflected an innate racism that might also explain the assassination of Dr. King. No such evidence was found.
>
> The committee's investigation at MSP, however, indicated that considerable discussion about "safe" countries occurred within the inmate population, and that Rhodesia was often mentioned in this regard. There is sound reason to believe, therefore, that Ray's inquires concerning Rhodesia in Mexico in late 1967, and in California in early 1968, stemmed from a desire to reach a safe haven, and not because of an interest in the country's politics. This interpretation is supported by Ray's post-assassination conduct. His frantic efforts to reach a variety of African countries probably reflected a simple desire to elude his pursuers.[52]

In 1978, a story surfaced about a bounty placed on King's life by two prominent (and by then deceased) St. Louis, Missouri, businessmen who had been supporters of Gov. George Wallace's campaigns for president.

The HSCA noted that there was "convincing evidence of a St. Louis-based conspiracy involving John Sutherland—a patent attorney—and John Kauffmann—an associate of Sutherland's involved in a variety of legal and illegal activities." The committee attempted to establish a link between these deceased, alleged conspirators and Ray, believing word of the bounty might have reached him through any one of several channels and thus providing a motive for which to murder King.

The plot was brought to the attention of the HSCA by Russell G. Byers, who alleged that Sutherland and Kauffmann offered him $50,000 in late 1966 or early 1967 to murder or arrange the murder of King.[53] Byers invoked his Fifth Amendment not to incriminate himself when questioned by HSCA but was compelled to testify with a grant of federal immunity.[54]

HSCA investigators questioned a number of other individuals in connection with Byers's allegation, including John Paul Spica, who was said to have been a convicted contract murderer. Spica and James Earl Ray worked in the prison hospital together for a brief period of time along with Dr. Hugh Maxey, the prison physician. Maxey was also an acquaintance of Kauffmann. Both Spica and Maxey denied ever knowing anything about Kauffmann's bounty on King's life.[55] Spica was murdered a year after his testimony to the HSCA when someone wired several sticks of dynamite into the ignition system of his car.

Although the HSCA identified four MSP inmates or former inmates who claimed to know of Ray's interest in collecting on a bounty on King's life, "the committee was unable to demonstrate a direct link between Ray and the St. Louis conspiracy through inmates or officials of the Missouri State Prison."[56]

Again, this represents another failed attempt by McMillan to establish Ray's motive to murder King as one of race. If HSCA investigators or anyone else had ever proven there was a connection between Ray and a bounty to murder King, they would have hung it around his neck like a noose. If there ever was a bounty and someone had collected the money, there would have been a money trail. But no one found any evidence that such a bounty ever existed, and there was no money trail to find.

To make a broad-brush assumption that thousands or tens of thousands of Americans who were opposed to civil rights are as equally guilty of the death of King as the assassin who pulled the trigger is to be guilty of the same false stereotypes King sought to destroy. This wide net of suspicion hardly singles out James Earl Ray as having a motive to assassinate King.

DID PEOPLE WHO KNEW RAY BELIEVE THAT RACE WAS A MOTIVE?

It is important to consider what various individuals who knew Ray thought about his supposed motive of racial hatred, especially since none of the four writers who wrote copiously on the subject ever met Ray. They were never in a position to make an in-person judgment of Ray's attitudes about race.

One of those who met Ray and spent several hours in conversation with him is John Jay Hooker Jr. Hooker's conversation with Ray changed his mind about whether he had a racial motive to harm King and perhaps even changed Hooker's view of his guilt.

Hooker was an unsuccessful candidate for the Democratic nomination for governor of Tennessee in 1966 from the left-leaning wing of the party, losing that year to Buford Ellington, who won a second non-sequential term as governor. In the mid-1960s, Hooker was one of the most prominent Tennessee politicians who supported the civil rights movement and full equality for black citizens. He believed that society

John Jay Hooker Jr. (Courtesy author's collection)

must change, even when it was not politically advantageous in the South to say so. He was a personal friend and political ally of King; his wife, Coretta Scott King; Andrew Young; and Jesse Jackson Sr.

Hooker met Ray in the early 1990s at the urging of Howard Bingham, Muhammad Ali's photographer. Hooker remembered, "He [Bingham] called me one day and said that he and a crowd out there [in Hollywood] wanted to do a movie about James Earl Ray, which I thought was sort of a bizarre thing in view of the fact that his crowd was all black."[57] Bingham was having trouble getting the prison authorities to allow him to see Ray and called Hooker to help.

Bingham believed that the two of them could get Ray to confess late in life, which would make a spectacular movie. "We went and spent three hours with [Ray] and I thought I could break him down. I thought it was in his best interest to say he killed him. I thought he had killed [King], and I couldn't understand why he wasn't willing to say he killed him."

Bingham confirmed that Hooker verbally worked over Ray pretty hard. "He looked him [Ray] right in the eyes, got right up in his face, and asked, 'Did you kill my hero?'"[58] Bingham said Ray told them he did not.

When I asked Hooker if Ray said anything to him or Bingham during the interview or indicated anything to him in any way that Ray was a racist, he explained that he felt that Ray probably thought black people were inferior, "but I don't think he hated black people, or at least if he did he covered it up very well because the man sitting next to me [Bingham] was black and wanted to make a movie about him."[59]

The long interview left Hooker questioning Ray's guilt.

Another individual who did not believe Ray was a racist is freelance journalist and screenwriter Mike Vinson of McMinnville, Tennessee. Vinson conducted the last in-person, published, question-and-answer interview of James Earl Ray. Vinson interviewed Ray on March 25, 1998, in the medical annex of Riverbend Maximum Security Prison in Nashville less than a month before Ray died. The interview was audio taped, as prison authorities would not allow video equipment. Ray was extremely weak and nearing death due to cirrhosis of the liver, thought to have been contracted when he was repeatedly stabbed by other prisoners years earlier. Vinson's interview of Ray was published on April 5, 1998, in three daily newspapers in Tennessee: the *McMinnville Southern Standard,* the *Murfreesboro Daily News Journal,* and the

Franklin Appeal Review. Vinson said that he "absolutely does not" consider James Earl Ray a racist. "Personally, I have not seen any hint that supports that at all."[60] He believes that McMillan and the other writers got it all wrong—likely deliberately.

Tennessee commissioner of correction Harry S. Avery was the only state official who conducted an independent, post-trial investigation of James Earl Ray, and he is the only contemporary official at any level of government who expressed the opinion that there was a conspiracy to murder King. Avery thought that Ray might have been involved in the assassination, but he completely rejected the notion that Ray acted merely due to the motive of racial hatred. "I am sure that James Earl Ray did not just get mad at Martin Luther King for what he was saying and go and slay him and bring the police forces of the world down on him when he was successfully an escapee for almost two years from the penitentiary with a twenty-year and six-month sentence hanging over his head. And we [Avery and Ray] talked all this out."[61]

Avery was also convinced that solving the King assassination case was all about the money—who paid whom to do what. Avery was convinced "beyond the bounds of reason" that Ray's participation in the events in Memphis—to whatever degree of participation it was—was bought and paid for by someone else.

Furthermore, Avery believed that there was money behind the effort to portray James Earl Ray as a virulent racist out to murder the leading black civil rights advocate in the nation:

> I figured these people that's been writing books and saying "Ray just did it," and that they were being paid to do this. Somewhere in the background there were finances being put up to educate the public to believe that James Earl Ray just killed Martin Luther King on his own, because he was a racist. That's so silly to me, based on my experiences of life that it's repulsive to even think about.
>
> A man that has escaped from a prison and gotten away and still has 20 years hanging over him or more would go and shoot somebody that the whole world is looking at, just because he don't like what he's saying. That is just far beyond anything that I can imagine after talking to James Earl Ray, that he did.[62]

Avery underscored his comments about Ray's motive by saying that perhaps he would have been capable of murdering King motivated only by racial hatred if Ray had been insane or had some other serious psychological problem. "Now if he was an insane person—he's not insane. If he were suffering from some degree of schizophrenia, or paranoid, or psychotic—maybe. But he's not a person like that. He's just a nitwit, two-bit felon, that's all."[63]

In the early 1980s, Harry Avery privately expressed skepticism that Ray was even the triggerman.

Retired prison warden Stonney R. Lane doesn't like talking about his most famous prisoner, James Earl Ray—perhaps because Ray escaped from his prison while he was on vacation at the beach. Lane refused to speak in detail about Ray other than to confirm that he considered Ray to be a quiet prisoner who got along with the other prisoners and caused no problems, racial or otherwise.

Lane was not Ray's only prison warden who did not believe he was a racist. Harold R. Swenson was retired from his position as warden of the Missouri State Prison when he was interviewed by HSCA staff investigators in 1977. A summary of that interview dated June 7, 1977, was introduced as evidence during the HSCA hearings and was available to committee members, but the file containing the interview notes (MLK Document 230037) is sealed until the year 2029. Fortunately, a reporter for the Associated Press spoke to Swenson the following day, and Swenson told the reporter the gist of his interview statement: "I never had any reason to believe he [Ray] was a racist," Swenson said, "but there are some things you may not know of course."[64] In 1968, when Ray was still on the lam and his identity had just been confirmed by the FBI, Swenson told the *New York Times* that Ray's record behind bars was "innocuous" and that his work reports in prison food service were "pretty good."[65]

Ray's original attorney, Arthur Hanes Jr., along with his father, former Birmingham, Alabama, mayor Arthur Hanes Sr., were contacted and asked to represent Ray by his London barrister, Michael Eugene, while Ray was still in an English jail prior to extradition to the United States. Hanes spent literally "hundreds of hours" interviewing Ray in preparation for trial and attempted to provoke Ray into blurting out an admission of hatred for King. "We tried everything we could think of, ranging from the extremes of Dr. King was a great American and whoever killed him should get the electric chair, to the other end, of what an evil menace he was and he deserved to die," Hanes said. The result was "nothing" of a racist nature out of Ray. Hanes reflected, "The King issue, that just wasn't on James Earl Ray's radar screen. . . . And believe me, we tried everything we could to get some kind of reaction out of him—nothing, ever."[66]

CONCLUSION

The HSCA investigation started and ended with the presumption that James Earl Ray's confession was truthful, accurate, voluntary, and not made under duress—that he alone assassinated King.

Ray was not an un-American, pro-Nazi, Hitler sympathizer as McMillan alleges. He was not active in any sort of politics, American or otherwise. There is no evidence to suggest that any sort of racial

Arthur Hanes Jr. (Courtesy author's collection)

prejudice or any aspect of the civil rights movement was the precursor to violent behavior seething just beneath the surface.

The widespread attempt to portray James Earl Ray as a man with a self-imposed duty to silence King due to racist tendencies does not hold up under close investigation. Memphis police didn't even know where King was going to stay—so how would James Earl Ray have figured it out?

One remaining possible motive—money—people dare not whisper because money means conspiracy—and conspiracy begs the question: Who wanted Rev. Martin Luther King Jr. dead? And furthermore, who then put up the money to "educate the public" that Ray had committed the murder out of sheer racial hatred?

The HSCA suggested the possibility of conspiracy. The final report attempted to finesse this issue by simply stating that James Earl Ray thought he would get paid to murder King—by someone, somewhere:

> In conclusion, the committee's investigation of Ray's motive revealed that while Ray's general lack of sympathy for Blacks or the civil rights movement would have allowed him to commit the assassination without qualms, his act did not stem from racism alone. The committee was convinced that while Ray's decision to assassinate Dr. King may have reflected a desire to participate in an important crime, his predominant motive lay in an expectation of monetary gain.[67]

So, the HSCA concluded that money was the likely motive behind King's assassination without ever identifying whose money it was and how Ray might have acquired it. After dissecting every aspect and detail of James Earl Ray's life—after considering the racial hyperbole of McMillan—the best the committee could do is say that Ray had a general lack of sympathy for the civil rights movement. Without the ability to establish a racist motive, the HSCA claimed that Ray thought he would get paid if he murdered King but didn't really know how much, when, where, or from whom he would get the cash.

The HSCA described the eleven-month period prior to King's assassination as the very best year of James Earl Ray's life without credibly identifying any crimes he committed that could have financed his lifestyle. HSCA investigators "traced Ray's steps over a worldwide path" without solving the question about how he got the money he lived on for those fifteen months.[68]

Several people who spent time with Ray and knew him personally (or at least met him several times) doubt Ray's guilt or discount it altogether. And no wonder: the physical evidence against James Earl Ray is exceedingly poor, and a racial motive is non-existent because Ray did not make overtly racist statements, even when provoked.

For many people, accepting the image of Ray as overcome with racist feelings soothes some troubled minds. But those feelings are not corroborated by hard evidence.

PART TWO: THE CONTEXT

CHAPTER 4
James Earl Ray and the US Intelligence Community

The connections to the assassination case of Rev. Martin Luther King Jr. among the various agencies of the US intelligence community are as mind-boggling as they are voluminous. Every thread in the fabric of these agencies' interest in James Earl Ray and Martin Luther King weaves a complex tapestry. Everywhere in this history is some agent of the CIA or its sister organizations in the US Army and Navy and the FBI. This great cloud of intelligence agents was not merely interested in the Ray case but also knew each other personally and shared intelligence responsibilities and duties. Their presence surrounding Ray is a strong suggestion of involvement in the plot to assassinate King.

Tellingly, of the most well-documented facts about the intelligence community's interest in James Earl Ray is whether or not he would succeed in obtaining a full trial. The CIA monitored this situation by opening a 201 (person of interest) file on April 18, 1968, under Ray's alias Eric S. Galt. Four days later, the name of the file was changed to James Earl Ray. The CIA agent who opened the 201 file was Richard Ober, the number two man in the CIA Office of Counterintelligence (CI), headed at the time by legendary counterintelligence agent James Jesus Angleton. Ober was a heavyweight at the CIA, and the case surrounding James Earl Ray begins with him.

RICHARD OBER, CIA COUNTERINTELLIGENCE OFFICER, AND OPERATION CHAOS

Ober was born in 1921 and graduated from Harvard *summa cum laude* in 1943. After Harvard, Ober joined the Office of Strategic Services (OSS), a predecessor of the CIA. In the OSS, Ober met Harvard law graduate James Jesus Angleton, for whom Ober worked as a CI officer for almost three decades.[1]

Ober is the highest-level CIA officer known to maintain a file on James

Earl Ray. When the CIA's 201 file was declassified and released in 1994, it was marked "MATERIAL REVIEWED AT CIA HEADQUARTERS BY HOUSE SELECT COMMITTEE ON ASSASSINATIONS STAFF MEMBERS."[2] The HSCA *Final Report* does not indicate whether the file was reviewed in full or redacted for the committee.[3]

The CIA's attempt to explain why Ober opened the 201 file on Ray raises troubling questions. The routing slip for volume III of the CIA's file on James Earl Ray states in the "remarks" section:

> Our files on Martin Luther King reveal that after King's killing that an attempt was made to locate James Earl Ray in various countries where it was suspected he might have fled. There is no written request from the FBI to do this but Mr. Ober had a number of conversations with Mr. Papich of the FBI, which are referred to in our files. It would be reasonable to conclude that our effort to locate Ray was done in close coordination with the FBI and probably at the FBI's specific request. A check of our files after the killing revealed nothing on Ray prior to the killing of King.[4]

Ray's 201 file of the CIA (Courtesy National Archives and Records Administration)

The statement appears to have the initials "JR" scribbled at the bottom, presumably belonging to John Reagan, a CIA official. Nothing is mentioned about volumes I and II of this file.

The "Mr. Papich" referred to as having a number of conversations

APPROVED FOR RELEASE 1994
CIA HISTORICAL REVIEW PROGRAM

The routing slip of James Earl Ray's CIA 201 file (Courtesy National Archives and Records Administration)

with Ober is FBI special agent Sam J. Papich. In the 1960s and 1970s, Papich was another heavyweight in the CI division of the US intelligence community, and he had direct access to FBI director J. Edgar Hoover.[5]

The CIA claims that Ober opened the file on Ray in an effort to locate him "in various countries where it was suspected he might have fled." This is a disingenuous if not deliberately false explanation, as the file was nothing more than newspaper clippings of the progress of Ray's effort to gain a full trial. It had nothing to do with the effort to capture James Earl Ray. Why would the FBI ask CIA CI to help them find Ray? The job of CI is to guard against penetration of the US intelligence agencies by hostile governments, not to find fugitives.

What security interest did Ober and the CIA have in James Earl Ray's appeals process? There does not seem to be legitimate interest— but as far as the record indicates, neither G. Robert Blakey nor anyone on his HSCA staff ever asked that question. It is likely that Ober was concerned that someone's cover might be blown if Ray got a full trial and evidence was examined in open court. The effort to ensure that there would be no real trial and thus no examined evidence was the same concern expressed by the staff of Tennessee governor Buford Ellington, as commissioner of correction Harry S. Avery overheard in a conversation in the governor's office.

Was the CIA concerned that Ray might be a national security risk? Obviously not. But it speaks volumes that Ober and the CIA had no documented effort to find Ray when he was a fugitive from justice but a great deal of interest and concern as to whether Ray might get a full trial.

Nowhere in the HSCA *Final Report* are the contents of Ray's CIA file or even its existence mentioned. The CIA's interest in whether James Earl Ray got a full trial apparently was never questioned by HSCA investigators.

In addition to opening the 201 file on Ray, Ober was in charge of the day-to-day management of one of the largest domestic spying programs ever conducted by the US government on its own citizens within its own borders.

Ober was picked to manage the CIA's Special Operations Group (or Operation MHCHAOS as it was known) by his boss, James Jesus Angleton. The letters "MH" are a prefix that classifies it as a worldwide operation, but it commonly was referred to simply as CHAOS. Ober led

CHAOS from its inception in 1967 to its termination in 1973. At its peak, CHAOS involved sixty agents. In December 1974, the *New York Times* exposed its existence; Angleton was forced to retire and Ober was reassigned to the National Security Agency.

The mission of Operation CHAOS "was to gather and evaluate all available information about foreign links to racial, antiwar, and other protest activity in the United States."[6] Counterintelligence investigations of this type generate databases that consist of the names and background information of Americans and aliens of interest. Ober testified before the Rockefeller Commission that no detail is too small to be irrelevant when obtaining background information on American citizens or others of interest. During that period, special emphasis was placed on activities that could have disrupted government goals in Vietnam, including anti-war and civil rights efforts. Ober told the Rockefeller Commission that all "tidbits" of information that could be obtained on Americans, whether or not they are suspected of anything, are needed to understand a potential threat: "I think that it is significant in any counterintelligence operations, that the meaning of information in the abstract, it is very difficult to determine. You have to measure it against other information and put it into context."[7] This is CIA talk meaning that no personal, medical, financial, political, social, religious, educational, sexual, or business information about a person is off limits. The CIA believed that it could not construct a proper scenario involving a citizen unless it gathered every detail about that person's life. It was Ober's job to do so.

It was Sam Papich's role as FBI liaison to Richard Ober's CI team to ensure that the CIA received all information that other domestic government agencies and departments shared with the FBI.

Operation CHAOS gave Ober the tools to monitor Ray and his requests for a full trial. As the CIA agent in charge of the day-to-day operation of Operation CHAOS he had the position, organization, resources, mind-set, and capability to uncover any information necessary—and he believed he had the authority to do so. He made it his business to know whatever he wanted to know about any American he chose, and it was special agent Sam Papich's job to make sure the FBI cooperated. With this wealth of information under his fingers, Ober had everything he needed to know about both King and Ray.

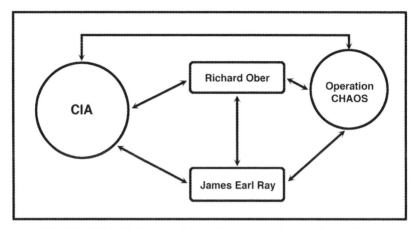

The CIA, CHAOS, Ober, and Ray (Courtesy author's collection)

JAMES JESUS ANGLETON, THE CIA'S NUMBER ONE COUNTERINTELLIGENCE OFFICER

James Jesus Angleton was born in Boise, Idaho, in 1917. He entered Yale University in 1937.[8] After graduating from Harvard law school in 1944, he was recruited to the Office of Strategic Services (OSS). With OSS, Angleton worked in the top secret X-2 counterintelligence (CI) office in London. X-2 was the only OSS organization that was cleared to receive raw data intercepted from the captured German encryption machine Enigma. Angleton worked for the CIA from its creation in 1947 until his forced retirement in 1974. In 1947, he became the CIA's liaison to counterpart security agencies with other Western nations. This gave Angleton extraordinary access to security data, including personnel files in other Western powers such as Canada. As the CIA's number one CI officer, Angleton also was allowed to keep extensive files outside of the CIA's regular document control system.[9]

Angleton's most notable spy cases (of the public's knowledge) involve two Soviet KGB agents. Angleton was responsible for the detection and capture of KGB colonel Rudolf Abel in 1957 and the interrogation and detention for three years of Yuri Nosenko, another KGB officer who defected in 1964. In 1962, Angleton traded Abel for CIA pilot Francis Gary Powers, whose secret U-2 surveillance plane had been shot down in Soviet Union airspace in 1960.

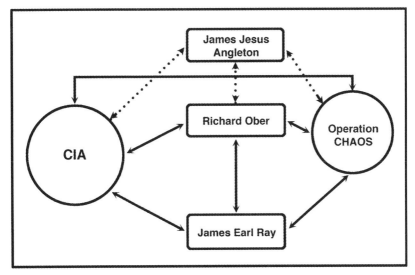

The CIA, CHAOS, Angleton, Ober, and Ray (Courtesy author's collection)

Based on his answers, Angleton most likely provided Ray's Canadian aliases.

CIA CONNECTIONS OF RAY'S FIRST BIOGRAPHER, WILLIAM BRADFORD HUIE

William Bradford Huie was Ray's original literary agent who owned the rights to James Earl Ray's story. After Arthur Hanes Jr. and his father agreed to represent Ray, Huie contacted them wanting exclusive access to Ray and his story. Huie was a prominent writer from Alabama who had a national audience from his novels, magazine articles, television appearances, and news coverage of the civil rights movement in prominent national publications. "He wanted in on it, and we for various reasons thought he would be the best one," Hanes said. Ray was being vilified by the national news media during the summer of 1968, and Huie was able to get some "good sympathetic publicity for James Earl Ray" through *Look* magazine.[10]

These events led to the three-party contract that called for Huie to write the James Earl Ray story as "They Slew the Dreamer." But when Huie's book was published in 1970, the title had become *He Slew the Dreamer*—an important alteration.

Huie's professional connections to the CIA were numerous and varied. Perhaps the best known connection was through William F. Buckley Jr. From 1951 to 1952, Buckley served in the CIA's Mexico City station under E. Howard Hunt (destined to become a household name in the infamy of the Watergate scandal). Huie hired Buckley to the staff of *The American Mercury* once he left the CIA. Under Huie and Buckley, *The American Mercury* became something of a CIA "rag," publishing numerous articles and book reviews by individuals who were CIA consultants, members of CIA front organizations, and out-and-out CIA agents. It would have been impossible for Huie not to be aware of at least some of these CIA connections, even though they were never attributed in any of the articles. CIA front men or agents were simply referred to as university professors or authors. Huie's CIA-related contributors at *The American Mercury* included Sidney Hook, who helped found two CIA front groups, the Congress for Cultural Freedom and the American Committee for Cultural Freedom; CIA employee James Burnham; Max Eastman, a friend of Burnham and also an influential member of the American Committee for Cultural Freedom; and William Phillips.[11]

Additionally, Huie had extensive intelligence contacts from a

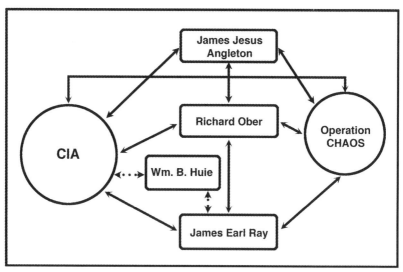

The CIA, CHAOS, Angleton, Ober, Huie, and Ray (Courtesy author's collection)

television-interview program he frequently co-hosted from 1951 to 1955 called the *Longines Chronoscope. Chronoscope* was broadcast on CBS-affiliate stations during a time when the integrity of the network was thoroughly compromised under the CIA's Operation MOCKINGBIRD. During this period, his co-host on fourteen programs was Donald I. Rogers, financial editor of the *New York Herald Tribune,* another news outlet compromised by Operation MOCKINGBIRD. Max Eastman also co-hosted one of the programs. A co-host of eighteen programs was Elliott Haynes, who, along with his father Eldridge Haynes, founded Business International Corporation (BIC) in 1953.[12] BIC was a CIA front organization.[13]

With this background, Huie had numerous connections that could have influenced his work with James Earl Ray.

GEORGE MCMILLAN, PROPAGANDA WRITER, REPORTER, AUTHOR, AND *FBI* NATIONAL ACADEMY GRADUATE

George E. McMillan was born in Knoxville, Tennessee, on March 11, 1913. After the US entered World War II, he worked for the news bureau of the Office of War Information (OWI), the government's war propaganda department. OWI and the OSS were the predecessor organizations of the CIA. In 1943, he joined the US Marines and served as a combat correspondent in the Pacific Theatre. This led to McMillan's first book, *The Old Breed,* a history of the First Marine Division, in which he served. Following the publication of his book, McMillan was awarded a Guggenheim Fellowship in 1950. The fellowship recognized McMillan's arrival as an establishment writer.

In the 1960s, McMillan's stature as a well-known writer was sufficient to garner a spot in the FBI's invitation-only National Academy, a training and indoctrination program for high-profile civilians.[14] There is also evidence that the FBI fed documents to McMillan. A 1969 memo from Cartha DeLoach, the number three man at the FBI at the time, indicated having passed on certain documents to McMillan.[15]

In 1965, McMillan married fellow author and propagandist Priscilla Post Johnson, who worked extensively with the CIA. The couple moved to Cambridge, Massachusetts, in the early 1970s, and each wrote a book on the most infamous assassins of the twentieth century: George on James Earl Ray in 1976 and Priscilla on Lee Harvey Oswald in 1977.

George McMillan at the Office of War Information news bureau in 1943, handing out material to the press (Courtesy Library of Congress)

Both books assert a "lone assassin" theory. Both books presume guilt of the alleged assassin without question and neither book addresses physical evidence. Both books present damning accusations about the assassins' motives, ostensibly as told to the authors by the assassins' family members. McMillan's most inflammatory allegations against Ray were told to him by Ray's brothers—though Ray's brothers deny they ever told McMillan any such stories. Jerry Ray told me that he often deliberately misled Georgie-pie (as he nicknamed him) because he sensed from the start that McMillan was no friend of his brother. Plus, McMillan had a generous expense allowance, and Jerry Ray tried to get as much as possible.[16] McMillan's book certainly seems to have been written to nail shut James Earl Ray's legal coffin and deliberately prejudice his effort to get the full trial he sought.

In 1969, before he started work on the book, McMillan told Jeremiah O'Leary of the *Washington Star* that he did not plan to investigate the King assassination. Rather, he planned to focus on Ray's life.[17] For whatever reason, perhaps at the suggestions of others, the book morphed into a huge denial of conspiracy that advocated an overwhelming racial motive and ignored the physical evidence as if those items were irrelevant artifacts. Suffice it to say that the 1978 HSCA investigation into the King assassination took some cues from the elaborate but flimsy accusations in McMillan's book but was unable to substantiate any of those allegations.

McMillan's intent seems to have been to poison the American public's attitude toward James Earl Ray—to transform him from a man into an inanimate symbol of evil: Ray, the racist who murdered the man who would make blacks equal to whites. Between McMillan, Posner, and Sides, Ray was characterized with just about every epithet and socially abominable label they could think of: racist, anti-Semite, Hitler sympathizer, jailhouse dope addict and pusher, homophobe, homosexual, bi-sexual, Rhodesia supporter, apartheid supporter, George Wallace supporter, half-wit, pro-KKK, neo-Confederate, and ultra-right wing gun-nut who was fascinated with pornography.

McMillan also publicly denounced the HSCA's investigation before it got started and wrote an op-ed in the *New York Times,* criticizing it as a waste of time and money. The article introduced the term "assassinologist" to label anyone who questioned the preconceived lone gunman theories about Lee Harvey Oswald and James Earl Ray.[18]

Similarly, in a laudatory review of McMillan's *The Making of an Assassin,* O'Leary wrote that McMillan had already "done a good deal of the committee's work," and his book affirms that "the world knows all there is to know" about James Earl Ray as King's murderer.[19] The very next year, O'Leary was outed as a CIA collaborator by the *Washington Post.*[20] In any case, McMillan's book became the centerpiece of HSCA efforts, as the book was released just before the committee launched.

PRISCILLA POST JOHNSON MCMILLAN, REPORTER, AUTHOR, AND CIA COLLABORATOR

Priscilla Mary Post Johnson McMillan worked on the staff of Sen. John F. Kennedy in the early 1950s and interviewed Lee Harvey Oswald, who, as a nineteen-year-old US Marine in Moscow, apparently attempted to defect to the Soviet Union in 1959. Johnson McMillan is the only evidenced individual who personally knew both Kennedy and Oswald before Kennedy's assassination in 1963.

Priscilla Post Johnson McMillan and husband George McMillan occupied an extraordinary position during the HSCA investigations. George avoided sworn testimony before the HSCA, even as his book served as their primer for the investigation into King's assassination. Priscilla was required to testify under oath in the investigation of the assassination of President Kennedy. Her testimony was classified and remains sealed until 2029. Because Oswald is dead, her word is all there is to confirm what she and Oswald discussed in Moscow four years before Kennedy was assassinated in Dallas and even that such an interview actually took place. Johnson McMillan was an employee of the North American Newspaper Alliance (NANA) when she traveled to the Soviet Union to interview Oswald. At best, NANA has a checkered past when it comes to providing cover to intelligence agents posing as reporters. NANA's owner, Ernest L. Cuneo, served in the OSS during World War II and was the liaison officer between OSS, the White House, the FBI, and British intelligence.[21]

While an undergraduate student in the late 1940s, Johnson McMillan joined United World Federalists (UWF), a one-world-government organization headed by Cord Meyer Jr., who served on Harold Stassen's staff at the United Nations (UN) organizational meeting in San Francisco in 1945. Alan Dulles recruited Cord Meyer to the CIA in 1949. After completing his PhD in history at Harvard in 1951, he became the principal operative of Operation MOCKINGBIRD.[22]

MOCKINGBIRD was a CIA propaganda project aimed at recruiting and paying individual journalists in all forms of media to skew their stories. MOCKINGBIRD also set out to compromise whole news organizations and outlets, including the American Broadcasting Company (ABC), Columbia Broadcasting System (CBS), and the National Broadcasting Company (NBC). At the height of MOCKINGBIRD's success, some four hundred journalists were on the CIA payroll to slant the news in such ways as the CIA instructed.[23]

In 1979, the HSCA *Final Report* noted that Johnson McMillan stated "she had never worked for the CIA, nor had she been connected with any other Federal Government agency at the time of her interview with Oswald." HSCA investigators reviewed CIA files and concluded, "There was no indication in these files suggesting that she had ever worked for the CIA."[24]

However, there were a number of situations, such as Johnson McMillan's 1952 application for a job at the CIA as an intelligence analyst, that the HSCA or Johnson McMillan simply explained away. She does admit being debriefed by the CIA in 1962 upon return from a trip to the Soviet Union. In addition, it is possible that the consular official in the US Embassy in Moscow who handled the Oswald case, Richard E. Snyder, was a CIA covert agent at the time. It was one of Snyder's direct embassy subordinates who suggested Johnson McMillan interview Oswald.[25]

There is some likelihood that Oswald was one of Angleton's fake defectors operating out of the Office of Naval Intelligence. Former Pennsylvania senator Richard Schweiker, a member of the 1975 Church committee, had access to documents that no one outside the CIA has ever been allowed to see, concluded that Oswald "was the product of a fake defector program run by the CIA."[26]

In more recent years, a great deal of direct evidence has surfaced that casts doubt on Johnson McMillan's denials of involvement with the CIA. Anthony and Robbyn Summers published a 1994 investigative story in which they revealed their review of a 1975 CIA document that listed Johnson McMillan as "Witting Collaborator OI, code A1" and described her as "a promising source."[27] In 2008, former Army Intelligence officer John Newman unearthed additional evidence of Johnson McMillan's CIA connections in a file released in 1994 that appears to be the cancellation of a request for a CIA security clearance. A related document identifies Priscilla Johnson by name, and says "the request for clearance was canceled according to [one or two words redacted] memorandum date 27 June 1958."[28]

Over a thirteen-year period, from 1956 to 1969, the CIA generated at least nineteen separate files or memoranda about Johnson McMillan in addition to her 1952 employment application.[29] Johnson McMillan repeated her denial of association with the CIA in email messages to the author but said that she "knowingly talked to a CIA official only once, Donald Jameson in the fall of '62."[30] Jameson evaluated Johnson McMillan in 1962 and noted that she "can be encouraged to write pretty much the articles we want."[31]

Additional telltale evidence of Johnson McMillan's ties to US intelligence work is found in an excerpt from a 1963 evaluation of Lee Harvey Oswald's address book by the FBI, in which Johnson McMillan's name is listed alongside that of another CIA agent, Richard C. Jacob. Both names were written in a sort of Russian/English code, the English equivalent of which read "Dzhonson, Prestsilla" and "Dzhekob, R."

In 1978, Bruce L. Solie gave secret testimony to the HSCA, identifying himself as a longtime CIA agent working for Angleton's CI. He stated that although Johnson McMillan was "compromised," "she did not compromise herself."[32]

All around Priscilla Johnson McMillan are connections to specific CIA agents and operations: Meyer, Snyder, Jameson, Jacob, Solie, MOCKINGBIRD, and Cuneo, her employer. There is a clutch of CIA documents on Johnson McMillan stretching from her application of employment in 1952 to 1969.

Furthermore, that both she and her husband would publish books in subsequent years on the assassins of the century seems more than merely coincidental. That the two books share the same modus operandi and the conclusion of the government's near-instantaneous solving of both crimes is even more suspect. There is no way of knowing whether either actually took payment from CIA as part of Operation

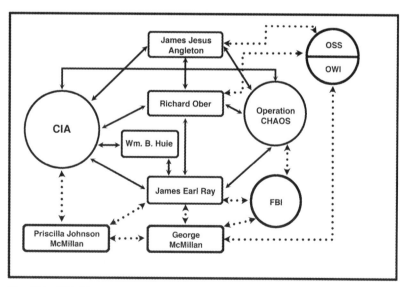

The CIA, CHAOS, Angleton, Ober, Huie, McMillan, Johnson McMillan, the OSS/ OWI, the FBI, and Ray (Courtesy author's collection)

MOCKINGBIRD, but their work is clearly in agreement with the official narrative on both Oswald and James Earl Ray. One author claims that Johnson McMillan's $100,000 book advance in 1964—thirteen years before her book was actually published—"was just a part of a series of CIA payoffs to Priscilla Johnson."[33] Her brushes with the CIA—or at the very least, CIA affiliates—are documented in NARA records: cold, hard evidence.

BERNARD FENSTERWALD JR. AND HIS CONNECTIONS TO THE CIA

Bernard Fensterwald Jr. served as James Earl Ray's attorney for a critical six-year period beginning around 1972. It was during this period that significant progress was made in the appeal process to get Ray a full trial. Fensterwald's connection to and relationship with the CIA raises questions as to how independent and complete his representation of James Earl Ray actually was, considering the CIA's interest in whether Ray was to get a full trial. Additionally, many of the CIA operatives and characters in Bernard Fensterwald's world, as with other individuals around James Earl Ray, have important connections to each other as well as to Ray. Fensterwald's representation of Ray also overlapped with the first couple of years of the HSCA investigation.

In the 1950s, Fensterwald worked in various positions, including as a staff member on investigative committees for US senator from Tennessee Estes Kefauver. He was also Kefauver's speechwriter during the 1956 presidential campaign, when Kefauver was Gov. Adlai E. Stevenson's vice-presidential running mate.

In spite of Fensterwald's refusal to accept the conclusions of the Warren Commission that Lee Harvey Oswald was the lone gunman in the JFK assassination, there was well-known speculation about his association with the CIA. When he died in 1991, the *Washington Post* raised the question of Fensterwald's association with the CIA in his obituary: "It was suggested from time to time that he worked for the CIA, and he seemed to relish the air of mystery that this created." The newspaper reported that when Fensterwald was asked about his involvement with the CIA, he answered "with vague statements" rather than a flat denial and that there was "no evidence" he was connected to the CIA.[34]

However, Fensterwald represented at least three CIA agents, former agents and/or employees, a State Department national security official, and one prominent journalist thought to be associated with the CIA in some manner. It is important to understand that when a CIA agent is called to testify before an investigating committee of Congress or is on trial for criminal activity associated with his/her official duties, that agent must hire a lawyer "acceptable" to the CIA. The CIA has the final say in who legally represented its agents. If only "acceptable" lawyers are allowed, it follows that some lawyers are unacceptable. It follows also that lawyers who want to represent CIA agents are required to accommodate the CIA as well as their clients. It also potentially compromises the ethics of every lawyer who participates in this system—and Bernard Fensterwald Jr. participated.

His most well known case was the representation of James W. McCord Jr., one of the Watergate burglars. Two other CIA agents whom Fensterwald represented include Richard Case Nagell and Maryann Paisley, wife of John Arthur Paisley, a CIA agent and a neighbor and lifelong friend of Fensterwald. At one point, Fensterwald represented Otto Otepka, the chief security officer for the State Department who studied American defectors to the Soviet Union, including Lee Harvey Oswald.[35] Fensterwald also represented Mitchell WerBell III, a former OSS agent who worked alongside E. Howard Hunt during World War II.[36] Another Fensterwald client was the journalist Andrew St. George, who published the first American interview of Fidel Castro in 1957. St. George's "rubbing of elbows with intelligence types led New Left conspiracy theorists to conclude that he worked for the CIA."[37]

Are all these relationships by and among Fensterwald's friends, associates, and clients random and meaningless? Was it merely a function of his high-profile law career? Is this web of CIA agents in which Fensterwald was tangled simply coincidence?

At the heart of it is Richard Ober and his 201 file on James Earl Ray that includes nothing other than press clippings about Ray's attempt to get a full trial.

It is impossible to know whether there was substance to Fensterwald's failure to deny his direct involvement with the CIA. If he was, his involvement as James Earl Ray's legal counsel could have been a deliberately managed maneuver by the agency to place him into a position to subvert the effort to have the guilty plea set aside should a federal court have appeared on the brink of ordering a full trial.

WHAT IS THE MEANING OF THE CIA CONNECTIONS?

The CIA had quite a lot of interest in James Earl Ray. The agency opened a 201 file on Ray when he was on the lam following King's assassination. The explanation given as to why the CIA opened that file was false and misleading. The CIA reported that the FBI "probably" asked for help in locating Ray overseas, to where it was suspected he fled. This explanation has the looks of placing their involvement on the FBI's shoulders. Whether or not the FBI asked for help, the contents of the CIA's file don't remotely support this explanation.

It is clear also that the CIA file was not opened as a routine request of some low-level federal functionary. The file was opened by Richard Ober, a relatively senior-level CIA officer who ran Operation CHAOS—the largest and most extensive domestic spy

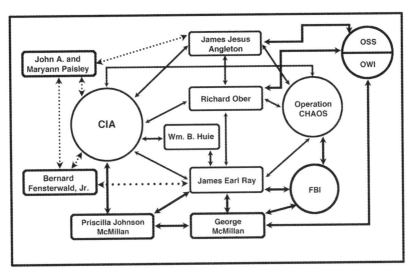

The cloud of government-affiliated people surrounding Ray (Courtesy author's collection)

program in public knowledge. Operation CHAOS had the ear and the attention of two presidents. Furthermore, Ober reported to Angleton, the powerful number-one man in charge of counterintelligence.

In addition to the CIA's direct interest in Ray, there is a web of CIA agents and collaborators who indirectly surrounded Ray. Those who wrote about Ray as well as Ray's own attorneys had extensive and suspiciously close degrees of separation from each other, the CIA, and agents Ober and Angleton.

The cloud of CIA agents around James Earl Ray—those who wrote about him, those who represented him in court, and even his jailers—is simply too extensive and too complete to dismiss as mere coincidence or irrelevance.

Furthermore, the CIA's sole documented interest in James Earl Ray—whether he would get a full trial, as evidenced by the contents of his 201 file—coincides with the interest Governor Ellington's office of coercing him into pleading guilty from the start, as expressed to the US Justice Department.

If government authorities were afraid that their flimsy evidence against Ray might fail the test of a full and fair trial in 1969, they were equally alarmed in subsequent decades and equally dedicated to ensure that this would never happen.

The existence of intelligence community's activities after the assassination to influence public opinion about the crime suggests the US intelligence community's involvement in the event from its initiation. Harry Avery's words are particularly resonant: "Somewhere in the background there were finances being put up to educate the public to believe that James Earl Ray just killed Martin Luther King on his own because he was a racist. That's so silly to me, based on my experiences of life, that it's repulsive to even think about."[38]

CHAPTER 5
The US Army and the Civil Rights Movement

In the 1960s, as manpower needs for the war in Vietnam were ramping up, the commanders of the United States Army feared Rev. Martin Luther King Jr. for what he could have said to two specific groups of the population: black soldiers in uniform and black youths about to turn eighteen and face mandatory registration for military draft.

Army commanders feared chaos in the ranks if King were to pronounce the war immoral and tell black soldiers to lay down their weapons and ignore orders. This would have re-segregated the armed forces along racial lines in terms of who fought whose battles.

An even more volatile scenario to both Army and civilian leadership was the upheaval that would result if King were to tell black youths to ignore draft registration and induction notices. This would have instantly shifted the burden of high manpower quotas throughout the nation to an all-white affair, potentially plunging the nation into divisive social bedlam.

And what did the Army do to keep abreast of these potential scenarios? It did what it had done in decades past: commissioned its own military to spy on American civilians.

The Army knew that the CIA was already spying on Americans through Operation CHAOS and that the FBI was spying on Americans through their own COINTELPRO. The Army decided to initiate its own domestic espionage program and eventually created "literally millions of dossiers" on Americans, leading North Carolina senator Sam Ervin to comment that the indiscriminate spying was as obviously unconstitutional "as the noonday sun in a cloudless sky."[1]

Decades earlier, during World War I, the Army spied on King's maternal grandfather, Rev. Adam Daniel Williams, who was pastor of the Ebenezer Baptist Church in Atlanta, fearing he was a subversive. During World War II, King's father, Rev. Martin Luther King Sr., was also a person of interest to Army intelligence agents. The government spied on the King family for at least three generations.

In the 1960s, it seemed that all branches of the military were spying on everyone. Some instances of spying are humorous in hindsight, such as candlelight peace vigils sponsored by church-affiliated colleges in Illinois. In Mississippi, agents of the 111th Military Intelligence Group (MIG) from Fort McPherson, Georgia, rented a pick-up truck and shadowed James Meredith's March Against Fear.

That same MIG unit was stationed in Memphis on April 3 and 4, 1968, quietly monitoring King's movements the day he was assassinated. The Army denied its presence in Memphis that day until a 1993 investigative story by Stephen G. Tompkins of the *Memphis Commercial Appeal* blew the story wide open.[2] Later, the Army tried to discredit the story by saying the newspaper "misinterpreted" the secret mission of its plainclothes men in Memphis that day.[3]

Considering the scope and breadth of Army espionage related to King—including waiting around his grave to hear what mourners said, listening in on conversations in his church office, and bugging motel rooms—it's insulting for the Army to suggest that its agents were in Memphis for reasons other than spying on King.

DOMESTIC SPYING IN THE 1960S

The Army's 1960s-era domestic spying on racial conflict in the South was first suggested by Maj. Gen. Creighton Williams Abrams Jr. In a detailed, eleven-page memorandum to Army chief of staff Gen. Earle G. Wheeler, Abrams recommended the need for intelligence to support "efforts to obtain equal rights and opportunities for Negro citizens and how the Army can best organize and function to accomplish that mission."

Abrams wrote the memo from Birmingham, Alabama, in May 1963, while his 101st Airborne troops were in the field in Oxford. He noted that in the previous six years, the Army had been called upon several times "to intervene or to prepare to intervene in a Negro civil rights situation." Each time, Abrams wrote, the Army cobbled together an "ad hoc organization, hastily improvised" without adequate intelligence or preparation. This type of Army response was wasteful and "potentially dangerous." (It is not clear whether Abrams believed the danger was to troops, civilians, or both).

Abrams recommended:

> We in the Army should launch a major intelligence project without delay, to identify personalities, both black and white, develop analyses of the various civil rights situations in which they may become involved, and establish a civil rights intelligence center to operate on a continuing basis and keep abreast of the current situation throughout the United States, directing collecting activities and collating and evaluating the product. Based upon this Army intelligence effort, the Army can more precisely determine the organization and forces and operation techniques ideal for each.[4]

Almost immediately, and apparently without waiting for authorization or orders, Abrams commenced his program of domestic surveillance, headquartered at Fort McPherson. Historian Joan M. Jensen recorded that Wheeler never officially approved Abrams's intelligence project, but neither did he curtail it.[5] The Army simply looked the other way until 1970, when a former Army captain, Christopher Pyle, went public, and Senator Ervin's subcommittee took note.

However, it is challenging to believe that top army brass was unaware of Abrams's efforts. First, Abrams put his recommendation in writing to Wheeler. It seems unlikely that such a detailed memo from a high-ranking general officer would go without discussion, much less any response. As Abrams had already implemented it, his commanders would have been faced with the decision of shutting it down, taking it away from him, or leaving it alone and letting him run it in accordance with Army regulation.

The Abrams initiative became known as an "early warning system," intended to give the Army a heads-up assessment for pending domestic deployment of troops to quell "ghetto riots" in big cities (mostly in the west and north) and enforce federal court orders on matters of civil rights (mostly in the South). By 1973, the Senate Judiciary Subcommittee on Constitutional Rights noted, "there is no indication that the intelligence was ever actually used in this way [pursuant to an early warning of deployment].[6]

In fact, the Army's domestic surveillance program was much like those of the CIA and FBI. They each treated King, the civil rights movement, black militancy, white supremacist groups, the Ku Klux Klan, and everyone who had contact with these groups as suspects.

After the Detroit riot of 1967, President Johnson's liaison to local officials, Cyrus Vance, issued a report that included the following recommendations: "The assembly and analysis of data with respect to activity patterns is also needed. I believe that it would be useful to assemble such data for Detroit, Newark, Milwaukee, Watts, etc. There may be 'indicator' incidents; there may be typical patterns of spread; there may be a natural sequence in the order in which several types of incidents occur. All of this should be studied."[7]

The job fell to the US Army to undertake the studies recommended by Vance. The Counterintelligence Analysis Branch (CIAB) in the Office of the Assistant Chief of Staff for Intelligence (OACSI) was directed to develop what the military bureaucracy cryptically called "elements of information," or EEIs, regarding ghetto riots. The Army's analysis of the intelligence was that "the assumption that ghetto riots were likely . . . caused by conspiracies." These conspiracies and conspirators also included those who were "behind or involved in mass demonstrations."[8]

The counter-insurgency theory was the ultimate justification for military spying on civilians. In reviewing notes about the Detroit riot of 1967, Gen. William P. Yarborough, the assistant chief of staff for intelligence, famously made the comment to his staff, "Men, get out your counter-insurgency manuals. We have an insurgency on our hands." Senator Ervin's subcommittee concluded that Yarborough "was wrong in that assessment."[9]

The longer these surveillance programs ran, the bigger the files and the more expansive the list of suspects and suspect groups became. As the Army discovered interaction between suspect groups and non-suspect groups or organizations, it simply added the previously non-suspect group to its records. The same is true for CIA and FBI operations.

Based on testimony, intelligence reports, and other evidence examined by the Senate Subcommittee on Constitutional Rights in 1973, ". . . no demonstration was too small or too peaceful to merit direct or indirect monitoring. No church meeting was too sacred and no political gathering too sensitive to be declared off limits. The picture is that of a runaway intelligence bureaucracy unwatched by its civilian superiors, eagerly grasping for information about political dissenters of all kinds and totally oblivious to the impact its spying could have on the constitutional liberties it had sworn to defend."[10]

Essentially, the subcommittee found that the military oath to protect and defend constitutional rights from all foreign and domestic enemies had been abused and disregarded by top commanders. The subcommittee, however, was engaged in a war of words, and nothing more than a stern admonishment was issued by the government. No generals were forced to resign, and Abrams had become the Army chief of staff by the time the story broke.

Years later, in 1993, the *Memphis Commercial Appeal* reported that Yarborough believed that communist governments, Soviet Union or China, were financing King and other black radicals due to an intelligence report from a friend in the Mexican Army, which said that the Cubans were providing military training to American black radicals.

Although none of this was proven to be true, Yarborough defended his actions in the 1993 article. He told the newspaper, "The Army was over a barrel."[11] That too, has proved to be incorrect, but clearly the top Army commanders of the day believed it, as this is what their intelligence analyses appeared to indicate.

It was during this volatile period that the US Army created its Intelligence Command (USAINTC). USAINTC had fifteen hundred plainclothes agents spying on members of the civilian population, including King. Additional plainclothes agents worked within Abrams's rump intelligence unit. This meant that there were two separate surveillance and intelligence systems within the Army, "one legal according to their directives, the other not."[12]

USAINTC was the Army's chief domestic intelligence agency. It divided the continental states into seven regions with more than three hundred offices scattered across the country. The command structure of this massive system reported to General Yarborough at Fort Holabird in Maryland. The agency even had a separate war room in the basement of the Pentagon.[13]

One of the USAINTC's regional organizations was the 113th Military Intelligence Group headquartered in Evanston, Illinois. John O'Brien was a three-year veteran of service in West Germany when he was transferred to the 113th MIG in September 1969.

O'Brien became suspicious of the mission when he saw a person of interest dossier labeled "Adlai Stevenson III" on his boss's desk. Stevenson's name was hardly that of an outsider or anti-establishment figure in Illinois. Stephenson's father was Adlai Stevenson II, a former

Illinois governor, US Ambassador to the United Nations, and two-time democratic candidate for the presidency.

Stevenson III was a lieutenant in the US Marine Corps and served in Korea during the war. He was elected to one term in the Illinois legislature in 1964 prior to becoming state treasurer in 1967, the office he occupied when O'Brien discovered his file in 1969. The following year, Stevenson won a seat in the US Senate in the special election to fill the vacancy left by Everett Dirksen's death. So why did the 113th have a file on him? Author Clay Risen noted in an article, "Because, O'Brien was told, Stevenson had expressed support for Jesse Jackson, who was then an activist in Chicago. Jackson had ties to a variety of civil rights and anti-war groups, and these groups were suspected in turn of having ties to violent radicals. That, apparently, was enough to qualify Stevenson as a subject of concern."[14] Jesse Jackson was associated with King's Southern Christian Leadership Conference (SCLC).

The Senate Judiciary Subcommittee on Constitutional Rights found that USAINTC had spied on dozens—perhaps hundreds—of organizations from one end of the political spectrum to the other, including American Civil Liberties Union (ACLU), Anti-Defamation League of B'nai Brith, Congress of Racial Equality (CORE), Hell's Angels of California, John Birch Society, Ku Klux Klan, League of Women Voters of the USA, Minutemen, National Association for the Advancement of Colored People (NAACP), Peace Corps, Presbyterian Interracial Council of Chicago, Southern Christian Leadership Conference (SCLC), United World Federalists Inc., Urban League, and Young Americans for Freedom.[15]

Information on all of these groups and associated individuals was fed from the seven group offices to the central data banks at Fort Holabird. Much of the information generated at each local office was also kept in duplicate files and databases at every office it passed through as it went up the chain of command.

What's more, data was shared indiscriminately with other military and even non-military organizations. "Some were swapped with municipal intelligence squads, state police, the National Guard, the FBI, the Navy, the Air Force, and other federal and state agencies," according to the senate's report.[16]

The Army's Counterintelligence Records Intelligence System (CRIS) was computerized in the late 1960s. The CRIS database had three components: a personality file, an incident file, and an organization file. The existence of the system, which contained details on at least seven thousand Americans, was withheld from civilian Army officials for at least two to three years. Once revealed, it was said to have been destroyed.

The information CRIS stored on individuals was extremely intrusive. The top of each dossier included the individual's name, address, date of birth, employment information, the source of the information contained in the dossier, along with a nine-digit CRIS identification number. Details stored beneath the headline information included ethnic group and race, religion, gender, and marital status, alias and arrest history, service status and citizenship, employment type and education, character, occupation, and annual income. The FBI was the data source about 80 percent of the time.[17]

The FBI also obtained data from the IRS, the US Post Office, the Secret Service, other branches of the military such as the Office of Naval Intelligence, and the CIA. It is safe to assume that some of the information CRIS sourced from the FBI actually came from other original sources and was merely shared by the FBI to the Army.

By the time the news story broke publically about the Army's massive spying network, civilian authorities had quietly put in place a series of new rules intended to protect against abuse. However, Ervin's investigation noted that all the files Pyle specifically referred to had been removed and destroyed so as to avoid detection by the Army inspector general's office.

The senate's committee found the Army's first public statement to be "patently misleading" and containing "just enough truth to mask an essential falsehood." Even the Army's general counsel had been deliberately misled about the biographical data kept on file. Furthermore, the various military intelligence groups "throughout the country began replacing all two and three-year agents . . . with career agents to guarantee still further that Congress, the public, and the Secretary of the Army would not learn of their activities."[18] It was a full-blown cover-up.

The Senate firmly determined that Army surveillance of individual civilians was unconstitutional, illegal, and intended to encourage silence. "Army surveillance was very real: its effects, while more subtle, are no less real. It was as destructive of the freedom of expression as an explicit law making it a crime to disagree with the government."[19]

KING'S TIES TO THE ARMY

The Army had a history of spying on King, as examined in the *Memphis Commercial Appeal* in 1993. This story demonstrates the connection between the CIA and the Army's espionage.

The US Army started a file on King in 1947 while he was a student at Morehouse College. King was a member of the Intercollegiate Council at Morehouse, headed by Mrs. Dorothy Lilley, whom the Army suspected was a communist. This occurred twenty years prior to his assassination.

By 1957, the Army described King as a "Communist tool" for speaking at the twenty-fifth anniversary of the integrated Highlander Folk School formerly of Monteagle, Tennessee. The school had been monitored by the Army for years, which took note of the "communist activities" of its director and other leading members.

The newspaper's article described the disconnect between the "almost exclusively white" US Army officers corps, which served in

Martin Luther King Jr. at the White House with President Lyndon B. Johnson (Courtesy Library of Congress)

the intelligence-gathering units, and "ordinary black Americans." The officers had virtually no contact with those upon whom they spied because they lived on military posts where racial diversity and integration was minimal. "Successive generations of Army leaders saw black Americans in the same light as Maj. R. M. Howell, assistant chief of staff for intelligence at Fort McPherson in Atlanta. 'Communism has chosen the Southern Negro as the American group most likely to respond to its revolutionary appeal,' Howell told the War Department in a December 5, 1932, intelligence report."[20]

The 113th MIG filed a report on King's activities in Chicago in January 1963. The report stated that at a dinner at the Edgewater Beach Hotel, King was overheard telling "two black men and a pretty white woman that Project C was ready to go." Project C has since been identified as King's plan to disrupt commerce and local government in Birmingham that began that spring.

When riots broke out in May, the Kennedy administration directed General Wheeler to send three thousand men from the Army's Second Division in Fort Benning, Georgia, to Birmingham to keep the peace. The commanding officer in Birmingham, Maj. Gen. Charles Billingslea, asked for more help because he had "a full-scale revolt on [his] hands down here."

In the mid-1960s, the Army received intelligence reports from Mexico that Cubans were training militant blacks and funding such operations through the Organization of Latin American Solidarity (OLAS), which was associated with Stokely Carmichael's Student Nonviolent Coordinating Committee (SNCC). During that time, Carmichael and King were increasingly seen together.

The "communist background" of some of King's advisors was the subject of a February 18, 1965, internal FBI memorandum with the subject line "MARTIN LUTHER KING, JR. SECURITY MATTER—COMMUNIST." The memo was prepared for FBI associate director William C. Sullivan and included the comment that Vice President Hubert Humphrey "ha[d] already been briefed" regarding the communist leanings of Bayard Rustin, an associate of King.

By 1967, the Army even had King's office in Ebenezer Baptist Church wired to eavesdrop. Of particular importance were conversations such as these:

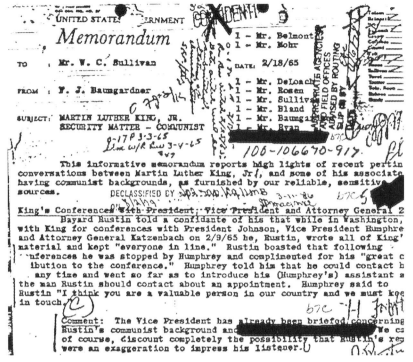

The 1965 FBI memorandum labeling King a communist (From FBI, *MURKIN*, vol. 21)

STOKELY CARMICHAEL: You making a lot of new enemies. Not sure [unintelligible] Birmingham as dangerous as people you're pissing off. The man don't care you call ghettos concentration camps, but when you tell him his war machine is nothing but hired killers, you got trouble.

MARTIN LUTHER KING: I told you in Los Angeles I can do nothing else.[21]

On April 4, 1967, one year to the day before he was murdered, King spoke at New York's Riverside Church at the invitation of its pastor, Rev. William Sloane Coffin. King spoke to congregants on the Vietnam War and Pres. Lyndon Johnson's Great Society poverty programs, which he said brought hope for the poor regardless of race:

And then came the buildup in Vietnam, and I watched this program broken and eviscerated as if it were some idle political plaything of a society gone mad on war, and I knew that America would never invest the necessary funds or energies in rehabilitation of its poor, so long as adventures like Vietnam continued to draw men and skills and money like some demonic destructive suction tube. So, I was increasingly compelled to see the war as an enemy of the poor and to attack it as such.

. . . And so we have been repeatedly faced with the cruel irony of watching Negro and white boys on TV screens as they kill and die together for a nation that has been unable to seat them together in the same schools. And so we watch them in brutal solidarity burning the huts of a poor village, but we realize that they would hardly live on the same block in Chicago. I could not be silent in the face of such cruel manipulation of the poor. . . .

Now, it should be incandescently clear that no one who has any concern for the integrity and life of America today can ignore the present war. If America's soul becomes totally poisoned, part of the autopsy must read: Vietnam.[22]

The speech changed the way the Army viewed King. Words such as "treason" began being thrown around in MIG units. Intelligence officers told commanders that the speech and its related fallout caused black troops in Vietnam to be "unsettled."

That summer, a riot in Detroit killed forty-three people and provoked Army deployment. A secret Army survey among black men arrested during the riot demonstrated King's growing influence, provoking the Army's fear of him.

Years later, Yarborough remembered, "Blacks were using the uncertainty of the Vietnam period and taking advantage of it." He said, "They [blacks] were attacking the weak point in the line, which is tactically a good idea, but you couldn't do it without arousing animosity of all kinds." Army commanders "were increasingly frustrated with top civilian Pentagon officials who ignored warnings that black unrest was Communist-inspired, damaging morale in Vietnam and leading to armed revolt at home."

Perhaps nothing scared the military as much as King's plan for a "poor people's march" on Washington. Army intelligence analysis in December 1967 described it as "a devastating civil disturbance whose sole purpose is to shut down the United States government." At a Pentagon meeting to discuss the march, Army officers planned "'target city priorities' in light of 'King's plans to ignite violence and mayhem' throughout the United States in April."

Army intelligence units used "Green Beret teams to make street maps, identify landing zones for riot troops, and scout sniper sites in thirty-nine potentially racially explosive cities, including Memphis."[23]

THE ALABAMA NATIONAL GUARD, THE CIA, AND JAMES EARL RAY

Some of the special forces veterans from Vietnam who had worked in clandestine operations with the CIA, the Special Operations Group (SOG), or the top secret Detachment B-57 were "dumped" into the Twentieth SFG for "safekeeping," according to "a former major with Army counterintelligence." The SOG in question was a CIA-related unit and/or operation.

Richard Ober, the CIA agent who opened the 201 file on James Earl Ray, also ran Operation CHAOS. The Rockefeller Commission was entrusted with gathering information on domestic CIA activities and reporting them to Pres. Gerald Ford, who authorized the commission by executive order on January 4, 1975. The commission had a whole chapter devoted to the SOG and Operation CHAOS.[24]

Ober testified twice before the Rockefeller Commission in early 1975, on January 27 and again on February 3. His testimony was "top secret" but declassified in 2002—with portions exempted from release. The details of Operation CHAOS were explicitly discussed both times Ober testified. The index of the Gerald R. Ford Library's files on Ober and his testimony states, "During his tenure as Chief of the [two or three words redacted] Ober had, at various times, four different chains of command."[25] The four chains of command described in the document referred to the publically known supervisors to whom Ober reported and his involvement as head of the SOG and his management of Operation CHAOS.

Furthermore, another participant in the Rockefeller Commission investigation and former member of the Foreign Intelligence Advisory Board, Wheaton B. Byers, also linked Ober as head of the SOG. Byers established this link in a March 12, 1975, interview with commission investigators when he told them he was not aware at the time that Ober's SOG activities included infiltrating domestic dissident groups with CIA agents, although that is precisely what Ober was doing.[26]

Some of the special forces soldiers who had worked SOG missions in Vietnam acted as if they were still there. They were "dumped" on the Alabama National Guard because the military had nowhere else to place them. "They couldn't let a lot of these crazy guys back into the States because they couldn't forget their training," a former Army intelligence officer noted for the *Memphis Commercial Appeal.* He said, "Birmingham became Saigon. The rural South was in-country and at times things got out of hand."

Former members of the unit who spoke to the newspaper under an agreement of anonymity said that they used a network of Klansmen to gather information about "n----- troublemakers" and passed it on to the Pentagon. "It wasn't any big deal." Some of the Twentieth SFG soldiers shared a training site with Klansmen in Cullman, Alabama.

Thus, in the months leading up to King's assassination, a group of special forces soldiers who performed clandestine intelligence operations for Richard Ober's CIA group in Vietnam and possibly Cambodia, were "dumped" into an Alabama National Guard unit because it was not safe for them to go unsupervised into the civilian population. These troops, at least some of whom had difficulty differentiating between the rural South and Vietnam, were stationed in a unit 260 miles from Memphis.

It may have been possible that one of the unassimilated soldiers from South Vietnam or a Klan operation decided to murder King. However, these scenarios are highly unlikely.

From a logical standpoint, the most substantial scenario is that someone in the CIA or Army intelligence gave the order to assassinate King, as it would dovetail perfectly with Richard Ober's documented interest in whether Ray got a new trial. If Ober's team murdered King and pinned it on James Earl Ray, he would certainly have a vested interest to ensure that Ray did not get a new trial and open the evidence that might lead to them. However, whether Ober's SOG or special forces soldiers associated with it (stationed near Memphis) was involved in any way with King's assassination may never be proven.

THE FBI, KING, AND THE LORRAINE MOTEL

One of the most shocking revelations about the 1968 events in Memphis did not surface until 2010. It came from another excellent news story in the *Memphis Commercial Appeal.*

Marc Perrusquia revealed in *The Commercial Appeal* that Ernest C. Withers, the famous black photographer and reporter, was a paid FBI informant from at least 1968 through 1970. The newspaper learned this from thousands of pages of documents that the FBI released in response to a Freedom of Information Act request.

Withers was an FBI "super-informant." FBI reports indicated that he was "most conversant with all key activities in the Negro community." He was "the perfect source" for the FBI because he could go into any of King's private meetings with his camera and report back to the FBI everything that was said.[27]

The information that Withers reported to his FBI handlers was typed up by the Memphis FBI office in a ninety-three-page, single-spaced document. The detail is mind boggling. In the days and weeks leading up to King's assassination, Withers provided intimate details about King's and others' activities in Memphis. He reported whom King saw, where they met, and what they discussed. He reported the comings and goings of the entire King entourage; when and where they ate and with whom; and what the plans were for the march to support the striking city-sanitation workers. Withers also reported King's travel plans and daily schedule as well as motel accommodations right down to the room number. He reported license plate numbers and supplied many of his photographs to the FBI.

King stayed at the Holiday Inn Rivermont during his previous trip to Memphis in late March 1968. "When violence broke out during the march King led in Memphis on 3-28-68, King disappeared. There is a first class Negro hotel in Memphis, the Hotel Lorraine, but King chose to hide out at the white owned and operated Holiday Inn Motel [Rivermont]."[28] When King left Memphis and returned to Atlanta on March 29, the FBI's CI program began a campaign to manipulate the King entourage to stay at the Lorraine Motel, where he was shot to death just six days later. The subject of the memo was "Counterintelligence Program . . . Racial Intelligence."

Obviously, the FBI tactic worked, because Withers informed the FBI on April 3 that King would stay in Room 306 of the Lorraine Motel. The feds in Washington had this information before the Memphis police department, according to testimony before the HSCA by Memphis police director Frank Holloman. In the FBI's report, Withers, "source two," is seen to have passed King's specific room number at the Lorraine Motel to the FBI.

MLK Exhibit F-451C

UNITED STATES GOVERNMENT

Memorandum

Mr. W. C. Sullivan   DATE: March 29, 1968

FROM : G. C. Moore

SUBJECT: COUNTERINTELLIGENCE PROGRAM
BLACK NATIONALIST - HATE GROUPS
RACIAL INTELLIGENCE
(MARTIN LUTHER KING)

PURPOSE:
            To publicize hypocrisy on the part of Martin Luther
King.

BACKGROUND:
            Martin Luther King has urged Negroes in Memphis,
Tennessee, to boycott white merchants in order to force
compliance with Negro demands in the sanitation workers'
strike in Memphis.

            When violence broke out during the march King led
in Memphis on 3-28-68, King disappeared. There is a first
class Negro hotel in Memphis, the Hotel Lorraine, but King
chose to hide out at the white owned and operated Holiday Inn
Motel.

RECOMMENDATION:
            The above facts have been included in the attached
blind memorandum and it is recommended it be furnished a
cooperative news media source by the Crime Records Division
for an item showing King is a hypocrite. This will be done on
a highly confidential basis.

Enclosure

TJD:ted
(7)
1 - Mr. C. D. DeLoach
1 - Mr. T. E. Bishop
1 - Mr. W. C. Sullivan
1 - Mr. G. C. Moore
1 - Mr. D. Ryan (Mass Media)
1 - Mr. T. J. Deakin

The initial FBI CI memo regarding Ray's presence in Memphis (From HSCA,
Hearings, vol. VI, 589)

BLACK ORGANIZING PROJECT (BOP)

      Lieutenant Arkin advised that his source learned later on the night of April 2, 1968, that Reverend James Orange of the SCLC staff had promised that BOP would have an office of its own in the Minimum Salary Office of the AME Church, 276 Hernando, by April 3, 1968.

      Also on April 3, 1968, source two advised that Cabbage, John B. Smith, Charles Ballard and Edwina Harrell were all staying in Rooms 315 and 316 of the Lorraine Motel.

      Later on April 3, 1968, source two stated that Dr. King, who was staying in Room 306 of the Lorraine Motel, had checked in there prior to going to a strategy meeting at the Centenary Methodist Church on April 3, 1968, and that he returned to the Motel on the afternoon of April 3, 1968, for lunch with members of his staff and various representatives of the COME and BOP.

      Later on April 3, 1968, source two stated that BOP representatives Charles Cabbage, Edwina Harrell and Don Neely, an Owen College dropout, all ate dinner with Dr. King and with Dorothy Cotton and Andrew J. Young, all of the SCLC staff, and that Harrell bragged that she had been living with some of the black power people at the Lorraine Motel for the past several days.

A portion of the ninety-three page FBI report on racial intelligence in Memphis, as supplied by Ernest C. Withers (Courtesy *Memphis Commercial Appeal*)

Neither the room number nor the name of the motel was reported in the April 3 afternoon newspaper, the *Memphis Press-Scimitar*, or in the April 4 morning newspaper, the *Memphis Commercial Appeal*. The only thing that the *Commercial Appeal* reported about King's whereabouts in the April 4 morning newspaper was that while he ate lunch at the Lorraine the previous day, he was served with a federal court injunction. "They found Dr. King and four other defendants [black ministers] named in the injunction . . . eating lunch at the Lorraine Motel."[29] The injunction enjoined them from organizing a mass rally and march to support the striking city sanitation workers.

With no public knowledge of King's location, James Earl Ray would have had no way of knowing where to find him. Ray didn't know where King was staying and did not have his room number when he checked into Bessie Brewer's flophouse on April 4 across the street from the Lorraine Motel—but the feds did.

According to Hanes Jr., one of Ray's initial lawyers, King was "not on James Earl Ray's radar" screen. Ray was in Memphis for the first time in his life because someone—Raoul—told him to be there. Raoul told him to buy the .30-06 in Birmingham and bring it to Memphis. The only thing Ray knew about this trip to Memphis is that it would put a little more money in his pocket.

Conclusion

Secret military spying on Americans was advocated by General Abrams as a means of responding to the role of enforcing federal court orders on desegregation in the South. Almost immediately, military intelligence officers identified virtually every black civil rights leader as a suspect. Its analysis of the "intelligence" it collected concluded that the civil rights leadership was guilty of disloyalty, acting under communist influence, and in some cases planning for out-and-out armed revolution. Such analyses only bred paranoia.

To many who watched the Detroit riot on the television, it looked like a local race riot confined mostly to the inner city. It looked like poor, urban blacks were destroying their own neighborhoods. But to General Yarborough, it looked like armed revolution that threatened the very existence of the federal government.

Pres. John F. Kennedy warned about secrecy in government, yet as US Attorney General, his own brother approved FBI surveillance of King .

The sad truth is that the US military and intelligence services considered Rev. Martin Luther King Jr. a threat to national security. They believed that he was a communist or working under international communist control and influence. They believed that his message of equality, change, and non-violent civil disobedience was a cover for the disruption of US military operations and perhaps even the government itself. They feared him just as they did any external enemy and planned how they might counter this threat—or eliminate it.

CHAPTER 6
Percy Foreman Is in the Building

How does one describe the late Percy Foreman? He was a man who loomed larger than life in the courtroom. At six feet four inches tall and 250 pounds, with a booming voice and an assertive personality, he cast a John Wayne-like presence.

Foreman was a man of great legal aptitude, keen instinct, masterful speaking ability, and astounding theatrical talent. He had both charm and venom, and he knew which to use at any given moment. He had a gift for reading the psyche of the jury and a knack for knowing which emotional buttons to push as well as when and how hard to push them. A powerful lawyer, Foreman was a riveting speaker on behalf of the high-society divorce clients and wealthy murder defendants he typically represented. He was a man of colossal vanity and ambition, with a touch of a messianic complex.

And, while representing Ray, Percy Foreman committed at least two felonies. Foreman suborned perjury by coercing and threatening Ray into pleading guilty and suppressing Ray's full testimony in Memphis. Second, while testifying to the HSCA, Foreman lied under oath about having received a letter from James Earl Ray that invited him to come to the Shelby County jail in Memphis to discuss the possibility of his representation.

These crimes were not Foreman's only deceptions while representing Ray. Foreman also made false statements to the court regarding his willingness to represent James Earl Ray without compensation, claiming that he no longer practiced law for money. Four days later, Ray signed over to Foreman his complete royalties in the original literary contract with William Bradford Huie.

FOREMAN'S BACKGROUND

Percy Eugene Foreman was born in 1902 in Polk County, Texas, about seventy-five miles northeast of Houston.

Over the course of his sixty-year practice, he defended fifteen hundred accused murderers, only one of whom was executed.

One of his most powerful clients was South Texas political boss George Parr, the "Duke of Duval." In 1948, Parr masterminded a plot to elect Lyndon Baines Johnson to the Senate with 202 "extra" votes that appeared in Jim Wells County the day after the Democratic primary for US senator. Johnson won the primary by a scant 87 votes statewide.[1]

In 1957, Foreman represented Parr when he was convicted of mail fraud, but the verdict was eventually overturned by the US Supreme Court. In 1953, Foreman represented Nago Alaniz, a man accused of murdering the son of Parr's main political opponent, attorney Jake Floyd. Floyd was targeted by a hit man, who apparently mistook Floyd's twenty-two-year-old son, Jacob Floyd Jr., for his father. Foreman succeeded in clearing his client of the murder charge after controversy arose surrounding the judges assigned to the case, thus clearing the Parr organization of a politically motivated murder.

FOREMAN ENTERS THE RAY CASE

Arthur Hanes Sr. and his son, Arthur Hanes Jr., were James Earl Ray's official attorneys when Foreman appeared at the Shelby County jail in Memphis on Sunday, November 10, 1968. Author William F. Pepper wrote that earlier that day, brothers Jerry and John Ray met Foreman at the Memphis airport with a copy of the literary contract between Huie, James Earl Ray, and the Haneses. After reviewing the contract, Foreman expressed confidence that he could break it, so the three went to the Shelby County jail to see James Earl Ray about hiring Foreman. Ordinarily, only the attorney of record can visit a jail prisoner.

Judge Preston Battle permitted Foreman's entry in to the jail. He was delighted to get rid of the Haneses. Hanes Sr., along with several news reporters, had been cited by Battle for contempt of court for violating his order not to discuss the particulars of the case in public. Battle appointed a committee of lawyers to help enforce his order. Hanes Sr. commented that they were just a bunch of "Harper Valley P. T. A. hypocrites," referring to a leading country music hit of the day, a line published in the *New York Times*.[2] Hanes Jr. explained to me that the apparent animosity between Judge Battle, himself, and his father was overblown. "That was the strangest thing," Hanes said. "The truth of it is that Judge Battle was in over his head, and he was almost paranoid about it." He continued, "The result of it was he [Battle] just didn't handle it very well."[3]

Ten years after meeting Ray—almost to the day—Foreman testified before the HSCA about his access to Ray. The person who questioned Foreman was Peter G. Beeson, who now practices "legal malpractice defense, professional disciplinary proceedings, ethics consultations and expert opinions for the legal profession." From the published transcript of Foreman's sworn congressional testimony on November 13, 1978:

> PETER G. BEESON: Would you give the committee your recollection, please, of how you came into the Ray case?

> PERCY FOREMAN: I refused several times—at least three times commencing in June at the arrest and before Ray had been returned to Memphis—I refused to go to Memphis to talk with Ray. I refused to go to London to talk with Ray. I was asked to do so by Jerry Ray, James Earl Ray's brother.[4]

Jerry Ray told me that this part of Foreman's story is "absolutely false" and that he had no contact with Ray while he was in jail in London nor knew how to reach him.

Jerry did not even mention Foreman to James Earl until after his meeting with William Bradford Huie in late October or early November 1968. It was then that Jerry called Foreman's office in Houston. Foreman answered the telephone himself and agreed to come to Memphis.

At no time did the HSCA investigators question Foreman about the month he first heard from the Ray brothers—whether it was June or November 1968. The investigators asked no questions about the specifics of Foreman's alleged June contact and whether it was through Ray's brothers or through his English barrister, Michael Eugene. Foreman asserted that the Rays had wanted him from the get-go, and that he had repeatedly refused them. At that time, no one questioned his assertion.

Foreman's comments in 1968 to reporter Kay Pittman Black of the *Memphis Press-Scimitar,* however, belie his sworn testimony and corroborate Jerry Ray's version of events. In a front-page news story

Jerry Ray (Courtesy author's collection)

on the afternoon of November 13, 1968, Black wrote that Foreman was "discussing for the first time how he got into the case."

Black reported: "Foreman said he talked to John and Jerry Ray, who called him from St. Louis last 'Thursday or Friday' asking him to take the case." That previous Thursday or Friday was November 7 or 8, just as Jerry Ray said, not the previous June as Foreman later claimed. The Black news story continued, "There were subsequent conversations with the brothers and later James Earl Ray himself on Sunday, when Foreman visited the jail, but he declined to say who was the final persuader."[5]

In Foreman's first public explanation of how he came into the case, there is no mention of a letter from James Earl Ray. Nor is there any hint that the Ray brothers had been trying to get Foreman to take the case for months.

The following year, Foreman repeated under oath this same story that he told to Black. During a deposition in John Hooker Sr.'s law office in Nashville on November 11, 1969, Ray's then-attorney J. B. Stoner asked Foreman to explain his meeting with the Rays. Foreman replied that Ray's brothers brought him into the case and that he "had talked to them from Texas and they in St. Louis. I had not met them officially or personally except over the telephone, in a telephone conversation prior to the Sunday morning that I came [to Memphis]."[6] This statement matches his previous story in Black's news article.

In Foreman's 1978 HSCA testimony, he changed his story to testify that, instead of the initial phone call from Jerry and John Ray in early November, he had received a letter from James Earl Ray via post:

PERCY FOREMAN: I was asked to come to Memphis to talk to him [James Earl Ray]. I told [Jerry Ray] that I would not go talk with James Earl Ray unless James Earl Ray himself wrote a letter asking that I come, and I did receive such a letter. It came to my office about the 8th—7th or 8th—of November, and—

PETER G. BEESON: Where was your office located, Mr. Foreman?

FOREMAN: Houston, Tex. I was in Waco or near Waco, trying a lawsuit when the letter came. It was read to me over the phone.

BEESON: Who read the letter to you?

FOREMAN: My secretary. I went back to my office, and I went by appointment with Jerry and John, who called me. Jerry Ray and John Ray, brothers of James Earl Ray, called me and arranged to meet me in Memphis, and we did meet at the airport. They met me. They were already there. We went to the Admiral Benbow Motel and thence to the Shelby County jail.

BEESON: Mr. Foreman, you said you returned to the office. You were in Waco when you were read the letter. You said you were in your office before going to Memphis; is that correct?

FOREMAN: Yes.

BEESON: Did you have an opportunity to see the letter at that time?

FOREMAN: I didn't catch your question.

BEESON: Did you have an opportunity when you returned to your office to see Mr. Ray's letter?

FOREMAN: Yes, I did.

BEESON: Mr. Ray has emphatically denied sending you a letter, Mr. Foreman, is he lying in his denial?

FOREMAN: If he is speaking, the chances are he is lying, and he is lying when he says he did not write me that letter.

BEESON: Where is the letter now?

FOREMAN: The letter with all of the files in the Ray case is in John Hooker's home in the suburbs of Nashville, Tenn., is where I last heard, delivered to my attorney, John Hooker.

BEESON: When did you deliver the letter to Mr. Hooker?

FOREMAN: When he directed that I bring him all of my files, suggested that I do so, and it was in connection with this suit that James Earl Ray had filed against Bradford—William Bradford Huie—and me; and I can't fix the time, but it was—we were served within a week after the service of citation on me in that suit.

BEESON: Have you made an effort to locate the files in the Ray case recently, Mr. Foreman?

FOREMAN: Yes, I have. John Hooker has died and his firm claims they do not have that set of files in the office. I don't know what disposition was made of it. At the same time I left my files, I left another briefcase and an overcoat, and I got the briefcase and the overcoat, but not the files.

BEESON: To the best of your knowledge then, you are unaware of the location of the letter at this time; is that correct?

FOREMAN: I have no idea where any of the papers—it was a large box; I guess 2 feet by 3 feet by 12 inches.[7]

Foreman told two lies in his sworn testimony: one about his files, the other about his contact with Ray's brothers. Foreman claimed that his files were lost after the death of John Hooker Sr. just before Christmas Eve, 1970, and that Foreman had attempted to recover them. He claimed under oath that he sent his original files of the Ray case to Hooker Sr.

Foreman's statement about the location of the files has been disputed by the young lawyer who was assigned by the Hooker, Keeble, Dodson, and Harris law firm to take up this case at the death of Hooker Sr. Gareth Aden, who "got assigned that case because [he] was the low man on the totem pole," had been licensed to practice law for barely a year when he was assigned the duty of defending Foreman in federal appeals court. Aden told me that he presented an oral argument in court "months later," following Hooker Sr. 's death. "To my recollection, there never was a controversy with any problem, or heard anything about those files being lost." He added, "nor do I have a recollection of anyone contacting the firm about [lost] files." Aden argued before the US Court of Appeals for the Sixth Circuit in Cincinnati and won. He certainly was not hampered by lost files, which, according to Foreman's timeline, were lost before Aden prepared for court.

What Aden recalls is that he prepared a winning oral argument using only the files he was handed at the death of Hooker Sr. He specifically recalled he had no conversations with Foreman prior to court and no conversations with Foreman at any time regarding the whereabouts of any files. Foreman had lied about contacting the Hooker law firm to locate the files.

G. Robert Blakey, head of the HSCA committee, noted that Foreman was "admittedly unethical" and that his statements are unreliable. "Frankly, I would not believe him about anything."

If Blakey didn't believe that Foreman had told the HSCA the truth, then why didn't his staff pursue it? Beeson was one question away from exposing Foreman's lie. All Beeson had to do was call Gareth Aden in Nashville to respond to Foreman's story.

Neither Blakey nor Beeson will say why they didn't ask, but if they had proven that Foreman perjured himself before the HSCA, it would have led to a reopening of Ray's appeals and Foreman's perjury would have been grounds for a full trial. Neither Blakey nor Beeson were prepared to do that.

John Jay Hooker Jr. doesn't buy a word of Foreman's story about the lost files. "I can't imagine anything happening to my father's files," Hooker Jr. told me. "My father was a meticulous man." He added, "No sophisticated lawyer, much less one with a *cause célèbre* client, would send his sole file to someone else without copying it."

At the heart of Foreman's lie are the questions of whether he sent Hooker Sr. the original files or a copy and if he kept a copy of his files. HSCA member and congressman Richardson Preyer asked these questions following Beeson's weak interrogation:

RICHARD PREYER: When you turned these files over to Mr. Hooker, did you make no copy of that letter to keep in your own files?

PERCY FOREMAN: No, sir, I didn't keep a copy of a single item in that file.[8]

This exchange—in fact, all of Foreman's testimony and depositions—must be understood in the context of his extreme tendency to retain records. Under questioning by Jim Lesar in a 1974 deposition for *Ray v. Foreman*, Foreman stated that he owned "eighty houses—more than that . . . [and] they are all for storage, that is what I use them for."[9]

The proposition that a man who filled more than eighty houses with case files sent his uncopied, original files on James Earl Ray to a third party and were subsequently lost is inconceivable. There are no facts that corroborate Foreman's testimony.

The second lie in Foreman's account to the HSCA was that Ray's brothers contacted him in June 1968, when James Earl Ray was still in jail in London. This is impossible, as Ray's brothers had no contact with Ray until he was extradited to Memphis. That Foreman was first contacted that summer stands in great contradiction to the practice of Ray's English legal counsel, Michael Eugene, as Eugene had written to the Haneses, who responded that they would take Ray's case.

Foreman also claimed that he refused an invitation to go to London to see Ray and to enter the case "several times." He said he only agreed to see James Earl Ray after he was sent a letter of invitation to his Houston office, but Foreman never told anyone what changed his mind. Foreman put the letter in his files, he claimed, and went to Memphis to meet Ray.

James Earl Ray denied sending Foreman a letter. He testified before the HSCA that Foreman appeared at the jail "unsolicited" and that it was his brother, Jerry Ray, who had made the contact and arrangements with Foreman.[10]

In late October and early November 1968, Jerry Ray was already talking to Memphis attorney Richard J. Ryan, who had been recommended to the Rays by Raulston Schoolfield, a state judge who had been impeached and removed from office by the Tennessee State Senate in 1958. Ryan promised Jerry Ray that he would take the case, but he wanted to associate it with a big-name criminal attorney. Jerry Ray and Ryan discussed Foreman. When Jerry called Foreman and spoke to him that November, Foreman indeed asked for a letter. Jerry told him that the trial date was the following Tuesday and that there was not enough time for a letter. Foreman consequently agreed to meet with the Ray brothers in Memphis.

Previously unpublished documents from the archives of Shelby County, Tennessee, released in 2011, including a letter written by Foreman, prove that Foreman used the death of his friend John Hooker Sr. to invent his plausible but false story as to why he can't produce the letter of invitation he insists that Ray sent him. He was never able to produce it simply because it never existed.

The first pertinent document from the Shelby County Archives about Foreman's entry into the Ray case is Sheriff William N. Morris Jr.'s statement, dated November 10, 1968 at 10 p.m. The statement had been typed but unsigned.

> Mr. Percy Foreman, attorney, arrived at the Shelby County Jail today with John Ray and Jerry Ray, brothers of James Earl Ray and requested to see the prisoner.
>
> This permission was granted and during the course of this visit, certain decisions were made and a letter was written to Mr. Arthur Hanes Sr., attorney, and signed by James Earl Ray. This letter was presented to me for reading by Mr. Foreman and it declared an intent by James Earl Ray to dispense with the legal services of Mr. Hanes and his son and of an intention to obtain new counsel and a Tennessee lawyer.
>
> Mr. Foreman has told me that it is his intention to appear before Judge W. Preston Battle Tuesday morning at 9:30 a.m. to request a continuance in the trial of the case pending against James Earl Ray.[11]

Sheriff Morris must have been quite uneasy about letting Foreman into James Earl Ray's jail cell when Ray's attorneys of record were the Haneses. Obviously, if Foreman had had a letter of invitation from Ray, there would have been no need for Morris's memorandum.

There is other evidence of what went on at the Shelby County jail. Jailers kept a daily activity log on Ray for every day he was in their custody from midnight on July 20, 1968, to 2:30 a.m. on March 11, 1969, when he was transferred to state officials for transport to the Tennessee State Penitentiary in Nashville. The log was typed and signed by a sheriff's department captain and included the names of the two jailers on observation duty around the clock. It noted all of Ray's daily activities, including when he woke up, took a nap, and went to bed; what sort of mood he was in; when and how long he read the newspaper; when he watched TV, what he watched, and his reaction to it; what he ate and when; what visitors he had; when the jailhouse physician checked in on him; when he showered; when he asked for aspirin and how many he was given; when he wrote; whether he expressed complaints to the jailers; when and what type of exercise he did; etcetera. These reports even note the date and time Ray asked for a change of bed linen and clean underwear. These daily logs also listed the letters he received and those he wrote and to whom. All correspondence was processed (censored) by the jailers, and the addressee's name was noted.

The daily log for November 10, 1968, read as follows:

> At 11:55 a.m., Ray was advised that Mr. Percy Foreman was in the building requesting to see him and he was asked if he wanted to talk with Mr. Foreman and he replied that he did. He walked in the block until Mr. Percy Foreman was taken inside the block at 1:40 p.m. While Mr. Foreman was in the block, Ray wrote a letter to Mr. Hanes telling him that he was dissatisfied with him and that he desired a Tennessee lawyer and one other attorney to represent him. Mr. Foreman also requested that Officers Hall and Weichert be witnesses to some questions that he asked Ray. These questions were: (1). Did I influence you to change lawyers? Ray answered, "No." (2). Did I solicit your business or come to you? Ray's answer was, "I contacted you."
>
> Mr. Foreman stated to officers that he wanted witnesses because he figured on repercussions from Mr. Hanes. At 3:30 p.m., Mr. Foreman was taken out of A Block and a supper of bologna, cheese, potato salad, fruit cocktail, bread and tea was served. Ray ate a good meal and appeared to be in good mood.[12]

The order of events raises an interesting timeframe. When Ray was advised at 11:55 a.m. that "Percy Foreman was in the building" asking to see him, Ray noted that he did want to take the visit. There would have been no need to record Ray's response in the daily log if Foreman had received a letter of invitation from James Earl Ray. Furthermore, if Ray had actually sent Foreman a letter, it would have been noted in the daily report. The jailers knew that Foreman's entry was controversial.

The log further noted that it was 1:40 p.m. when Foreman entered James Earl Ray's cell. Approximately one hour and forty-five minutes elapsed between Ray agreeing to see Foreman and his admittance to Ray's cell. This gave ample time for the head jailer to contact Sheriff

Morris, for Morris to call Judge Battle, and for Battle to think it over and instruct Morris as to his decision.[13] This is the same story separately corroborated by Jerry Ray and Arthur Hanes Jr.

Foreman knew that, without a prior letter of invitation from Ray, he had to cover for himself in order to deflect the criticism he expected from the Haneses for stealing their client in such a high-profile case.

Getting James Earl Ray to deny that Foreman persuaded him to dump the Haneses and hire him doesn't make it fact. Foreman was one of the most persuasive lawyers in the country.

Another miscue by Foreman created yet a third version of his story about receiving a letter of invitation from Ray. In an article in *Look* magazine entitled "Ray Wanted to Win Recognition," Foreman stated, "last November, the brothers of James Earl Ray sought me out and handed me a letter from him, beseeching me to represent him . . ."[14]

Foreman was questioned about the details of this version of events during his HSCA testimony. He had previously told the committee that a letter was mailed to him, and he quickly denied the "hand-delivered" version, blaming it on William Bradford Huie's artistic freedom as an author:

> PETER G. BEESON: I wonder if I could direct your attention, please, to the second paragraph in the [*Look*] article, and if you would follow along with me, I will read that for the record: "When, last November, the brothers of James Earl Ray sought me out and handed me a letter from him, beseeching me to represent him . . ."

> PERCY FOREMAN: That language is not mine; that language is Bradford Huie's. He wrote this. I wrote it as a lawyer would write it and I did not say the letters were handed me by the brothers, but that was the way it appeared here, but it was rewritten for the public by Bradford Huie, but it was my language. Go ahead.

> BEESON: My question as you are clearly anticipating, is an attempt to resolve the conflict in this article—which is dated 1 month after the guilty plea—and your current testimony before the committee concerning the method in which you received the letter from Mr. Ray. You have testified today that this letter was mailed from Mr. Ray to your office in Texas, that you were notified about it by your secretary over the phone—

FOREMAN: That is correct.

BEESON: [continuing] and that you went back to your office and reviewed the letter at that time.

FOREMAN: I do so represent; that is true.

BEESON: And your explanation for that contradiction, Mr. Foreman?

FOREMAN: I wrote this article and actually my agreeing to write the article came through a vice president of *Look* magazine who was also a lawyer, and from him through William Bradford Huie. When I wrote the article, I was in Tennessee, Peabody Hotel, and I gave it to William Bradford Huie, and he undertook to make it more readable. This is the first time I have read the article since it first appeared. But he took poetic license there several times in telescoping and translating into idiom, but the essence of the article is true, and the bringing of the letter, it was not brought by the brothers; it was mailed to me at my office.[15]

There was no letter from Ray to Foreman processed by the Shelby County jail in the weeks leading up to Foreman's arrival on November 10. Foreman said that he received the letter November 7 or 8. According to the signed daily log reports in the three weeks prior to those dates, Ray wrote five letters. None of the letters were to Percy Foreman. Three letters went to his brother Jerry, one letter went to his attorney Arthur Hanes Sr., and one letter went to Judge Battle. The signed daily logs eliminate any doubt about whether James Earl Ray sent a letter of invitation to Percy Foreman. He did not.

In answer to the question of when Foreman delivered all of his James Earl Ray files to John Hooker Sr., Foreman said, "I can't fix the time, but it was—we were served within a week after the service of citation on me in that suit."[16] The suit to which Foreman was referring was *James Earl Ray v. Percy Foreman, William Bradford Huie, et al.*, in federal court in the Nashville, Tennessee, district (filed April 11, 1969). Foreman said that it was "within a week" after being served that he claims to have delivered his files to Hooker Sr., but this too is a lie.

On May 10, 1969, Foreman replied to an April 30 letter from Ray's attorney, Richard J. Ryan, who had written Foreman requesting access to "whatever files you have in your possession" on James Earl Ray.

If Foreman had indeed sent all of his files to Hooker Sr. in the week following April 11, even allowing for a few days for the process servers to catch up with Foreman, his files would have already been in Hooker's possession.

Foreman declined to provide Ryan with his files on James Earl Ray for two reasons. First, he said that his files were "essential to the defense" of additional suits in which he was involved. Second, Foreman bizarrely claimed that "My own investigation and interviews with witnesses are in a cryptic form of shorthand, being a combination of Gregg, Pitman, Percy Foreman and Alabama-Coushatta Indian hieroglyphics. In other words, no living human being except myself can decipher whatever has been reduced to writing by me as a result of interviews in the James Earl Ray case."[17]

This peculiar claim says nothing about the Ray files no longer being in his possession, since they had, as alleged, already been delivered to Hooker Sr. by the date of the letter. Indeed, Foreman's letter makes it clear that he intended to retain possession of the files. In Foreman's own words—assuming there is a word of truth to his claim of cryptogrammic shorthand—what use would the files have been to Hooker Sr. if he

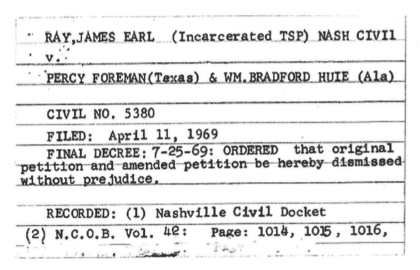

Index card showing Ray's filed suit regarding the literary contract with Huie and subsequently Foreman (Courtesy United States District Court, Middle District of Tennessee)

couldn't read them? If Foreman had shared his "hieroglyphics" with him, it would have defeated the reason for developing it.

The evidence strongly suggests that Foreman used his friend's untimely death as a cover for the destruction of all of his Ray files. The key question is what was this lie all about?

FOREMAN'S FEE

William Bradford Huie claims in his book *He Slew the Dreamer* that he and Percy Foreman first met in Ft. Worth, Texas, on November 27, 1968. The purpose of the meeting was to discuss Huie's literary contract with Ray. Foreman was interested in rearranging it so that he would own 60 percent of it, Huie 40 percent, and James Earl Ray none.[18] Huie could not see Ray in jail—as he was not Ray's attorney. Nor could Huie get uncensored material. Ten weeks after Foreman's first discussion with Huie, he prevailed. The new contract was signed on February 3, 1969.[19]

The dates of the meeting with Huie and the new contract are important milestones. On December 18, 1968, three weeks after first discussing these arrangements with Huie, Foreman misled the court, stating that, "there is no money whatever available in this case for either investigating expenses or attorney fees as of now." He made no mention to the court that he had already demanded more than half of the literary contract with Huie, who by then had published and been paid for two lengthy, feature articles in *Look* magazine as a means of obtaining the money needed to pay the legal fees of the Haneses.

Foreman told the court that day that he was in receipt of "numerous offers by publications, magazines and writers [without naming any of them] to underwrite [Ray's] fees." He said that he declined the offers "because most of them have a hook in them," without elaborating on what he considered to be a "hook." It was probably that no writer or publisher wanted to give Foreman a 60 percent cut.

Foreman also pledged to the court that day, "I will keep this court advised if any contracts of any kind are signed or agreed upon."[20] The court ruled that Ray was indigent and appointed the public defender's office to assist Foreman in the case. Judge Battle noted that "Foreman has volunteered and donated his services to Mr. Ray."[21] Foreman offered no caveat to the court to revise or correct Battle's statement.

His misrepresentations to the court worsened. On February 5,

1969, two days after signing the new literary contract with Huie, he filed a motion with the court to have the State of Tennessee pay for court reporting expenses on the basis that Ray was financially indigent. Foreman declared that he "does not contemplate he will receive any" fee to represent Ray. On February 7, 1969, he not only failed to report the new contract to court as he had pledged to do, but he also told the court that "as of today I have no reason to believe that anything else will be paid."[22] If Foreman did not think Huie would generate any more income under the new contract, why did he bother drawing it up? In fact, Foreman referred to this same contract in his March 9, 1969, letter to Ray as "my own property," indicating he attached monetary value to it.

The Texas Bar Association confirmed that the ethical guidance in force ("applicable disciplinary rules") in the years in question was the American Bar Association's *1908 Canons of Professional Ethics*.[23] Foreman appears to have violated Canon 22, "Candor and Fairness," which states: "It is unprofessional and dishonorable to deal other than candidly with the facts in taking the statements of witnesses, in drawing affidavits and other documents, and in the presentation of causes."

Whether Foreman was professionally obligated to reveal his negotiations and contract with Huie to the court as he pledged but failed to do, or whether he technically violated Canon 22, is irrelevant. No charges were brought to the Texas bar regarding Foreman's conduct in Tennessee. Judge Battle lived only three weeks after Foreman's final court appearance in Memphis, and nothing of his behind-the-scenes maneuvering surfaced until after Battle's death. What is important is that Foreman, by deliberately withholding and distorting relevant information, and by allowing the court's mistaken impression of his intentions and actions to go uncorrected, demonstrated his deceptive nature. In his representation of Ray, he disregarded his obligation to report to the court concerning contracts and fees; he lied to the HSCA about how he became involved in the case and how his case files on Ray were lost; and he solicited and coerced Ray to commit perjury at the sentencing hearing.

"They've Got Nothin' on Your Brother"

On November 12, 1968, the court permitted Ray to change lawyers but admonished him that no more changes would be favorably entertained.

This change was made over the sharp objection of state prosecutors, who wanted the court to order the Haneses to stay in the case, appoint Foreman only as a member of the defense team, and proceed that very day with the trial. But Ray and his brothers got their wish: the Haneses were out, Foreman was in, and the trial was delayed until the following March.

A few days later, Jerry Ray was back in Memphis. Foreman, in the mood to celebrate, invited Jerry up to his room at the Peabody Hotel. Jerry said that Foreman gave him money to get a bottle of whiskey, which he purchased and brought to Foreman's room. "He stripped down to his shorts and paced back and forth talking about how great a lawyer he was," Jerry Ray said. When Jerry poured Foreman about two fingers of whiskey, Foreman told him that he wanted a real drink, so Jerry filled the glass. Before the night was over, Jerry said, Foreman had drunk the whole bottle. He drank for hours, strutting around the room and talking about the lack of evidence, lack of a murder weapon, and how easy it was going to be to get James Earl Ray off. Foreman said, "They've got nothin' on your brother. They've got nothin' on your brother."

Jerry said that the experience of that evening magnified his shock when, later on, Foreman began pressing him and other family members to get his brother to plead guilty. The euphoria of having the famed Percy Foreman in the case and Foreman's assurances that he would get James Earl Ray cleared did not last long. Ray was soon having second thoughts about firing the Haneses and hiring Foreman.

Arthur Hanes Jr. told me that James Earl Ray soon called Hanes's father and said, "My God guys, I've made the biggest mistake I've ever made in my life. All this fellow wants me to do is plead guilty." He said that Ray asked them to get back into the case, "but by then things were so bollixed up we weren't about to get back into it." He was not surprised to hear that Foreman wanted Ray to plead guilty. "We knew immediately that when that blowhard Percy Foreman came through Birmingham, that something like that was afoot." Nor was Hanes surprised to hear that James Earl Ray was actually going to plead guilty. "Ray was canny enough and knew enough about the system to know that if he had gone to trial with Percy Foreman, who never lifted a finger to prepare or defend the case, that he would be much worse off with a sham trial and getting convicted than he would be with a plea of guilty and recanting it immediately."

Ray quoted Arthur Hanes Sr. in his book, *Who Killed Martin Luther King, Jr.?*, stating that Foreman "never prepared" and "never investigated" the case once he took it over. Hanes Sr. concluded that Foreman "never considered giving James Earl Ray a trial."[24] In reality, Foreman did initially intend to go to trial—he simply changed his mind. When, forty-two years after the fact, Hanes Jr. heard that Jerry Ray said that Foreman hinted that he would not do his best job if James Earl Ray refused to plead guilty, he replied: "I believe that. I believe that. That's the first I've heard that, but I believe that."[25]

Jerry Ray is not the only witness of Foreman's betrayal. Attorney-turned-journalist Sidney Zion wrote for the *New York Daily News,* the *New York Post,* and other publications. In 1996, years after Foreman died, Zion published a story about conversations he had had with Foreman on the James Earl Ray case in a *New York Daily News* column titled "Ray of Truth in King Plot." Zion said that he had known Foreman for many years when he told him, in the winter of 1968 to 1969, in his room at the St. Regis hotel in New York, that the James Earl Ray case was "the biggest story of our lives." He told Zion to be patient and promised to give him the scoop that will "take the top off the country" and perhaps deliver his long-awaited Pulitzer Prize. Foreman told him that Ray was innocent, that indeed there was a conspiracy to murder Reverend King, and that either Lyndon B. Johnson or J. Edgar Hoover—perhaps both—were implicated. Could it be that Foreman thought such an acquittal would be sufficiently disruptive to ponder a betrayal?

Zion described the revelation a "shocker" because it was not only completely different from what Foreman had already told him, but also it was not Foreman's way of doing business, especially in high-profile cases. In any case, a criminal defendant doesn't need Percy Foreman in order to plead guilty.

Zion tried to learn more about what had happened, but Foreman never again took his calls. A few months after Ray's sentencing hearing, the two men ran into each other at the bar in Sardi's (one of Zion's notable New York hang-outs). Zion said he attempted to question Foreman about the earlier conversation, but Foreman denied that any such conversation had ever taken place, hurriedly put down a $20 bill for his drink, and left.[26]

Foreman Coerces Ray

Shortly after coming into the case, Percy Foreman began preparing James Earl Ray to plead guilty, which neither Ray nor the Haneses had wanted to do. In early 1969, Foreman obtained Ray's written consent to negotiate a guilty plea with the district attorney general's office in exchange for waiving the death penalty. Ray didn't have much choice other than to go along with Foreman; the Haneses were not going to return to the case, and the court had already told Ray that he could not change lawyers again.

Apparently, the best that Foreman could do—or at least the best he was willing to do—was to reaffirm district attorney general Philip Canale's offer to waive the death penalty and agree to a ninety-nine-year sentence that would have made James Earl Ray eligible for parole in thirty years. (Ray died in the twenty-ninth year of his sentence). This is a strange turn of events, especially considering that the Haneses had spurned a guilty plea in exchange for a life sentence that would have made Ray eligible for parole in thirteen years.

Hanes Jr. told me that he, his father, and Ray were looking forward to a plea of innocence in order to attack the state's weak evidence. He said he, his father, and Ray were all confident of an acquittal. But Ray wanted to testify, and Hanes Sr. did not want Ray on the witness stand. The disagreement about putting Ray on the stand was the first of two instances that brought Ray's brothers to consider replacing the Haneses. The second was Jerry Ray's meeting with Huie in the fall of 1968, when Huie offered to pay Jerry cash money to keep James Earl Ray off the stand. Huie explained to Jerry that they would lose control of the story if he told it in open court. Jerry Ray told me that Huie frightened him and his brothers into believing that he, rather than the Haneses, was calling the shots in the case. Jerry immediately began looking around for another lawyer. He now admits that firing the Haneses and hiring Foreman was the worst mistake they made.

Ray's incarceration in the Shelby County jail was unusual, if not unconstitutionally cruel, under both the US and Tennessee constitutions. In prison, Ray was surrounded with lights and cameras, so he was constantly watched and even his sleep was disturbed. Battle ruled that the lights and cameras could stay after a hearing on September 30, 1968. An investigator associated with the case claimed that the lights and cameras created a condition of confinement prone to breaking down the health and will of its inhabitants.[27]

Sheriff Bill Morris refused to make any comment, but Sheriff Roy Nixon, who worked under Morris, was much more cooperative. Nixon told me that the idea had come from federal authorities at the US Bureau of Prisons

James Earl Ray, dressing in his Shelby County jail cell, circa 1969 (Courtesy Shelby County Archives)

(BOP). He said that the BOP sent someone down "to work with us on it," and that the idea for the lights and cameras "came up with discussions, sitting around talking, that that is something we needed to do."[28]

For Ray's entire period of incarceration in Shelby County, his cell was brightly lit with TV studio-type lights round-the-clock, monitored by two surveillance cameras, recorded by a microphone, and watched by at least two jailers, even when he was asleep. The outside windows were covered with plate steel and sealed so that Ray could see neither daylight nor darkness. He never breathed any fresh air. He had no privacy, even when he used the toilet, since one jailer was inside his cell at all times. Sheriff Morris testified to these facts in court on September 30, 1968.

ARTHUR HANES SR.: In addition to the television cameras there in the cell, and the microphones, are there any personnel in that cell with Mr. Ray?

BILL MORRIS: Yes sir.

HANES: At all times?

MORRIS: Yes sir.

HANES: Twenty-four hours a day?

MORRIS: Yes sir.

HANES: They watch everybody's moves?

MORRIS: Supposed to.

HANES: Every time he breathes, everything he does, they watch that, is that correct?

MORRIS: That is correct.[29]

The daily activity logs show Ray's erratic sleep patterns, sleep deprivation, and a physical and emotional toll from the lack of privacy, deliberate humiliation, round-the-clock lights.

Morris testified that he had never before used the surveillance system to which he subjected Ray, nor was he using it on other inmates charged with first degree murder. In addition, Judge James C. Beasley, who was an assistant district attorney at the time and subsequently served for many years as criminal court judge, had no knowledge of the use of the surveillance system for any inmate after Ray.

It was in this context that Foreman worked on badgering James Earl Ray into pleading guilty. Foreman told Ray that if he did not plead guilty, the FBI would arrest his aged father, George Ray, and return him to prison in Iowa for a parole violation from the 1930s; at least, this is what Ray told the HSCA in 1978.[30] Jerry Ray corroborated this account—but how could Foreman have known about Ray's father unless the FBI had fed him this information?

Foreman also told Jerry Ray that he and his brother John would be arrested on conspiracy charges in the King assassination unless James Earl pleaded guilty. Foreman told James Earl Ray that he faced the death penalty, even though no one had been executed in Tennessee in nine years due to executive clemency exercised by then-governor Buford Ellington and governor Frank Clement, who preceded him. In fact, no one convicted of murder in Shelby County had been put to death in Tennessee's electric chair since 1948. In spite of these facts, Foreman told Ray he would probably be "barbecued."[31] One of Ray's attorneys in the early to mid-1970s, James H. Lesar, told me that Percy Foreman put Ray under "incredible pressure to plead guilty. There's no question about that."[32]

Foreman also used his connections to Hooker Sr. to pressure Ray. Foreman apparently told Ray that if he pleaded guilty, John J. Hooker Jr., who was a shoe-in to be the next governor of Tennessee, would pardon him in a couple of years. Foreman denied ever discussing this story with Ray. In any case, even if Foreman did tell Ray this story, it makes more sense to go trial and hope for an acquittal knowing you have a pardon up your sleeve than it does to plead guilty without trying for acquittal in the first place. The details and context of this story have all the earmarks of a sophisticated thinker such as Foreman—and certainly not Ray.

Hooker Jr. said that the talk about pardoning Ray was ridiculous. He had no way of knowing what Foreman may have said to Ray, but that his "father never mentioned it to me, nor would he have." Hooker Jr. told me that he had gotten overwhelming support from black voters in his previous run for governor, "and the idea that I would pardon James Earl Ray is about as remote as me joining him in his cell in the state penitentiary."[33]

Foreman gave Jerry Ray cash money more than once and offered James Earl Ray additional future compensation through the literary contract—under the condition of a guilty plea. Foreman told Ray that the press had already convicted him and that the government had bribed witnesses who would place him at the scene.[34]

Hanes Jr. refused to speculate on whether Battle should have accepted Ray's plea had he known what was going on between the Ray family and Foreman, especially Foreman's last-minute letters to Ray about money. However, as a former judicial officer and one who spent many years training other judges, Hanes told me, "If Ray had, in any way, let me know [about Foreman's letters], I personally would have never accepted such a plea."[35]

Indeed, in just a few years, another court would find that Foreman's conduct in representing Ray "reek[ed] with ethical, moral, and professional irregularities," according to federal appeals court judge William Ernest Miller, the second jurist to die with a plea from James Earl Ray pending on his docket.[36] Hooker Jr. knew Miller "extremely well" and described him as an "excellent judge" who first served at the federal district court level and then on the Sixth Circuit appeals court. "I don't think any lawyer in Middle Tennessee or in the circuit who's ever appeared before [Miller] would deny that he is highly competent." For Miller to make such a "far-reaching" statement about Foreman's conduct, he said, "indicates he smells a rat."

NOT HIS STYLE

Sidney Zion noted that pleading a client guilty was simply not Percy Foreman's way of doing business. His reputation of holding the keys to the jail was not built on guilty pleas. Foreman had argued much tougher cases than James Earl Ray's and not only refused to plead his clients guilty but also won acquittals.

Further evidence of Foreman's deceptive behavior in Ray's case comes from his own sworn testimony. In his November 11, 1969, deposition in *Ray v. Foreman*, J. B. Stoner asked Foreman if Ray "fire[d] Mr. Hanes and hire[d] you just to plead him guilty." Foreman's answer was tangential to the question: "When a man hires me, I do the thinking."[37] Later in the deposition, Stoner asked Foreman, "did he [Ray] hire you to enter a plea of guilty?" Foreman replied: "People don't hire me, sir, to do anything. I do what I think is right. If they [Ray and his brothers] are going to run it they can get a Western Union messenger boy for two dollars."[38]

The HSCA said almost the same thing in a lengthy staff report on the validity of Ray's guilty plea. The HSCA staff concluded the guilty plea was Ray's own voluntary act. Right in the middle of that twenty-four-page report, however, is a comment that indicates the opposite: "Foreman's decision to plead Ray guilty did not appear to turn on his expectation that it would increase the value of the interest that he held in the literary contract."[39] Note that the language used indicates that it was Foreman's decision, not Ray's. This is also known as coercion.

SUBORNING RAY'S TESTIMONY

The essence of Foreman's second deception is the subornation of James Earl Ray's testimony, coercing him into a guilty plea, and ensuring the court would not know about it. The last thing Foreman wanted Ray to do was to march into Battle's courtroom and say something that might have caused the plea-bargain deal to unravel.

The day before Ray entered his guilty plea and was sentenced, Foreman sent Ray two letters that unmistakably connect his testimony in Battle's courtroom with payment of money. One letter addressed a cash money payment of $500 to Jerry Ray; the other letter addressed an adjustment of Foreman's fees charged to James Earl Ray based on the plea he enters. Foreman had James Earl Ray countersign both letters.

The first letter from Foreman on March 9, 1969, revealed that Ray had asked him to advance $500 to his brother Jerry Ray. Foreman explained the accounting of the $500 in the first two paragraphs of his letter. In the third paragraph came a quid pro quo. Foreman wrote that the $500 advance "is contingent upon the plea of guilty and sentence going through on March 10, 1969, without any unseemly conduct on your part in court."

In other words, Foreman reduced to writing a contract to plead guilty and to affect Ray's conduct and testimony in court the next day in exchange for payment of cash money to his brother. It was a felony bribe.

The second letter from Foreman to Ray explicitly linked the amount of his fees as well as his willingness to assign any overage from the

The cancelled bribery check to Jerry Ray (Courtesy US District Court, Western District of Tennesse)

contract proceeds to Ray, above Foreman's dues. He paid, or at least promised to pay, Ray future literary revenue in exchange for his guilty plea and good behavior in Battle's court the next morning: "If the plea is entered and the sentence accepted and no embarrassing circumstances take place in the court room, I am willing to assign to any bank, trust company or individual selected by you all my receipts under the above assignment in excess of $165,000.00. These funds over and above the first $165,000.00 will be held by such bank, trust company or individual subject to your order."

In the mid-1970s, as Ray's attempt to get a new trial seemed to be gaining ground, the US Court of Appeals, Sixth Circuit, considered an appeal of the refusal of a federal district court to give Ray a hearing based on the evidence. The two March 9, 1969, letters from Foreman figured prominently in the appeals court's hearing on Ray's claims of constitutional violations. The federal district court had previously found that Foreman's advice to Ray "was within the range of competence demanded of attorneys in criminal cases." The Sixth Circuit strongly disagreed. In reversing the district court and ordering an evidentiary hearing, it said that, if Ray's assertions are true, "the actions of his attorneys made his defense 'a farce and mockery of justice that would be shocking to the conscience of the court.'" The ruling continued:

> If the allegations are correct, petitioner's counsel [Foreman] not only did not properly advise him but deliberately misled and coerced him. It is inconceivable to us how a plea entered under these circumstances could be either intelligent or voluntary. . . . in light of the total circumstances preceding his sentencing . . . Ray could easily have believed that he had no other choice. He could follow the scenario prescribed by Foreman in his letter of March 9, 1969—enter the plea and accept sentence without creating any 'embarrassing circumstances . . . in the court room'—or he could have gone to trial with the reasonable belief, if the contentions are accurate, that a fair hearing would be impossible.[40]

Unfortunately for Ray, federal district court was no kinder to him after it was reversed on appeal than it was for the first hearing. The second hearing ended at the same legal dead end, and by the time of the next appeal, Miller, perhaps the most sympathetic jurist to Ray in any court, was dead. Bernard Fensterwald Jr. was Ray's attorney at the time.

In spite of the appearances to the contrary, the credibility of the State of Tennessee, the US Justice Department, and the FBI were used to make Ray's plea look legitimate. Subsequent to his guilty plea, a propaganda campaign commenced to smear Ray and transform him from a man into the symbol of a dirty racist.

Hooker Jr. personally knew Foreman through his father, although only "superficially." Regarding the March 9 letters to Ray, Hooker Jr. reacted, "I'm astonished that Percy Foreman, who was a sophisticated lawyer, would have put something like that in writing, because it's obviously a bribe."

Hooker said that if he had been the judge in court that day and had known about Foreman's letters to Ray (which Battle did not), "the first thing I would have done is to put Percy Foreman in contempt of court, because basically Percy Foreman was trying to influence testimony in court." Hooker also noted that he would "want to know what Ray knows that would be embarrassing to Foreman."

The deceptive nature of the letters was "extremely hostile to the administration of justice," Hooker continued. "[It's] an offense against the court. I can't overemphasize how preposterous it is that I think any lawyer of substance would admit he's paying a bribe in a pending criminal case."

Likewise, Tennessee commissioner of correction, Harry Avery, believed Ray's plea was coerced. In fact, it was Avery's investigation of Ray once he was in his custody at the state penitentiary on the wee hours of March 11, 1969, which revealed the existence of Foreman's letters. This would be the last investigation of the King assassination by any incumbent Tennessee official.

Avery said that it was a "well-known fact across the country" that two successive Tennessee governors—Frank Clement and Buford Ellington—had commuted death sentences rather than carry out any executions in the electric chair. Thus, Foreman's claim that Ray was in danger of a death sentence was not only false, it was contrary to Foreman's knowledge and not offered to Ray in good faith. Furthermore, Avery indicated that the payment of cash money to Jerry Ray was another type of duress. In a taped interview in 1978, Avery said, "I know as a lawyer that if I do my client that way, that that client is going to say 'I was under duress and led into pleading guilty.' And I think Ray was led into pleading guilty out of fear of the [electric] chair and out of the things Foreman was doing for his brother. That's how I feel about it."[41]

REMOVING DOUBT OF FOREMAN'S GUILT

After Ray pleaded guilty on March 10, 1969, Judge Battle explained his rights as well as all the rights he waived by entering the plea. Then Battle asked Ray the following:

W. PRESTON BATTLE: Has anything besides this sentence of ninety-nine years in the penitentiary been promised to you to get you to plead guilty? Has anything else been promised to you by anyone?

JAMES EARL RAY: No, it has not.

BATTLE: Has any pressure of any kind by anyone in any way been used on you to get you to plead guilty?

RAY: Now, what did you say?

BATTLE: Are you pleading guilty to Murder in the First Degree in this case

because you killed Dr. Martin Luther King under such circumstances
that it would make you legally guilty of Murder in the First Degree under
the law as explained to you by your lawyers?

RAY: Yes, legally, yes.

BATTLE: Is this plea of guilty to Murder in the First Degree with an
agreed punishment of ninety-nine years in the State Penitentiary freely,
voluntarily and understandingly made and entered by you?

RAY: Yes, Sir.

BATTLE: Is this plea of guilty on your part the free act of your free will
made with your full knowledge and understanding of its meaning and
consequences?

RAY: Yes, Sir.[42]

Now, there is a discrepancy between the two separate transcripts
in the Shelby County, Tennessee, archives, when Ray answers Battle's
question about "pressure of any kind." The transcript of the Shelby
County district attorney's office recorded Ray's response to the question
above as "No. No one in any way."

Ray never answered the question of whether any outside pressure
compelled him to plead guilty, and Battle simply moved on to another
question without repeating and requiring Ray to answer it. The second
transcript falsely records a negative response by Ray.

Ray lied in response to every other question. Whether he also lied
in answer to the question about "any pressure of any kind by anyone"
as recorded in the second transcript is immaterial. He did exactly what
Foreman wanted and expected him to do. He entered the guilty plea
and kept his mouth shut about Foreman's activities. Ray covered
for Foreman's because, as the federal appeals court would later
conclude, he "could easily have believed that he had no other choice."[43]
Furthermore, Ray lied when asked if anything else had been promised
to him other than the ninety-nine-year sentence, as there is evidence
that Foreman gave Jerry Ray $500 and the promise of revenue from the
literary contract. Foreman's assurance that Ray would be pardoned when
John Jay Hooker Jr. was elected governor also constitutes a promise. In

addition, there were threats for the arrest of his brothers, the return of his aged father to prison, and the insinuation that he would be barbecued in the electric chair. Ray lied when he said that the guilty plea was the free act of his own free will. Ray never wanted to plead guilty, and he and the Haneses had already turned down a better offer. Why wouldn't a man acting of his own free will insist on the much shorter sentence previously offered to him?

Ray was cornered, and Foreman knew it, because it was Foreman who set it up this way. At this moment, Ray became as much a prisoner of Percy Foreman as he was a prisoner of Shelby County. By paying Jerry Ray $500 cash, promising James Earl Ray additional literary revenue, and threatening Ray's family members, Foreman secured this secret from the court.

PECULIARITIES IN THE COURT

In 1969, Tennessee law required any plea of guilty in a murder case to be approved by a perfunctory jury, even when there was not an actual trial. After the perfunctory jury had been selected and seated, James Earl Ray unexpectedly stood up and announced to the court that he had something to say.

JAMES EARL RAY: Your Honor, I would like to say something. I don't want to change anything that I have said, but I just want to enter one other thing. The only thing that I have to say is that I can't agree with Mr. Clark.

PERCY FOREMAN: Ramsey Clark.

W. PRESTON BATTLE: Mr. who?

RAY: Mr. J. Edgar Hoover, I agree with all these stipulations, and I am not trying to change anything.

BATTLE: You don't agree with whose theories?

RAY: Mr. Canale's, Mr. Clark's, and Mr. J. Edgar Hoover's about the conspiracy. I don't want to add something on that I haven't agreed to in the past.

FOREMAN: I think, that what he said is that he doesn't agree that Ramsey

Clark is right, or that J. Edgar Hoover is right. I didn't argue that as evidence in this case, I simply stated that under riding the statement of General Canale that they had made the same statement. You are not required to agree with it all.

BATTLE: You still, your answers to these questions that I asked you would still be the same? Is that correct?

RAY: Yes, Sir.

BATTLE: There is nothing in these questions that I have asked you and your answers to them, you change none of them at all. In other words, you are pleading guilty to, and taking ninety-nine years, I think the main question that I want to ask you is this: are you pleading guilty to Murder in the First Degree in this case because you killed Dr. Martin Luther King under such circumstances that it would make you legally guilty of Murder in the First Degree under the law as explained to you by your lawyer. Your answer is still yes? Alright, Sir, that is all, you may swear the jury.[44]

The elephant in the room was the question of conspiracy, and what Ray might have known about others that he never told anyone. Battle had a confessed killer standing before him who had just disagreed with the comments of the director of the FBI and the US attorney general, who had said that there was no conspiracy. Obviously, Ray had something on his mind, but Battle was too focused on accepting the plea and disposing of the case to find out. Had Battle questioned Ray about what his comments really meant regarding conspiracy, it might have blown the guilty plea deal out of the water.

Battle, however, did not follow up, nor was there any note in the nine-page stipulation prepared by the district attorney's office about Ray having acted alone in the murder. It merely said that Ray fired the shot that fatally wounded King, making him "legally guilty" of murder. The stipulation was silent on the issue of conspiracy. Ray seemed to understand this fact better than Battle when he said that he didn't want to "add something on" to the stipulation that he had previously signed.

Foreman interjected in the unanticipated exchange between Ray and Battle in order to smooth things over and keep in place the guilty plea that he had forced Ray to make. Researcher and author Harold

Weisberg suggests that, in doing so, Foreman was working more for the prosecutors than he was for his client.[45]

During the selection of the perfunctory jury, both the prosecution and defense questioned each juror as to whether they would accept the guilty plea with the ninety-nine-year sentence that had been agreed to by the state and Ray. The court adjourned for lunch and the jury returned to inform the court they agreed with the plea deal.

Battle passed the agreed-upon sentence without ever asking two direct questions: "Did you murder Dr. Martin Luther King?" and "Did you act alone?"

FOREMAN AND THE FBI

Another unconscionable act by Foreman was the consent he gave to the FBI to interrogate Ray after he had entered the guilty plea. Foreman not only consented to an interrogation, which was conducted for the purpose of implicating Ray in other crimes he might have committed, but he agreed to withhold Ray's access to legal counsel during the interrogation.

Ray was interrogated in his prison cell in Nashville on March 13, 1969—the day he wrote Battle and fired Foreman—by FBI agent Robert Jensen and assistant attorney general Fred M. Vinson Jr. He was not read his rights. The report of the interrogation has been sealed along with other HSCA evidence.[46]

Jerry Ray told me that he doubts his brother agreed to speak to them. He said he and his brother had a rule never to speak to the FBI, especially when two agents were present and could support each other's version of what was said. That any lawyer would agree to any client speaking alone to two FBI agents shows incompetence or gross neglect of the client's interests.

THE LOOK MAGAZINE ARTICLE

Ray arrived at the Tennessee state penitentiary in the early morning hours of March 11. Two days later, he fired Percy Foreman. Almost immediately, Foreman began speaking ill of his former client. On April 15, Foreman authored an article in *Look* magazine.

In the article, Foreman wrote that he assumed Ray was guilty in the same way a doctor summoned in the middle of the night to a man's bedside assumes the patient is sick. Foreman admitted elsewhere that he had never directly inquired of Ray whether he was guilty.

Foreman also claimed that he spent forty hours attempting to convince Ray that he knew more about the law than Ray. Foreman never claimed to have spent even a single hour investigating or preparing the case—just as Hanes Jr. noted.

Towards the close of the article, Foreman claimed that if Ray had not pleaded guilty after Foreman had negotiated a death penalty waiver, it would have been Foreman's "duty" to turn on his client and offer testimony against him. This act would constitute an unconscionable violation of Ray's right to have privileged communication with his attorney. Hooker Jr. also told me that such an occurrence would have been an "inconceivable" violation of attorney-client privilege. Foreman knew this, but in his confusion of going back and forth between his roles of lawyer, dramatic actor, psychologist, provocateur, and carnival barker, he might have simply gotten carried away. Perhaps this is what the federal appeals court had in mind when it labeled Foreman's bizarre behavior as "a farce and mockery of justice that would be shocking to the conscience of the court."

Foreman closed the *Look* article with the assertion that Ray murdered King because he wanted attention.[47] Even if that were the case, why did the assassin fire from a concealed, distant location and run away immediately? The circumstances indicate that the assassin wanted—needed—to get away, not to get caught.

So, Why Plead Guilty?

I have little doubt that the question on the minds of many readers is, "Why would anyone, including James Earl Ray plead guilty if he were truly innocent?" It is a reasonable question that must be addressed.

Ray was offered two plea "deals." The first one was a "life" sentence offered to the Haneses that they and Ray turned down. Ray would have served much less time with a life sentence (less than fifteen years) than with the ninety-nine-year sentence (thirty years) negotiated by Foreman before leaving jail for parole. But James Earl Ray is not the only defendant who has accepted a plea "bargain" arrangement when he did not commit the crime. The problems associated with plea-bargaining are complex and pervasive, and a full explanation is a book-length topic.

According to the Innocence Project, an organization aimed to correct wrongful convictions, one out of four falsely convicted criminal defendants either made incriminating statements to police, gave confessions, or pleaded guilty to crimes they did not commit. The organization notes a variety of factors as to why innocent people confess, including duress, coercion, and the threat of a harsh sentence—all of which were factors in Ray's situation. Some guilty pleas can be explained by the mental state of the defendant—another factor affecting Ray due to nearly eight months of incessant lights, cameras, and invasive, dehumanizing surveillance.

Several books address this question: are only the guilty punished and are the innocent freed? In former Ohio attorney general Jim Petro and his wife Nancy's 2011 book *False Justice: Eight Myths that Convict the Innocent,* the authors include "false confession" as one of their eight myths. Nancy Petro stated that among the "primary contributors to wrongful conviction," they rank "mistaken eyewitness as the most prevalent, then government misconduct, and then perhaps false confession." She added that the factors are often interdependent. "For example, government misconduct can prompt a coerced, false confession."[48]

The rigors of imprisonment can also break people. Former US attorney Hal D. Hardin described how convicted murderer Ronald Harries "wanted to die because it was just horrific what he was living under." Harries told him that "I'd rather die than live in a situation like this."[49] Harries and Ray were both imprisoned at the main penitentiary in Nashville during this period.

When James Earl Ray pleaded guilty, he was under physical and emotional duress from his rigorous confinement in the Shelby County jail, his family was threatened with prosecution, he was threatened with execution, and, even if he was acquitted of murdering King, he was going to have to go back to prison in Missouri for a long time. Furthermore, Foreman had threatened to throw the case unless he pled guilty. Ray was cornered. What real choice did he have? His decision to plead guilty is no different than many other criminal defendants who admitted committing crimes for which they were not responsible.

"How Did It All Happen?"

Foreman provided neither a competent nor honest defense on behalf of his client and coerced, berated, and threatened Ray to achieve a guilty plea in court.

Foreman entered the case at the invitation of Ray's brothers in order to get the Haneses out of it. At first, Foreman clearly believed that he could get Ray acquitted. But something changed. Was it the presentation of physical evidence, the testimony of eyewitnesses, or the revelation of a motive?

The evidence against Ray, as both the Haneses and Foreman knew, was extremely weak. The state never proved it had the murder weapon. The Haneses had the green army jacket that was too small for Ray and a witness who said he saw a man wearing it in the flophouse right after the shot. If it doesn't fit, you must acquit, after all. Foreman had it too, but his actions indicate that he was more interested in silently dispatching Ray than he was in defending him. Moreover, the Haneses—and, subsequently, Foreman—had a witness, Guy Canipe, who was going to dispute the state's entire timeline of the crime.

Without eyewitnesses, the murder weapon, or opportunity, motive alone doesn't prove anything. The HSCA tried to determine Ray's motive to kill King, but it never verified anything that established one. It would be closer to Foreman's known defense style to have put almost every white male in the South on trial to prove that there were millions of people with a motive to kill King, not just James Earl Ray, if the state relied on race to prove its case.

There is also the matter of Foreman's two perjuries. It is not just important that Foreman lied about how he got into the case; it is also significant that he later changed the story to include receiving a letter from Ray. There may be several reasonable explanations as to what happened, but it is obvious that someone forced him to revise his story. Foreman wanted the world to know that it was his case to refuse from the time Ray was apprehended in London, even though all the evidence suggests the contrary. Both James Earl and Jerry

Ray initially believed Foreman was going to mount a credible defense. It was only after Foreman was hired that he changed his course.

After Ray was railroaded by his own attorney, the Haneses shook their heads in wonder. Hanes Jr. told me, "My Dad and I speculated afterwards, how did it all happen?"

Was Foreman's relation to the case and its outcome merely chance? Hanes Jr. didn't think so. He revealed that he and his father felt pressure from something outside of the court that they suspected was local. "We [Haneses Sr. and Jr.] think there was a component in the establishment in Memphis that worried that we would in fact, win it, with bad consequences to Memphis." Hanes Jr. said, "Foreman being what he was, I can imagine Foreman getting sucked into that."[50]

CHAPTER 7
One Too Many Transcripts

There are two competing transcripts of James Earl Ray's sentencing hearing in Battle's court on March 10, 1969. One of the transcripts is a legitimate record of the questions Battle posed to Ray and the answers Ray gave. That transcript was "typed up that same day," according to James A. Blackwell, clerk of Shelby County's criminal court at the time. "We had about twenty-five reporters that were waiting for a copy of the transcript."[1] Blackwell's deputy clerk, Charles E. Koster, was the typist. Koster noted, "I started working on it about ten minutes after we got out of court." He said that it was completed and distributed that afternoon.[2]

The other transcript is not an accurate record of those proceedings. It was deliberately altered to conceal the truth of Ray's replies to Battle's question about pressure and Battle's resulting legal gaffe. Furthermore, the evidence indicates that the transcript was changed in the Shelby County district attorney's office—not the clerk's.

A shocking aspect of the altered transcript is that the HSCA almost certainly knew that two versions existed. HSCA general counsel G. Robert Blakey had copies of both transcripts, yet Blakey and his staff failed to determine which was the true text before the committee.

To add insult to injury, the HSCA staff made additional alterations of its own in its 1979 published findings in order to implicate Ray more than by the words he actually spoke during his guilty plea hearing. Blakey glibly dismisses any significance to the altered transcript: "If it exists, and it was material, it was not, in any event, brought to my attention." The doctored transcript was not only material, a federal court found it "central and determinative" in keeping Ray in prison. Furthermore, Blakey's denial that it wasn't brought to his attention is an admission that his staff was incompetent and his investigation inadequate because the valid transcript was published in two books listed in the HSCA bibliography.

James A. Blackwell with Charles Koster's original transcript (Courtesy author's collection)

The rulings by the Tennessee Court of Criminal Appeals and the Tennessee Supreme Court were limited to procedural, not factual, aspects of the case. As far as the Tennessee courts were concerned, it mattered not how Ray answered—or in this case refused to answer—Battle's questions. Their primary concerns were whether Ray had legal counsel (which he did), whether Ray agreed to waive his right to a jury trial (which he did), whether Ray agreed to waive his right to appeal (which he did), whether Ray entered a guilty plea (yes), and whether Ray entered his guilty plea because someone pressured him to do so. This ultimate question Ray refused to answer and Battle failed to pursue.

The federal court reluctantly looked at both the procedural and factual aspects of Ray's appeal, but, like the courts in Tennessee, they rejected it based, in part, on their understanding of the altered transcript.

It is unlikely that there would have ever been an alternate transcript if Battle had lived. In 1969 and until 1978, there was no clear authority in Tennessee courts to certify a transcript of a court proceeding other than the judge who actually presided over it. Battle, however, died before certifying a transcript of Ray's sentencing hearing.

Had Battle lived, he would have certified the transcript of the proceedings of his court, and that would have become the official version of events—right or wrong. Any appeals court reviewing the matter would have used the court-ordered certified transcript exclusively. There would have been no room in the process for any altered transcript to compete with the one that was officially certified by the court.

THE ORIGINAL TRANSCRIPT

The Shelby County Archives holds both the original transcript of Ray's March 10, 1969, sentencing hearing and the altered one. Koster transcribed the original, the authenticity of which is proven by the sworn affidavits from Blackwell and himself. There are three early accounts of the sentencing hearing, published in books after the fact, which agree with each other and with Koster's original transcript in the Shelby County Archives. Two of the three authors of those books were in the courtroom that day and no doubt obtained a copy of the transcript that Koster distributed. Blackwell also kept his own personal copy of the transcript and showed it to me in his home on April 17, 2013. Lastly, there are voice recordings of the hearing in question, and it is clear on those recordings that Ray equivocated, giving a non-answer that matches the original transcript. In spite of all of this, it only took about ten weeks for the altered transcript to surface.

Ray's first appeal to Shelby County Criminal Court of May 26, 1969, was heard by Battle's designated successor, Judge Arthur C. Faquin Jr. The Shelby County district attorney's office introduced the altered transcript as "Exhibit 4" at this hearing. Since neither Blackwell nor Koster had made any changes to the transcript once it was completed and distributed, the alteration must have occurred in the district attorney's office. The district attorney called Blackwell as a witness and had him read the court's Minute Books as evidence. He also had Blackwell read a portion of Exhibit 4, in which the official transcript was embedded. Blackwell clearly says on the audiotape that it begins on "page 208." The eighty-six-page altered transcript in the Shelby County Archives shows a stamp on each page, with page 1 of the transcript stamped with the number 208. Thus, it is clear that the stamp originated when Exhibit 4 was created.

AFFIDAVIT

I, James A. Blackwell, having first been duly sworn, do upon my oath state:

I served in the office of Clerk of the Criminal Court of Shelby County, Tennessee from 1953 to 1990.

I was present on March 10, 1969 for the entire guilty plea hearing of defendant James Earl Ray.

As part of my duty as Clerk, I supervised the personnel who made audio recordings of said hearing.

Under my direction, and using the recordings thereof, my deputy Clerk, Charles E. Koster, typed an 86-page transcript of said hearing; page four of which represents the original transcript that was prepared and distributed to news reporters the afternoon of March 10, 1969 as shown in Exhibit 1 to this affidavit.

After said transcript was distributed to news reporters on said date, I made no changes to, nor did I authorize any changes.

Witness my signature this day, April _19_, 2013.

James A. Blackwell
James A. Blackwell

State of Tennessee
County of Shelby

Sworn and subscribed before me this April _19_, 2013 in Shelby County, Tennessee.

Notary Public

My seal and commission expiration date: _____   MY COMMISSION EXPIRES AUG 15, 2015

James A. Blackwell's signed affidavit confirming the authenticity of Koster's original transcript (Courtesy author's collection)

Faquin accepted the district attorney's tactic, and Blackwell cannot remember why the transcript was presented in this way. When he listened to his own voice from forty-four years prior and followed along on his own yellowed copy of the transcript, he shook his head at the altered line and

AFFIDAVIT

I, Charles E. Koster, having first been duly sworn, do upon my oath state:

I served as deputy Clerk of the Criminal Court of Shelby County, Tennessee from 1964 to 1986.

I was present on March 10, 1969 for the entire guilty plea hearing of defendant James Earl Ray.

As part of my duty as deputy Clerk and court reporter, I made audio recordings of said hearing.

Using the recordings thereof I transcribed an 86-page transcript of said hearing, which was typed on one typewriter; page four of which represents the original transcript that was prepared by me and distributed to news reporters the afternoon of March 10, 1969 as shown in Exhibit 1 to this affidavit.

After said transcript was distributed to news reporters on said date, I made no changes to, nor have any knowledge of changes to said transcript.

Witness my signature this day, May 6 , 2013.

Charles E. Koster

State of Tennessee
County of Chester

Sworn and subscribed before me this May 6 , 2013 in Chester County, Tennessee.

Barbara C Cole
Notary Public

My seal and commission expiration date: 3/14/17

Charles E. Koster's signed affidavit confirming the authenticity of the transcript that he transcribed (Courtesy author's collection)

said, "No, no, that's not what he said."[3] However, because Blackwell was not a lawyer and was reading something the district attorney had handed him to read, and because Ray had fired Foreman three days after the March 10, 1969, hearing and hired new attorneys, no one disputed the transcript at the appeals hearing. Judge Faquin probably would not have been prepared for the legal significance of the altered transcript even if he had caught the change.

Clay Blair Jr. was physically in the courtroom the day Ray was sentenced. He was part of the crowd of reporters and writers waiting for a copy of the completed transcript. His version of the transcript, which he printed verbatim in a book published within days of Ray's 1969 hearing, is corroborated word for word by a subsequent book by John Seigenthaler, James D. Squires, Jack Hemphill, and Frank Ritter.[4]

The second book considered the peculiarities of the cases against various accused assassins, including James Earl Ray. Like Blair, Squires was present in the courtroom and witnessed Battle's questioning. Squires also included the verbatim transcript of the proceedings.[5] The transcript as printed agrees word for word with Blair's book and the one in Blackwell's possession.

Squires further corroborated his transcript's accuracy: "This has to be the original [transcript] because if we had used it out of Blair's book, and copied it and just took his, then we would have put it in the bibliography." He also observed that the length of the passages must have come from the court reporter. "I didn't do that off my notes. . . . This has got to be the one that happened that day."[6] He expressed confidence that the transcript that both he and Blair separately published was the real thing.

Michael Dorman's book about Percy Foreman, published in 1970, has only one brief chapter on Foreman's participation in Ray's defense, but it too published a transcript wording that matches Squires, Blair, and Blackwell's transcripts.

Shelby County district attorney Phil Canale avoided the issue of the lack of a certified transcript at the May 26, 1969, hearing of Ray's motion for a full trial.

Canale did not want Ray's actual words entered as evidence at the hearing. Ray's new lawyers would have used his non-answer to argue that Battle's acceptance of the guilty plea was in error. After firing Foreman, Ray was represented by Memphis attorney Richard J. Ryan, Chattanooga attorney Robert W. Hill Jr., and Savannah, Georgia, attorney J. B. Stoner. Unfortunately, none of these attorneys had been at the March 10 hearing, and apparently none had listened to the audio recording of the hearing itself.

What follows is the entire original transcript of the questions posed by Battle and the responses Ray gave. This is from the original Koster transcript in the Shelby County Archives; it is what Blackwell and Koster have sworn is true; and it is the word-for-word reprint in Blair's, Squires's, and Dorman's books, which were each written independently. On March 10, 1969, Criminal Court was called to order:

THE COURT: The calendar has been transferred to Division I. Alright, I believe the only matter we have pending before us is the matter of James Earl Ray.

MR. FOREMAN: Would your Honor give me just a minute?

THE COURT: Yes, Sir.

MR. FOREMAN: May it please the Court, in this cause, we have prepared the defendant and I have signed and Mr. Hugh Stanton, Sr. and Jr., will now sign a Petition for Waiver of Trial and Request for Acceptance of Plea of Guilty. We have an order, I believe the Clerk has this.

THE COURT: This is a compromise and settlement on a plea of guilty to murder in the first degree and an agreed settlement of 99 years in the Penitentiary, is that true?

MR. FOREMAN: That's the agreement, your Honor.

THE COURT: Is that the agreement? Alright, I'll have to voir dire Mr. Ray, James Earl Ray, stand. Have you a lawyer to explain all your rights to you and do you understand them?

A [JAMES EARL RAY]: Yes, Sir.

THE COURT: Do you know that you have a right to a trial by jury on a charge of Murder in the First Degree against you, the punishment for Murder in the First Degree ranging from death by electrocution to any time over 20 years. The burden of proof is on the State of Tennessee to prove you guilty beyond a reasonable doubt and to a moral certainty and the decision of the jury must be unanimous, both as to guilt and punishment. In the event of a jury verdict against you, you would have the right to file a Motion for a New Trial addressed to the Trial Judge. In the event of an adverse ruling against you on your Motion for a New Trial, you would have the right to successive appeals to the Tennessee Court of Criminal Appeals and the Supreme Court of Tennessee and to file a Petition to Review by the Supreme Court of the United States. Do you understand that you have all these rights?

A: Yes, Sir.

THE COURT: You are entering a plea of guilty to Murder in the First Degree as charged in the indictment and are compromising and settling your case on an agreed punishment of 99 years in the State Penitentiary. Is this what you want to do?

A: Yes, I do.

THE COURT: Is this what you want to do?

A: Yes, Sir.

THE COURT: Do you understand that you are waiving, which means giving up a formal trial by your plea of guilty although the laws of this State require the prosecution to present certain evidence to a jury in all cases on pleas of guilty to Murder in the First Degree? By your plea of guilty, you are also waiving your right to one, your Motion for a New Trial; two, successive appeals to the Supreme Court, to the Tennessee Court of Criminal Appeals and the Supreme Court of Tennessee and three, Petition to Review by the Supreme Court of the United States. By your plea of guilty, you are also abandoning and waiving your objections and exceptions to all the motions and petitions in which the Court has heretofore ruled against you in whole or in part among them being one, Motion to Withdraw Plea and Quash Indictment; two, Motion to inspect the Evidence; three, Motion to Remove Lights and Cameras from the Jail; four, Motion for Private Consultation with Attorney; five, Petition to Authorize Defendant to Take Depositions; six, Motion to Permit Conference with Huie: seven, Motion to Permit Photographs; eight, Motion to Designate Court Reporters; nine, Motion to Stipulate Testimony; ten, Suggestion of Proper Name. You are waiving or giving up all the rights. Has anything besides this sentence of 99 years in the Penitentiary been promised to you to get you to plead guilty? Has anything else been promised to you by anyone?

A: No, it has not.

THE COURT: Has any pressure of any kind by anyone in any way been used on you to get you to plead guilty?

A: Now, what did you say?

THE COURT: Are you pleading guilty to Murder in the First Degree in this case because you killed Dr. Martin Luther King under such circumstances that it would make you legally guilty of Murder in the First Degree under the law as explained to you by your lawyers?

A: Yes, legally, yes.

THE COURT: Is this plea of guilty to Murder in the First Degree with an agreed punishment of 99 years in the State Penitentiary freely, voluntarily and understandingly made and entered by you?

A: Yes, Sir.

THE COURT: Is this plea of guilty on your part the free act of your free will made with your full knowledge and understanding of its meaning and consequences?

A: Yes, Sir.

THE COURT: You may be seated.[7]

The previous day, Ray had agreed to answer the question about pressure ("Has any pressure of any kind by anyone in any way been used on you to get you to plead guilty?") with a simple "no." He went off-script by giving an equivocal non-answer. This was changed in the altered transcript to an unequivocal negative response: "No, no one in any way."

Ray spoke only twenty-five words during this three minute and forty-three second exchange. His longest statement was just five words. The effort to pressure Ray into pleading guilty, in part by prior systematic humiliation and complete deprivation of privacy for eight months in the Shelby County jail, ensured that the world would never hear more than these few words from James Earl Ray in open court.

BATTLE'S BLUNDER

Battle had no business accepting James Earl Ray's guilty plea without first exploring why Ray failed to answer the question about pressure. He further stumbled with the question he put to Ray about whether he actually murdered Reverend King. Battle's rambling, technical question did not definitively establish whether Ray murdered King "under such circumstances that it would make you *legally guilty* of murder in the first degree under the law as explained to you by your lawyers." Battle's question was as obscure to non-lawyers as a schematic drawing of the inside of a computer is to non-engineers. It consisted of a question ("did you kill King?") wrapped inside two other questions ("did your action meet the legal definition of murder" and "is that the way your lawyers explained it to you?").

Whether Ray actually understood the question or not, he seized upon Battle's use of the term "legally guilty" to answer "yes," admitting that he was "legally" guilty. This could have been Ray's way of recognizing that he was cornered and going to receive the legal consequences of the charge of murder without truly admitting that he pulled the trigger or knowingly participated in a murder plot. It was Ray's way of distinguishing between actual guilt and legal guilt.

Battle's failure to explore Ray's words is compounded by the fact that the questions Battle asked Ray were not only scripted but also written and virtually rehearsed the previous day.

"On the day before the guilty plea, Ray was shown a written copy of the questions which were to be asked him by Judge Battle, at the time of the plea. Ray initialed and signed each page of this document to indicate that he had read and approved this document," according to court pleadings filed by William J. Haynes Jr. and William Henry Haile of the Tennessee attorney general's office.[8]

The document to which Haynes and Haile refer are in the Shelby County Archives. It consists of a petition for waiver of the death penalty in exchange for a plea of guilty; a court order accepting the guilty plea; and the questions to be posed to Ray the following day. Ray's scripted answers were to be a simple "yes" or "no," and they were already written into the document. Both Ray and Foreman initialed or signed every page.

On March 10, 1969, Percy Foreman told Battle that he had "prepared the defendant" to follow the script. Battle took his cue, told Ray to stand and began reading his scripted questions as Ray faced him in open court. In all likelihood, Battle read from the actual *voir dire* document that also contained Ray's scripted answers, which he had signed the previous day. When Ray deviated from the script on the question about pressure and again with his answer about being "legally guilty," Battle simply continued slogging through the script without missing a beat.

One of Ray's attorneys for much of the 1970s, James H. "Jim" Lesar, told me that Battle "blew it in all sorts of ways." He told me, "There was incredible pressure on Ray to plead guilty. There's no question about that." Lesar says that the pressure came from Ray's former attorney Percy Foreman.[9]

The entire episode of Battle's questions and Ray's answers (as well as the previous day's rehearsal) was more akin to a dramatic performance than a tribunal of justice. It was a sham, a hollow counterfeit of the law and a cheap knock-off of the truth. It was a charade written and practiced in secret and revealed to the public in open court as if it were the real thing. In reality, a great deal of effort had already gone into ensuring that nothing would go wrong once the reporters were in the courtroom. "The show must go on," as they say in the entertainment business. It certainly did in Memphis that day.

THE ALTERNATE TRANSCRIPT

Doctoring a transcript is a serious offense. Any lawyer who introduces doctored evidence, even unknowingly, is on a fast track to professional disciplinary action. It is an offense against justice as well as the integrity of the court. The party or parties responsible for doctoring the transcript resided in the Shelby County district attorney's office, although the Tennessee attorney general also used the altered transcript, knowingly or unknowingly.

The only page that was changed in the altered transcript had obviously been typed on a different typewriter. Here is what the doctored transcript recorded:

THE COURT: Has any pressure of any kind by anyone in any way been used on you to get you to plead guilty?

A [JAMES EARL RAY]: No, No one, in any way.

In the original version, Ray's answer was "Now, what did you say?"

As previously indicated, the first use of the alternate transcript surfaced in the May 26, 1969, hearing for a new trial in Judge Faquin's court. It was subsequently used in every court hearing, unchallenged by Ray's string of lawyers. It also was used in the federal courts beginning with the case of *James Earl Ray v. J. H. Rose, Warden,* which originated in federal district court in Nashville in 1973. Ray's attorneys filed a writ of habeas corpus, which was subsequently denied and the case dismissed without a hearing by Judge L. Clure Morton.

Morton justified his decision by citing specifically from the altered words of the transcript, just as Faquin had done. In fact, Morton said that the counterfeit words were "central and determinative" in his decision:

> It appears to the [federal] court that the specific central and determinative issue raised by the massive pleadings in the case is this: Were illicit pressures placed upon the petitioner [Ray] to such an extent that he did not voluntarily enter the plea of guilty? . . .
>
> The record of the March 10, 1969, proceedings, considered alone, shows that the petitioner [Ray] entered a voluntary, knowing and intelligent plea of guilty . . .
>
> To summarize this order, the factual allegations of the petitioner . . . are insufficient to justify a holding that petitioner's plea was not voluntary, knowing and intelligent.[10]

Morton had no knowledge that his decision was based on a doctored, false transcript that was entered into evidence in his court by the Tennessee attorney general's office, which represented the State of Tennessee in federal court. Ray's attorneys not only allowed this version of the transcript into evidence without objection, they never raised the issue of what Ray did or did not say to the question about pressure.

Jim Lesar told me that he had no recollection of an altered transcript, although he thinks it may be true that were was one. He said that Robert Livingston (one of Ray's Memphis attorneys) "particularly did not trust" the transcript introduced by the state.[11] Another attorney associated with Ray's legal team, Stephen C. Small of Nashville, was a court-appointed attorney in a prisoners' rights case. Small told me that he was not directly involved in Ray's federal appeals process and was not aware of any controversy about the transcripts.[12]

Ray's attorneys appealed to the US Court of Appeals for the Sixth Circuit. The Sixth Circuit reversed Morton's ruling and ordered a full

```
THE COURT:   Has any pressure of any kind by anyone

             in any way been used on you to get you to

             plead guilty?

A            Now, what did you say?

THE COURT:   Are you pleading guilty to Murder in

             the First Degree in this case because you

             killed Dr. Martin Luther King under such

             circumstances that it would make you legally
```

```
THE COURT:   Has any pressure of any kind by anyone in

             any way been used on you to get you to

             plead guilty?

A            No, No one, in any way.

THE COURT:   Are you pleading guilty to Murder in

             the First Degree in this case because you

             killed Dr. Martin Luther King under such

             circumstances that it would make you legally
```

A comparison of Koster's original transcript (top) *with the altered transcript* (bottom) (Courtesy author's collection)

evidentiary hearing. Thereupon, Morton transferred the case to the west district federal court in Memphis, where more of the witnesses were located. Judge Robert M. McRae Jr. conducted an eight-day hearing in Memphis from October to November 1974.

For the hearing in McRae's court, Charles E. Koster ironically certified the doctored transcript as "a full complete, true and perfect copy of the transcript of March 10, 1969." Koster's certification is not equivalent to the court's routine certification of a transcript, which in this case never occurred. Furthermore, a "certified" document can be changed before it is filed with the court.

When a court certifies a transcript, it allows the lawyers on both sides to review the draft and note any discrepancies, changes, or objections. If these differences cannot be amicably resolved among the lawyers, then the court steps in and may allow oral arguments or written pleadings before deciding. A voice recording can be consulted at the court's discretion. None of this happened with Ray's sentencing hearing transcripts because Judge Battle had died.

The fact remains that the Shelby County district attorney's office deliberately changed Ray's answer and created the alternate transcript in order to deceive the courts and the public and ensure that Ray would never receive a full trial.

Following McRae's hearing, the Tennessee attorney general filed a seventy-one-page memorandum with the court in summary of its argument that Ray's case should be dismissed. This document was prepared and signed by two assistants in the attorney general's office, Haynes and Haile.

What is interesting about the altered transcript is that whoever doctored the longhand version likely was aware of the audio recordings or at least was present in the courtroom on March 10, 1969, and near enough to Ray to hear what he said. The writer penned "legally yes" into Ray's answers in the wrong place. Ray did not, as this document shows, say the words "legally yes" in response to the ninety-nine-year sentence and guilt plea question. Rather, he answered "legally yes" to the question about killing King.

Arguing in this memorandum that Ray's plea was entered voluntarily and without undue pressure, Haynes and Haile stated: "The highest and best evidence of the voluntariness of a plea of guilty are [sic] Ray's statements at the time the plea is entered . . . Some of these statements are worth repeating." Haynes and Haile referenced the alternate transcript of Ray's responses.

The memorandum referred to the alternate transcript as "Exhibit 87," indicating that it was introduced as evidence at McRae's evidentiary hearing in Memphis. The page that contains Ray's altered response is

JUDGE "Has anything besides this sentence of ninety-nine years in the penitentiary been promised to you to get you to plead guilty? Has anything else been promised you by anyone?"

DEFENDANT "No" *It has not.*

JUDGE "Has any pressure of any kind, by anyone in any way been used on you to get you to plead guilty?"

DEFENDANT "No" *No one in any way*

JUDGE "Are you pleading guilty to Murder in the First Degree in this case because you killed Dr. Martin Luther King under such circumstances that would make you legally guilty of Murder in the First Degree under the law as explained to you by your lawyers?"

DEFENDANT "Yes"

JUDGE "Is this Plea of Guilty to Murder in the First Degree with agreed punishment of ninety-nine years in the State Penitentiary, freely, voluntarily and understandingly made and entered by you?"

DEFENDANT "Yes" *legally yes*

JUDGE "Is this Plea of Guilty on your part the free act of your free will, made with your full knowledge and understanding of its meaning and consequences?"

DEFENDANT "Yes"

JUDGE "You may be seated."

The handwritten, incorrect transcript (Courtesy US District Court, Western District of Tennessee)

typed on a different typewriter and inserted into the document. The other eighty-six pages appear to have been typed on the same typewriter. Haile doesn't recall anything about the source of the transcript used in federal court: "I wouldn't know one way or the other." He added that Ray's lawyers didn't complain about its introduction as evidence. "They complained about every other thing. I'm surprised they overlooked that." He said, "They questioned the authenticity of everything, but not this [transcript]."[13]

Koster, on the other hand, firmly recalls the details of his original transcript and knows he did not change anything about it. Even if he had changed a page, he had his own typewriter at his desk and would have retyped it on the same typewriter. As for certifying Exhibit 87, Koster said: "Of course, you know, when I certify something and give it to somebody there's nothing that says they can't retype it and copy it and make it look like it is part of the original. I'm not saying they did, but that's what it sounds like."[14]

This is substantiated by both Blackwell's and Koster's affidavits and proves that the genuine transcript was finalized on March 10, 1969, and unchanged by either of them afterwards. Blackwell's affidavit says, "After said transcript was distributed to news reporters on said date, I made no changes to, nor did I authorize any changes."[15] Koster's affidavit added that he not only made no changes after the transcript was distributed but also he had no knowledge of any changes.[16]

Judge McRae held that Ray's guilty plea was entered voluntarily, that he was "not coerced by impermissible pressure by Foreman," and that he "coolly and deliberately entered the [guilty] plea in open court" based in part on the false transcript used as evidence.[17]

Ray's lawyers again appealed to the Sixth Circuit. This time, Judge William Ernest Miller, who had twice previously sided with Ray, unexpectedly died of a heart attack after hearing the oral arguments. His death left Chief Judge Harry Phillips (a Tennessean) and Judge Anthony J. Celebrezze (former mayor of Cleveland, Ohio) on the court. The court quoted the altered line in the transcript when it gave its ruling. "As stated, Judge Battle very carefully questioned Ray as to the voluntariness of his plea before it was accepted on March 10, 1969. Ray specifically denied at that time that any one had pressured him to plead guilty. His responses and actions in court reveal that he was fully aware of what was occurring."[18]

Whoever doctored the transcript accomplished his or her intentions: Ray was kept in jail as the murderer of Martin Luther King. The federal district courts in Nashville and Memphis and the Sixth Circuit never knew Ray's actual answer. The US Supreme Court's refusal to hear Ray's petition in 1976 was final.

The altered transcript created in the Shelby County DA's office was introduced as evidence in federal district court in Nashville in 1973. Very little else of the paper trail of that case file remains today, either in the district court or in the National Archives.

FORENSIC ENHANCEMENT OF THE AUDIO RECORDING

The audio recordings of Ray's sentencing hearing also are located in the Shelby County Archives. The audio quality is very poor for several reasons. The recordings were made with Edison Voicewriter machines that cut vinyl-like records that, in playback mode, ran in the slow, 15-rpm range. The technology behind the Voicewriter was forty years old at the time the recordings were made and probably was not suited to the recording of court proceedings due to the fact that it had only one microphone. The phonograph-type records "obviously had been played so many times that it is a wonder we were able to get anything listenable off of them at all," according to Vincent Clark of the Shelby County Archives.[19] Further diminishing the quality of the audio recordings is the fact that James Earl Ray was nowhere near the microphone when he gave his answers to Battle's question. A few of the answers are reasonably clear, but the disputed response to the question about pressure is hard to understand.

When Sean Coetzee, owner of Prism Forensics LLC of Los Angeles, California, and a certified forensic consultant by the American College of Forensic Examiners, forensically enhanced the audio recording of Ray's voir dire, the audio file became much clearer, much less noisy, and much easier to understand—especially where Ray's responses are concerned. Two things are quite clear about the disputed answer regarding pressure. First, Ray most certainly did not give the unequivocal negative answer to the question about pressure as the doctored transcript records. Second, Ray clearly gave a non-committal answer. In the exchange between Battle and Ray, the enhanced audio revealed:

THE COURT: Has any pressure of any kind by anyone in any way been used on you to get you to plead guilty?

A [JAMES EARL RAY]: I don't know what to say.

Because of the challenges with such audio files, the last word is open to interpretation. Ray either said "I don't know what to *say*" or "I don't know what to *think*."

If anything, Ray's spoken answer was even more ambiguous than that which is recorded in Koster's original transcript. Koster, however, had the advantages of being present in person and only a few feet away from Ray as well as a having a much clearer recording than remains today. In either case, Ray never answered the question about pressure. If that question was important enough for Battle to ask—if it was important enough for the district attorney and Ray's own lawyer, Percy Foreman, to give him a scripted, negative answer a day in advance—then it was important enough for the court to stop and elicit a full answer.

Battle's task was to make sure that Ray's guilty plea was admitted in good conscience. His decision to accept Ray's "answer," while alarming, is not necessarily surprising. Arthur Hanes Jr. noted that it seemed like Battle was under enormous pressure from outside of the courtroom. Perhaps Lesar put it best when he said that Battle "blew it."

THE HSCA'S ANALYSIS

G. Robert Blakey's HSCA staff had it within their power to discover the altered transcript and stop the judicial charade that had kept Ray in prison without a trial and obscured the truth from the rest of the nation. Instead of investigating fully, Blakey's staff failed—or perhaps refused—to discover the original transcript.

Blakey's staff compiled a bibliography of ninety-three book and magazine titles on the MLK assassination by the time they had finished their work in early 1979.[20] Blakey refused to say whether any staff members were assigned to read the selections, but the bibliography is still evidence of the published material that was in Blakey's possession. Among these titles are Blair's and John Seigenthaler's and Squires's books. Both books pointed to the true transcript.

If Blakey had actually assigned someone to read those books, he or she would have discovered the discrepancies. It is inconceivable that no one on the HSCA staff knew there was a problem. In addition, if Blakey had assigned someone to listen to the audio recordings of the March 10, 1969, hearing, he or she would have likewise discovered the problem.

Perhaps someone on the HSCA staff discovered the altered transcript, and there was a deliberate order to cover it up. Blakey's refusal to say inspires suspicion. Yet, if Blakey had revealed that the courts had ruled against James Earl Ray based, in part, on altered evidence, this would have triggered a new round of appeals that most likely would have considered Ray's guilty plea invalid and thus require a full trial. The government's failure to prove that it had the murder weapon would have been tested in open court. The evidence planted against Ray would have been re-analyzed. If the defense could prove that the evidence was planted rather than real, a conspiracy to frame Ray would have been exposed. Blakey was not willing to let that happen. Whether the case against Ray was too big to fail, or whether the truth was too just explosive to expose, Blakey turned his back. Furthermore, it cannot be disputed that the HSCA used the altered transcript in its evaluation of the evidence against Ray. After all, they quote from it right in the middle of their final report.[21]

WHERE WAS RAY'S LEGAL TEAM?

It is difficult to consider the creation and introduction of a false transcript as evidence without wondering why Ray's legal team didn't object to it. Why didn't they listen to the audio recordings and challenge the altered transcript for what it was—falsified evidence?

Ray's three lawyers at the May 26, 1969, hearing were new to the case and had not been present at the guilty plea hearing ten weeks earlier. The judge, Faquin, was also new to the case. These circumstances made it possible for the Shelby County DA to introduce the altered transcript. Only the prosecutors and Ray were present at both hearings, and Ray was not schooled enough in the law to know that his answer to the question about pressure was key.

More inexplicable is the failure of Ray's later lawyers to figure out the transcript discrepancy, as the genuine transcript was published in three successful books. Jim Lesar only vaguely remembers that Memphis attorney Robert Livingston was suspicious about the transcript. Bernard Fensterwald Jr., another of Ray's attorneys, died in 1991.

The haunting fact is that public documents released by the Assassination Records Review Board (ARRB) prove that the CIA was interested in whether Ray received a full trial. Did the agency turn its "interest" into action and have a hand in the further concealment of the transcript by the staff of the HSCA? Blakey has refused to comment in depth on the subject. This, however, tells us nothing about how much Blakey may have known about it at the time.

THE IMPLICATIONS

The presence of an altered transcript has profound meaning for our comprehension of the King's assassination and James Earl Ray's role. The fact that this transcript was introduced as evidence at every court hearing subsequent to Ray's sentencing hearing has undeniable implications.

Simply put, the creation and use of the doctored transcript means there was an active, thoughtful, and highly effective cover-up in operation that lasted for years. The conspiracy kept Ray in jail. The complexity of the cover-up suggests that others were involved in the assassination. To boot, Blakey now admits that questioning HSCA conclusions is no longer ludicrous. "Thoughtful people" now have questions, "not just nuts," Blakey said publicly in 2013.

Constructing the history that James Earl Ray stalked King, located him in Memphis, aimed his rifle, and squeezed off the single shot without any assistance meant that no one else had to worry about being implicated. If, on the other hand, Ray was only a scapegoat whose guilty plea, if overturned, would open a new investigation that might have implicated others, this was an infinitely more serious matter.

Someone altered the sentencing hearing's transcript to secure the failure of Ray's appeals.

CHAPTER 8
Lyndon, Buford, and the Boys

This chapter will reveal the 1960s-era relationship of the "Texas political mafia" of Pres. Lyndon Baines Johnson and its closely related eastern affiliate in Tennessee, headed by Gov. Buford Ellington. It will also discuss the significance of this unusually close relationship between Johnson and Ellington in the context of:

- Harry Avery's investigation into a possible conspiracy to kill Rev. Martin Luther King Jr.;
- Avery's refusal to drop the investigation and his subsequent firing by Ellington;
- The evidence Avery compiled and the mysterious disappearance of the both the original and a duplicate files;
- What Avery knew about the improper three-way contact between Ellington (or his senior staff), Percy Foreman, and the US Department of Justice; and
- How the legal system in Tennessee prevented James Earl Ray from acquiring a trial.

Buford Ellington was a close personal friend and political ally of Lyndon Johnson. The closeness of the relationship between the two was "something to behold," according to Hudley Crockett, Ellington's press secretary during his second term.[1] During Ellington's second term as governor in 1967, he and LBJ often discussed national political matters on the phone. "They talked on the phone quite often, went hunting out in Texas once or twice," according to William L. "Dick" Barry, a former speaker of the Tennessee House of Representatives who served as Ellington's legal counsel during his second term.[2] Another Ellington senior staff member, Samuel "Bo" Roberts Jr., told me that Ellington stayed at the White House every time he visited Washington.[3]

Ellington was in his first term as governor of Tennessee when LBJ ran for the democratic nomination for president in 1960, losing to John F.

Buford Ellington, governor of Tennessee from 1959 to 1963 and from 1967 to 1971 (Courtesy Tennessee State Library and Archives)

Kennedy at the convention. Ellington not only delivered the Tennessee delegation to his Texas friend, he was LBJ's floor manager at the national convention in Los Angeles. In between Ellington's separate terms as Tennessee governor (1959-63 and 1967-71), he served as LBJ's director of the federal Office of Emergency Preparedness from 1965 to 1966.

Ellington was LBJ's go-to guy on matters of race relations and Southern politics in the mid-1960s. Furthermore, LBJ's Texas political mafia, including Houston attorney Percy Foreman, was right in the middle of the case against James Earl Ray.

The last thing President Johnson wanted—the last thing Governor Ellington wanted—was for weak evidence to be revealed in court that could suggest the involvement of a person or persons other than Ray.

THE RACE ISSUE

Ellington and LBJ's private phone calls regarding the security of the Selma civil rights marchers in the spring of 1965 indicate the depth of their relationship. At that time, Ellington was serving as director of the Office of Emergency Preparedness, a precursor to the present-day Federal Emergency Management Agency (FEMA), for LBJ.

In a taped 1965 phone call to the White House, US attorney general Nicholas Katzenbach expressed his frustration to President Johnson on the inability to make any meaningful personal contact with Alabama governor George Wallace. Katzenbach told LBJ that he did not even know a potential intermediary who might approach Wallace in his stead. Johnson suggested Buford Ellington. Speaking to Katzenbach on the phone, Johnson said,

> This would have to be mighty quiet, but Buford Ellington is a man of extremely good judgment, and he was born in Mississippi, raised there, and then identified with the rural elements of Tennessee. He handles disaster problems and stuff like that on emergency planning. It could be that he knows Wallace. It could be that he could sit down with you, and you could give him some leadership and direction. Might be [Wallace] won't talk to him. I'll ask him if he knows him and how well he knows him, and if it looks like there's any . . . he has any confidence—Wallace has any confidence in him—he might be a go-between. . . . [Ellington] knows both sides of the coin, and I guess he's been on both sides.[4]

Apparently, Ellington called Wallace that very day, had a positive rapport with him, established direct communications, and defused the situation. Katzenbach expressed to LBJ the next day how impressed he was.

The President's candor in speaking freely and openly in private and decision to give Ellington the authority to make commitments in the his name in order to resolve complicated race relations speaks volumes about the trusting relationship between Buford Ellington and Lyndon Johnson.

ELLINGTON RE-APPOINTS HARRY S. AVERY

Shortly after winning his second term, governor-elect Ellington announced he would retain Harry Avery in the job as commissioner of correction. Avery had been appointed commissioner in January 1963 by Ellington's predecessor and political ally, Gov. Frank G. Clement, who was also a long-time ally of the Averys of Crockett County, Tennessee.

Frank Clement and Harry Avery were both progressives when it came to the matter of race. In 1963, Clement appointed the first black to serve on the Pardon and Parole Board, which Avery chaired. In 1965, Harry Avery oversaw the desegregation of the state's juvenile institutions. A state prison school was established and accredited that year. In 1966, Avery instituted the desegregation of all cellblocks in Tennessee's adult penal institutions.[5]

When Ellington announced Avery's reappointment on December 21, 1966, he praised him for the job he had done under Clement. "He has brought about improvements in various phases of our penal system, especially those areas attempting to rehabilitate the young first offenders," Ellington said. "I feel sure that under [Avery's] leadership the Department will continue to show substantial improvement."

AVERY INVESTIGATES THE KING ASSASSINATION

The evening after entering his guilty plea, James Earl Ray was transported to the main prison in Nashville. Harry Avery was in charge of and legally responsible for every prisoner in the state system. The position of commissioner made Avery the ex officio chairman of the Pardon and Parole Board. In this capacity, Avery interviewed virtually every adult male prisoner in the state system. He already had a plan in place to investigate Ray and what he believed might have been a conspiracy to murder King. He put that plan into action as soon as James Earl Ray was delivered into this custody.

Before Ray arrived at the prison, Avery approached the warden of the main prison, Lake F. Russell, with the idea that the two of them should collaborate on a memoir of prison management with a chapter on James Earl Ray. Originally, Russell seemed to acquiesce to Avery's wishes. After all, Avery was his boss, until it occurred to Russell that he could ingratiate himself with the governor and perhaps move Avery out of the way and take the commissioner's job in one stroke. Avery described,

> We started out on a planned program to extract a confession if possible from this character [Ray] along the lines which I had outlined. To wit:
> Make Xerox copies of all incoming mail.
> Make Xerox copies of all outgoing communications involving James Earl Ray.
> Make notations as to all visitors, and try to win his confidence and point out to him that if he had entered a plea of guilty and had tried to bargain with the district attorney for a life sentence rather than a ninety-nine-year sentence, that he would be subject to probationary parole in twelve years and seven months with good behavior. Whereas under the present sentence of ninety-nine-years, that a minimum of thirty years would have to be served before he could be even considered by the [Parole] Board.
> And if [his] sentence was commuted by the governor from ninety-nine-years to life that the same principle just enunciated would be applicable. But it would require recommendation by the Pardon and Parole Board before he [the governor] would even consider it.[6]

Avery first met with Ray on March 12, 1969, and introduced him to warden Russell and the chief records clerk of the Department of Corrections. Avery had three lengthy interviews with Ray during which he took notes. Two of the interviews were in private with no one present other than Avery and Ray. The final interview was conducted in late April or early May.

No sooner had Avery's investigation begun than Ray renounced his guilty plea. He sent a letter to judge Preston Battle on March 13, 1969, advising him that he had fired Percy Foreman and intended to petition the court to withdraw his plea. This did not alter Avery's investigation, but when Avery saw the letters Foreman wrote to Ray on the eve of the trial (March 9), it raised his suspicions as to why Ray was badgered into pleading guilty by his own attorney.

THE EVIDENCE ROLLS IN

In a matter of days, some "significant letters" began coming into the prison for James Earl Ray, and in keeping with the plan, these letters were copied and placed into Avery's file.[7] There were at least five significant letters that Avery believed should have been investigated, and he had intended to conduct that investigation until Governor Ellington fired him. These significant letters came from Birmingham, Alabama; New Orleans, Louisiana; Brussels, Belgium; McGill University in Quebec, Canada; and San Diego, California. In an audio-taped interview from 1978, Avery noted:

> It was apparent that the author of that particular anonymous letter [from Birmingham] had been in consultation with James Earl Ray prior to the assassination of Martin Luther King. And I thought this was highly significant to set up an overt act in the furtherance of a conspiracy. . . .
>
> There was a letter also that came from a woman in New Orleans that was not an anonymous letter. And on its face it revealed that she had formerly been a friend of James Earl Ray, and the last sentence in that letter: "I'm still as poor as a church house mouse," quote. I thought that perhaps proper investigation might reveal that she was saying to him that any monies that you instructed to be delivered to me have never arrived. I don't know the meaning of that unless you take it on its face. Why would somebody write a person in the penitentiary and say I'm as poor as a church house mouse when they had no way of helping them, financially? I thought that was significant. . . .
>
> There was another letter that was not anonymous, came from Brussels, Belgium. It was written in the Flemish language . . . So I had a lady in Nashville who is now the assistant librarian, foreign language division of the Vanderbilt library to translate this for me. And it talked about international conspiracy to kill Martin Luther King and also President Kennedy. . . .
>
> There was also a letter that came on the letterhead of McGill University from Canada, that to me, was significant. I felt the author of that letter might have been instrumental in helping to plot the course of getting the passports that were used by Ray, of the alias names who were Canadians. . . .
>
> There was also a woman from San Diego that [sic] wrote Ray every day. Every day there was a letter that came in to Ray. She was apparently a member of a choir out there in a church, and the salutation in that letter was a musical bar that the notes spelled out: "Hello my dear James Earl Ray." . . .

Avery identified these five letters as ones that he believed were important to an investigation, "And I felt that ultimately should be thoroughly investigated to develop the conspiracy if one existed." Avery added that as he was working from memory, these five letters were "not all of them" that were significant, "that's just all of them that I remember for the moment."

ELLINGTON WARNS AVERY

Some days after Avery first interviewed Ray on March 12, 1969, in the presence of Russell, Russell tipped off the governor or his staff. Around the end of that month, Ellington ordered Avery to drop the investigation.

Avery ignored the governor's warning and continued his investigation with at least one interview with Ray's brother, Jerry Ray.

By early May 1969, negative news stories about Avery began appearing in Nashville's daily Republican newspaper, the *Nashville Banner*, which also was allied with the conservative wing of the Ellington's Democrat party.

On May 16, 1969, reporter Larry Brinton reported in a front-page news story, "Avery Writing Book on Ray." Avery lived another twenty years after leaving the Ellington administration, but he never wrote any such book.

The key part of Brinton's news story is that the factual details could only have been leaked by Russell or someone on Ellington's staff. Brinton wrote that he got the information from "informed sources both inside and outside the walls" of the main prison. The way Brinton worded his resources gave the story great credibility and could not more perfectly describe the facts. He correctly reported that Avery had interviewed Ray three times, two of which were private. The first interview with Ray included Avery, Russell, and the chief records clerk. Avery took notes at of all the interviews.

Brinton wrote that he had called Avery that morning and that Avery first denied he was writing a book. According to Brinton, Avery "admitted" that he wouldn't write a book while he was commissioner, and that Avery eventually "confirmed" that he was thinking about a book.[8]

Who was Brinton's source? It is highly unlikely that Russell would have taken the initiative on his own to embarrass Avery unless instructed by the governor's staff. An attack on one of the governor's cabinet members was an attack on the governor—unless the attack was arranged by the governor's office to accomplish ulterior purposes.

It is more likely that the nimble minds of the governor's staff had handed Brinton the story with the intention of setting Avery up with allegations of misbehavior in office. The charge of writing a book on Ray that was never actually written is hardly misbehavior. At the very least, they stoked the fires of the *Nashville Banner*'s newsroom with enough fuel for other news outlets to pick up the story, thus making it appear that Avery had become such an embarrassment to the governor that he would have to go.

Five days later, the staunch Democratic newspaper, the *Nashville Tennessean*, picked up the story *and* named the source: the governor's news secretary, Hudley Crockett.

Under the lead-story headline "Ray-Avery Ties Studied," reporter

Hudley Crockett, circa 1968 (Courtesy Tennessee State Library and Archives)

John Haile questioned the veracity of Avery's statement that he had received and traced an anonymous call that warned of a conspiracy to murder Ray in his prison cell. Haile reported that the telephone company said that it was not aware that any such call had been traced, and Tennessee Bureau of Investigation (TBI) director W. E. "Bud" Hopton would not comment as to whether he had been called in to investigate.

"Bud" Hopton, director of the Tennessee Bureau of Investigation in 1969 (Courtesy Tennessee State Library and Archives)

Regarding rumors that Avery might have been planning a book about James Earl Ray, Crockett told Haile that Ellington had been looking at the Avery "situation" since the book rumor was first reported five days earlier. Crockett further stated that Ellington would receive a "full report" before making any statement about Avery, other than the governor would not tolerate any use of an official position "for personal gain."[9] Years later, Crockett told me he couldn't recall any details of that report.[10]

That same afternoon, Larry Brinton reported, "Avery Quizzed 'At Length' By TBI Director." Brinton, again relying on an unnamed source described as a "high state government" official, reported that the governor had sicked the TBI on Avery.

It seems that the governor feared that Avery might have discovered a conspiracy to kill King, and Ellington wanted to know what Avery knew. The official investigation into Avery's activities was ostensibly to learn whether he had actually discovered a conspiracy to kill James Earl Ray in his cell or whether Avery had made up that story, presumably to deflect any criticism about his activities.

Brinton reported that, the previous day, Hopton had questioned Avery "at length" about the conspiracy to kill James Earl Ray and reviewed "all the notes taken by Avery" during interviews of Ray. Brinton, citing Crockett as the source in a lower part of the story, indicated that Governor Ellington ordered TBI director Hopton to conduct an investigation into Avery's "alleged attempts at coercing Ray."[11]

This allegation of coercion originated earlier in the week with one of Ray's attorneys, Robert W. Hill Jr. of Chattanooga. Reports indicated that Hill was concerned that Avery might pressure Ray to cooperate with his planned book. Avery released a letter from Hill that dismissed any "personal charges" of coercion. The hoopla, however, was enough to make Avery's ouster seem as reasonable as it was inevitable.[12] In any case, Harry Avery had concluded that there was in fact a conspiracy to murder King.

The whole series of news stories in the Nashville newspapers was contrived to discredit, silence, and remove Avery from office to stop any investigation.

On May 23, the front-page headline of the *Nashville Tennessean* read, "Avery: No Resignation Plans." Haile's lead paragraph announced that Harry Avery's job was "threatened by his involvement with James Earl

Ray." Haile noted that there was "increased speculation" that Avery would be asked to leave his post as commissioner. The story also recorded that Avery was called into a conference earlier in the week in the governor's office to discuss "the entire matter" with TBI director Hopton and the governor's legal counsel William L. "Dick" Barry.

A report on Hopton's investigation of Avery was due to the governor within a matter of days, Haile reported.[13]

ELLINGTON FIRES AVERY

Six days later, the deed was done and announced to the press at the end of Ellington's daily morning meeting with his three senior staff members: Barry, Crockett, and Roberts. The afternoon newspapers across the state got the news first, thus rewarding Brinton for discrediting Avery.

The May 29, 1969, *Nashville Banner* eight-column, "second coming" headline in all capitals read "ELLINGTON BOOTS AVERY," followed by a smaller headline that stated, "Lake Russell Named Commissioner." It appears that Russell got his reward for squealing to the governor's staff. Brinton wrote that the primary cause of the firing was the "relationship" between Avery and Ray as reported in the memorandum to the governor by the TBI.[14] According to Crockett, "there were reports the governor got from the TBI and the FBI for that matter." Although there was no mention of FBI reports in any news story from that time, it doesn't mean that the Feds weren't involved.

Years later, Crockett reiterated in an interview the oft-repeated criticism of the book Avery planned to write about Ray. "Harry stepped out of bounds when he started interviewing James Earl Ray for a book," Crockett told me. "I think it just caught everybody by surprise." Avery, however, didn't believe there was anything untoward regarding his interviews of Ray. As commissioner and chairman of the Pardon and Parole Board, he interviewed thousands of prisoners during his six-and-a-half year tenure, often one-on-one and in private to help those who had been treated unfairly and to ensure the accuracy of their stories "I talked to seventy-two hundred inmates, why in the hell wouldn't I talk to James Earl Ray?"[15]

At some point before the afternoon newspaper deadline, Ellington was out in public, where Brinton and perhaps other reporters could pose questions. Ellington told Brinton that he had his secretary call Avery and asked him to come to his office that morning. Instead of coming in person, Avery called the governor's office and spoke to Ellington on the telephone.[16]

Ellington's legal counsel, Barry, who was the only other person privy to that conversation, said that the governor's office "had reports" about Avery's activities regarding James Earl Ray that came from the governor's snitch, Russell, and the TBI. While Barry was telling the story of Avery's dismissal, he interrupted himself mid-sentence and asked me, "Now, do you want me to tell you the truth?" When I answered in the affirmative, Barry related:

> No one else was there [with the governor] but myself. We had had reports that Harry [Avery] had gone to see Mr. Ray in prison, and that he had told him that if he needed any particular assistance or aid or anything of the sort just to let him know.
>
> When the governor heard this he called Harry and told him, "Harry, don't go to see [James Earl Ray] again." Harry did go see him again and allegedly told him if he [had] any money or anything he wanted protected he would be glad to take care of it for him—that if he ever wanted to write a book he would help him with it.
>
> As soon as the governor heard that, he called Harry and I was sitting right next to the desk, and he said, "Harry, I want your resignation." Harry said, "I'm not going to resign." Then the governor said, "You are dismissed," period. That is what happened because I saw it.[17]

What Barry's story confirms is that whether or not Avery was going to write a book, Ellington was concerned that Avery would learn things he shouldn't have known—in particular, anything related to a conspiracy to assassinate King.

The largest afternoon newspaper in the state, the *Memphis Press-Scimitar,* ran the firing as the lead story in an eight-column headline: "Prison Chief Fired Over Ray Case." A two-column subheading announced, "Ellington Acts After Probe." The news story carried the by-line of Null Adams, the *Press-Scimitar* political editor at that time. Adams wrote that Avery's firing came "following the completion of an investigation into Avery's handling of the James Earl Ray case." As with almost all the other news stories on the firing, four things were repeated: the allegation of Avery's intended book, the TBI report to the governor, the allegation of Avery's offer of special treatment for Ray, and the report of the International Association of Police Chiefs (IAPC) critical of the management of the Tennessee prison system.[18] The IAPC report criticized Avery's administration of correctional facilities, and cited "appalling and deplorable conditions," including personnel practices that were "predicated upon political patronage."

Another second-tier afternoon daily newspaper, the *Jackson (TN) Sun*, circulated in much of West Tennessee, including Avery's hometown of Alamo. The newspaper ran a simple, one-column headline on the front page above the fold: "Avery Fired By Ellington." The newspaper ran the Associated Press (AP) story about the firing that was on the state wire. The comment that Avery was born and raised in Crockett County was the only change they made to the AP story.

The next morning, May 30, the news of Harry Avery's dismissal made headlines across the country. The *Memphis Commercial Appeal* ran a two-column, three-line headline lead story, titled "Ray Case Theory Is Labeled Reason For Avery Firing." That news story quoted a member of the state legislature, Jack Comer of Knoxville, who expressed his opinion that the "primary reason" Avery was fired is because he was getting too close to unraveling the conspiracy.[19] The *Chattanooga Times* also ran an article, quoting Comer as saying that "all over the state," people believe Avery was fired because he was "getting too close to the conspiracy" in the King assassination and that "someone wanted him fired."[20]

Other headlines came much closer to telling the real story behind Avery's firing. The *Hartford (CT) Courant* ran, on page seven, "Fired Official Insists Ray Was Not Alone." The *Pittsburgh Press* reported, "Ray Told of Plot, Interviewer Says." The *Dubuque (IA) Telegraph-Herald* ran, in their Sunday edition, "Official Admits Attempted 'Deal' with Ray to Get 'the Full Truth.'" Hendersonville, North Carolina, reported, "Former Official Says Ray Part of A Conspiracy," and the *Middlesboro (KY) Daily News* announced, "Fired Corrections Commissioner: Ray Spoke of Conspiracy."

The lead story in the May 30 edition of the *Nashville Tennessean* read, "Avery Says His Side Not Heard." Political reporter Larry Daughtrey wrote that Avery was scheduled to appear at a state House subcommittee hearing to discuss the state penal system the day he was fired. When Avery showed up for the hearing, an impromptu news conference began. Avery told reporters that he is "positive" Ray was involved in the King's murder and "equally positive he is not the only one implicated." With this pronouncement, Avery placed himself 180 degrees across from the law enforcement and political establishment at the state and federal levels.

Avery also revealed that the *Nashville Tennessean* had attempted to hire his nephew, former state senator J. B. "Buck" Avery Jr., to represent James Earl Ray as a way of using family relations to obtain access to Ray and get his exclusive story.[21] Buck Avery saw through this rather transparent proposal and turned it down.

Brinton, however, had yet another news scoop handed to him for the *Nashville Banner* that afternoon. Under the front-page headline "Avery Questioned Ray About Cash," Brinton revealed that he was given access to Hopton's TBI report for Governor Ellington regarding Avery's investigation of Ray. Brinton did not reveal who gave him the report—or, at least, allowed him to read it. Brinton wrote that Avery had agreed to retrieve any money Ray may have hidden, presumably the payment for his involvement in the King assassination, and deposit it in a trust account for Ray. The report also contained Avery's offer to sell Ray's story to the highest bidder and turn all of the money over to him. The report, however, was not made public.

When asked about his Harry Avery news stories from May 1969 and whether he was fed information on Avery from the governor's staff, Larry Brinton's reply was strange: he mentioned that no one had tipped him off in his series of news stories, yet he added that "even though these stories happened forty-two years ago [as of 2011], I couldn't violate a reporter's code not to reveal my sources." Brinton said that he was not connected to the governor's staff even though he said he "grew up" with Hudley Crockett, "but to my memory neither Hudley, Bo [Roberts], or [Barry] ever tipped me to a story, not on Avery or anything else."

Nevertheless, information in Brinton's first news article about Avery on May 16 was provided by "informed" but unnamed sources "inside and outside" the prison walls. Brinton's final news story of May 30 specifically quoted Hopton's "highly secret report," to which Brinton says he was given access by unnamed sources.

WHAT HAPPENED TO HOPTON'S REPORT?

When asked about Hopton's TBI investigative report on Avery, Bo Roberts, Ellington's senior aide, told me, "I don't remember the details of the report, but I was dealing with some of it." Roberts elaborated, "It was one of those things that when you open the lid a little bit and start looking into it; the more you got into it the worse it got. And it became quite evident to several of us pretty quickly that a change [of commissioners] needed to be made."[22]

Roberts's comments support the timeline and the analysis that Ellington and his staff decided to dump Avery "pretty quickly" when the James Earl Ray conspiracy investigation came to their attention. When asked about Hopton's memorandum to the governor, Crockett indicated that he could not recollect any details about it. Barry likewise remembered nothing about it. "I never saw that [report]," Barry told me. "If it existed, I'm not aware of it." When I explained to Barry that Hopton's memorandum is not to be found in Ellington's collection of papers in the state archives but that its existence is authentic because it is described and mentioned in a footnote on page 658 of the HSCA *Final Report,* Barry readily agreed that it must have existed at one time. Then he suggested, "It must have been destroyed."

However, the memorandum must have been located in the Tennessee state library and archives from the end of the Ellington administration in January 1971 until at least 1976 in order for the HSCA to have obtained a copy it.

Ellington died in early 1972, so it could not have been in his possession later in the decade. Nor is it likely to have been in Hopton's possession in the late 1970s because he left the TBI in 1971.

When the HSCA issued its final report in 1979, all of its evidence files—including the Hopton memorandum—were sealed for fifty years.

The fact that the document was lost from the state archives raises the troubling question about whether the report was deliberately removed at the time the HSCA got their hands on it. The memorandum may have contained information embarrassing to the Ellington or even LBJ administrations. If Hopton saw and reviewed Avery's full evidence file, including James Earl Ray's correspondences, then this document is the only remaining record of key pieces of evidence.

THE PLAN IN THE GOVERNOR'S OFFICE

A couple of months or more before Ray's March 10, 1969, sentencing hearing in Memphis, Harry Avery overheard a conversation in the governor's office that should never have taken place. The exact date of the conversation is lost, but context places it during the brief period when Percy Foreman represented Ray, most likely in December 1968 or the first couple of weeks of January 1969, before Richard Nixon was sworn in as the new president on January 22.

In 1978, Harry Avery told me the story of arriving a little early at the state capitol for an appointment with the governor and was seated in the reception area of the governor's office just outside the huge, ornamental doors that open into the governor's private office suite. He took a seat beside those doors, waiting to be called in to meet with the governor. The doors were open and someone on the governor's staff could be overheard on the telephone. He could only hear the Nashville end of the conversation but he said it was obvious the person was talking to "a high official of the US Justice Department, perhaps even the Attorney General himself." Avery did not identify the governor's staff member by name. Given the topic of the conversation and that they were communicating with a high federal official, the person Avery overheard is almost certainly Barry, Crockett, or Roberts.

Avery overheard this anonymous person say, "Don't worry, Ray is going to plead guilty; there won't be any evidence put-on by the prosecution, there won't be any evidence that is tested in court—there won't be a trial."[23]

Avery told me also that he had come to the conclusion that King was assassinated in Memphis because those behind the conspiracy knew Ellington could control the state investigation, and they would not have to worry about a genuine federal investigation with LBJ in the White House and Ramsey Clark at the Justice Department. Buford Ellington appointed the judge, Preston Battle, who accepted Ray's guilty plea and sentenced him to ninety-nine years. US attorney general Ramsey Clark was part of LBJ's Texas political mafia who pronounced "no conspiracy" the morning after King was murdered. When the Ray brothers brought Percy Foreman into the case to represent Ray in Battle's court, it all aligned like an astrological chart.

WHAT HAPPENED TO AVERY'S EVIDENCE FILE?

When the HSCA committee was commissioned in 1976 to relook at the Kennedy and King assassinations, Avery wrote its first chief counsel,

Richard Sprague. He informed him that he was commissioner when Ray was received at the prison, that he had interviewed Ray and his brother Jerry Ray, and that he had kept the correspondence file on Ray and that he would be glad to share it with him. Sprague called Avery and told him he would send investigators down to interview him and go over the file. The investigators came to Avery's home and interviewed him on December 3, 1976, and again on June 14, 1977. It was during that time that Avery discovered that his files were missing from his home. But that was not all that turned up missing. "These letters that I've mentioned, they've disappeared regretfully. . . . When they sent the investigators here from Washington I thought I was just going to walk down and go in my [home] office and pick up a file just like I did those little old poems I showed you a while ago."[24]

The investigators headed to Thomas Steele's office in Nashville to pick up the duplicate file, but it too was missing. Avery said that the investigators from the HSCA worked in Steele's office trying to find the duplicate file, but the only thing they found in his file was the retainer letter.

Did Avery's original evidence file on James Earl Ray and a duplicate file some seventy miles apart just happen to be mislaid, misfiled, or inadvertently discarded? To suggest that someone took these files is to suggest the existence of an elaborate cover-up nearly ten years after the King assassination. When one considers that Percy Foreman's entire James Earl Ray file was "lost;" that William Pepper, one of Ray's attorneys, said he had files that disappeared; that journalist Steve Tompkins had missing papers; and that Gary Revel, a special investigator for another of Ray's attorneys, Jack Kershaw, had his entire Nashville apartment turned upside down and his Ray files stolen or destroyed, it seems that Avery's papers met a similar fate. The common factor with each of these missing bordereaux is the potential for exculpatory evidence that either would have benefitted James Earl Ray's appeals to get a full trial or indicated a conspiracy to murder King—or both.

WHY IT WAS IMPORTANT TO SILENCE HARRY AVERY

Ellington administration officials knew that it was important to silence Harry Avery for several reasons, but not before the TBI found out what he had learned from Ray or Ray's correspondence. Although the Ellington staff had effectively used its local newspaper connections to embarrass, discredit, and marginalize Avery, the headlines in the aftermath of his firing didn't look good from their perspective. State and federal law enforcement agencies cringed at headlines that used words such as "plot" and "conspiracy" or phrases such as "Ray was not alone."

In a taped interview in 1978, Avery expressed his candid views: "I know there was a lot [about] the assassination of Martin Luther King— there's been a lot of that that's been covered up or tried to be covered up. . . . And I know from Governor Ellington's reaction that he was disturbed greatly about what was going on . . . and I know that he was afraid I would get a full detailed confession from James Earl Ray in such a way that it would blow the whole thing out of the water."[25]

Ray was manipulated into position in Memphis with the gun he was told to buy in Birmingham with the money he was given with which to buy it. They used Percy Foreman to berate and coerce him into pleading guilty and accept a lengthy sentence. The conditions Ray suffered in the Shelby County jail for nearly eight months broke any stubbornness or will.

The *New York Times,* publishing houses, the highest law-enforcement officials, and eventually a congressional committee assured the public that James Earl Ray was the lone killer. Harry Avery would not be permitted to unravel the tapestry, even if he could prove that the weave was made of lies. That's why he had to go, and that's why his evidence files likely were taken years later when he first attempted to get them into the hands of HSCA investigators.

ELLINGTON SEALS THE DEAL

Within forty-eight hours of his transfer out of the Shelby County jail to state custody—at the end of the first two cycles of normal daylight that Ray experienced in almost eight months—he fired Percy Foreman. His March 13, 1969, letter to Judge Battle advised him of the firing and that he intended to renounce his guilty plea with plans to seek a full trial. A second letter on March 26, 1969, asked Battle to consider it as a request for a full trial. But Battle never filed either letter with the clerk of the court.

Battle died in his office on the afternoon of March 31, 1969, slumped face down in his own file on James Earl Ray. One source in Tennessee indicates that Battle had made up his mind to view Ray's correspondence as a motion, but this is disputed. James H. Lesar, one of Ray's attorneys in the mid-1970s, claims that he found a sheet from a notepad in Battle's papers that were secured shortly after he died that "clearly evinces Judge Battle's intent to grant Ray a trial."[26]

It is entirely possible that Battle sympathized with Ray and would have granted a motion for a full trial, but it is unlikely that he would do so until Ray had a new attorney of record. Jerry Ray contacted Memphis attorney Richard Ryan about a week after his brother's first letter arrived in Memphis, on or about March 17. It wasn't until approximately March 24 that the two of them spoke, and Ryan agreed to come into the case. Lesar confirmed that Ray's new legal team was having problems getting into the state penitentiary to see Ray and confirm his intention to retain them.

Ray's letters to Battle were filed with the clerk of the court the day after his death. The press recorded a public debate between the soon-to-retire chief justice of the Tennessee Supreme Court, Hamilton Burnett, and a Court of Criminal Appeals judge, Charles Galbreath, about the legal meaning of Ray's letters in light of Battle's death. Galbreath said that state law automatically granted any motion for a new trial for any cases pending before a judge who dies before acting on such a motion. Burnett contradicted him publicly and said that the law only applies to defendants who enter a not guilty plea. Burnett retired later that summer and Ross Dyer, a senior staff member during Ellington's first gubernatorial term, was elevated to chief justice.

The law in question, Tennessee Code Annotated (TCA) 17-1-305, stated at that time that when a judicial office is vacated by death or other causes (by law or constitutional provisions) following a verdict and after a petition is filed for a new trial but before the petition is heard, "a new trial shall be granted to the losing party if the motion has been filed within the time required by the rule of the court, and the motion is pending when the vacancy occurs." The time period was thirty days from the March 10, 1969, sentencing hearing. Battle died on March 31 in possession of both of Ray's letters. Yet, none of the court rulings against Ray, even at the appellate level, mention this section of the code. They did not attempt to explain it away—they simply ignored it.

It is clear that Ellington did not want to see the courts grant Ray

17-1-305. New trial in event of vacancy in office. — When a vacancy in the office of trial judge exists by reason of death, permanent insanity as evidenced by adjudication, impeachment and conviction under article V of the Constitution of Tennessee, or removal under article VI, section 6, of the Constitution of Tennessee, after verdict, but before the hearing of the motion for new trial, a new trial shall be granted to the losing party if the motion has been filed within the time required by rule of the court, and the motion is pending when the vacancy occurs. [Acts 1945, ch. 21, § 2; mod. C. Supp. 1950, § 9949.2; T.C.A. (orig. ed.), § 17-117; Acts 1994, ch. 833, § 1.]

Tennessee Code Annotated 17-1-305 (Courtesy author's collection)

a new trial. After Battle's funeral, Ellington announced that Arthur C. Faquin Jr., a pre-selected alternate judge, would hear Ray's case.[27] The hearing on Ray's request for a new trial was scheduled for May 26— coincidentally, the week Harry Avery was fired.

Faquin decided the law on two points: that Ray's guilty plea "precluded him from filing a motion for a new trial," and that Ray "knowingly, intelligently and voluntarily expressly waived any right he may have had to a motion for a new trial and/or appeal." Faquin's memorandum stated that "either one of these two decisions" were sufficient to deny Ray's request for a new trial. Neither basis for Faquin's decision is mentioned in TCA 17-1-305.

The last week of May 1969, Ray's appeal in trial court was denied, and Harry Avery was sent packing.

BATTLE'S DEATH

There is a troubling footnote to this episode. The front-page news story of Judge Battle's death mentioned a puzzling absence from his office during part of the afternoon of March 31, 1969, as well as time spent with an unknown visitor. His secretary told assistant attorney general James C. "Jim" Beasley that Battle was "apparently with *someone else*" while she and others attempted to locate him.[28] This situation strongly suggests that the unknown visitor was in Battle's office at some point or his secretary would have known only that Battle was not in. Furthermore, the situation also suggests Battle left his office with this unknown visitor because his secretary and others looked unsuccessfully for him in the jail complex of buildings. The attempt to find Battle would not have been necessary if he was in his office all afternoon. Battle did return to his office, however, because that is where his body was found.

The *Memphis Commercial Appeal* reported that when Beasley was leaving the building that evening, he noticed the lights were still on in Battle's office and it drew his attention. Jim Beasley doesn't quite remember it the same way. "Let me tell you as well as I can, exactly what happened. There was an opening between my building and the old jail building where Judge Battle's office was located on the ground floor." Beasley said that Battle had asked him early that morning to contact the warden of the state penitentiary and verify that the letters Battle received from Ray were genuine. This seems like a rather strange request for Battle to make because Battle had a meeting with one of Ray's attorneys, Richard J. Ryan, at 9 a.m. the morning of his death.[29]

Beasely's explanation is not precisely the way author and investigator Harold Weisberg described, but neither is it inconsistent. Weisberg swore in a 1974 affidavit that Battle instructed Beasley to confirm Ryan's inability to get into the state penitentiary in Nashville to see Ray and to obtain his signature on the motion for a full trial.[30] Nevertheless, Beasley said that he called the warden and determined that the letters were genuinely from Ray. He said he tried several times to find Battle to let him know what he had found out, but by the end of the workday was unsuccessful.

As he was leaving for home that evening, Beasley noticed that Battle's car was still there. "When I saw his car, I turned and went back because I didn't want to go home without telling him what I had heard from the warden," and that it had nothing to do with seeing lights on the building. When he entered the old jail building, Battle's office "was dark" and "wasn't lighted as I recall. It could have been, but I don't recall it being lighted."

When Beasley knocked on Battle's door, "nothing happened." He said the entire building was quiet, "everybody had gone home, and after I knocked again I tried the door knob." Beasley opened the door and stuck his head in the office and called Judge Battle's name a couple of times. "Without even entering I looked over and saw him. He was sitting at his desk, his head was on one of his arms like he had laid his arm down and laid his head on it as if, maybe, he was taking a nap."

Beasley immediately went to the sheriff's dispatcher on the same corridor and told him he had just looked in Judge Battle's office and that Battle "could be dead." Suspecting the possibility of foul play, he instructed the dispatcher to "get the chief of homicide over here immediately." Beasley told the dispatcher to call Attorney General Canale at home and tell him what's going on "and tell nobody else" until Battle's family was notified. The mysterious *someone else*," who was likely the last person to see Battle alive, was not seen by anyone that afternoon and remains unidentified.[31]

The news reported that Battle was found "seemingly dead," face down on top of his James Earl Ray file with his pen on the floor beside him. With the file open on his desk, it raises the possibility that Battle had discussed the case with the unidentified visitor. Battle was reviewing the Ray file in his last moments of life. Was Battle's unknown visitor somehow connected to the case, or was it simply a harmless visit by a friend? There is no evidence that Ryan returned again to discuss the case with Battle, so it almost certainly was not him. Besides, as a local lawyer, Ryan would have likely been known and recognized by Battle's secretary, especially if he had returned later in the day. Furthermore, it is unclear why Battle would review the file after Ryan's visit unless he considered that Ray's letters constituted a motion. Having met with Ray's attorney in the morning, it is extremely unlikely that Battle would have drafted a letter to reply to Ray's correspondence.

The medical examiner performed an autopsy that evening and concluded that Battle had died of a heart attack. The police shut down their investigation and never looked for Battle's unidentified visitor. Likely, there was no lingering suspicion of foul play at that time, and Battle's death was accepted as a dramatic, untimely, somewhat mysterious, but quite natural event. The mystery of who turned off the lights to Battle's office could be nothing more than a harmless detail or an indication that something else was going on.

Seven years later, in 1976, a second judge (William Ernest Miller of the US Court of Appeals for the Sixth Circuit), who also had a Ray motion pending before his court, died of a heart attack. The unexpected death of two judges is quite a coincidence and gives pause for thought. By 1976, it was probably too late to re-open Battle's death and attempt to identify the mysterious visitor to his office. The deaths of two judicial officers in the James Earl Ray case apparently raised no suspicion with the HSCA. Miller is mentioned nowhere in the *Final Report*.

The news story also said that Judge Battle was "obviously" keeping his schedule clear "for future hearings concerning this case." Was

Battle about to treat Ray's letters as a motion for a full trial? Was that the business the unidentified visitor had with Battle? In a 1998 letter to the editor published two months after James Earl Ray died, Judge Galbreath claimed that in the hours preceding Battle's death, he had already decided to consider Ray letters to be a "motion for a new trial." Galbreath's letter boldly asserted, "A new trial was necessary to comply with the law. Being an enactment of the legislative branch of government, neither the courts nor the executive branches had power to prevent it. But they both did, by refusing to recognize and obey the law they had sworn to uphold."[32]

The ugly question that cannot be avoided is whether Battle's death was a murder. The technical capability to induce a heart attack existed in 1969 but was not known until it was revealed in Church committee hearings in 1975. *Time* magazine reported that the CIA developed a "heart attack gun" that shot (almost silently) a tiny frozen needle the diameter of a human hair and a quarter of an inch long. The needle penetrated the skin after passing through clothing and thawed in the body, releasing a toxin. After the needle thawed both it and the substance disappeared, leaving nothing more noticeable than a mark like a mosquito bite. The toxin was a shellfish-based substance that induced a heart attack, but was completely denatured and undetectable at autopsy.[33] This technology was secret at the time of Battle's death, so it would have been unknown to the medical examiner. He had no reason to look for a fatal mosquito bite, and so it is uncertain if Battle's death was natural or not.

FUTILE APPEALS IN STATE COURTS

It took the court system in Tennessee only nine months to conclusively reject Ray's motion for a trial. Nine months in the appeals process is lightning speed for three separate levels of the court system to consider and decide any legal matter. Between March 31, 1969 (Battle's death), and January 9, 1970, the criminal court in Shelby County, the Tennessee Court of Criminal Appeals, and the Tennessee Supreme Court each ruled against Ray. It shows just how anxious the state court system was to put it to rest.

After Faquin ruled that Ray had waived his right to appeal, Ray's lawyers filed an appeal with the Tennessee Court of Criminal Appeals

(CCA) in Jackson, Tennessee, on June 25, 1969, and the court heard the oral arguments in Knoxville on July 15. The appeals court sided with the lower court against Ray, and issued and signed an order the same day. The clerk of the Appellate Courts found only the order, so it seems that the CCA listened to the attorneys' arguments and denied Ray's petition without explanation. All the order said is that the petition was "not well taken," and "is hereby denied."[34]

After Burnett's late-summer retirement, the Tennessee Supreme Court consisted of four members: chief justice Ross Dyer (an Ellington protégé), Allison B. Humphreys, George F. McCanless, and Larry B. Creson. Creson was the only non-Ellington appointee on the court.

Before the court heard James Earl Ray's appeal, Governor. Ellington selected a fifth member of the court, a special justice on a temporary basis, solely for the purpose of having a full, five-member court hear Ray's case. The special justice was Erby L. Jenkins, a prestigious Knoxville attorney and jurist, who was selected to write the court's unanimous opinion.

Most court opinions are written in a very neutral, mundane, matter-of-fact style of prose. Jenkins's opinion rings with shrill, condescending, emotional hostility towards Ray. It notes that Ray pleaded guilty to "a cold blooded murder without an explained motive," and that granting his petition for a trial "would be permitting [Ray] to toy with the courts," leaving the gates to Tennessee penal institutions "ever ajar to those incarcerated therein." The opinion continued:

> We are not deciding on the defendant's guilt or innocence. He and his retained counsel made that decision themselves. . . . We are simply deciding whether or not, after he entered a plea of guilty and received a sentence of ninety-nine years, he can thereafter have a change of heart and make a motion for a new trial. We think not. . . .
>
> In Tennessee, a reasonable person does not shoot and kill an unarmed, unsuspecting and innocent victim without just punishment and retribution under our law. The defendant, by his own voluntary and uncoerced action received such, or what he thought was then just punishment, and will now not be heard to complain. . . .
>
> In Tennessee, as in all other liberty loving civilized countries, ambush killers are not looked upon without much favor, to say the least. . . . one does not shoot down his fellow man unless that man has committed an overt act that would justify the defendant in so doing . . . this Court cannot

sit idly by while deepening disorder, disrespect for constituted authority, and mounting violence and murder stalk the land and let waiting justice sleep.[35]

It would have been impossible for the Tennessee Supreme Court not to have seen the national news stories that circulated in the days following Ray's sentencing. Reports stated that Ray's plea was the "result of lengthy and closely guarded negotiations" between the prosecution and defense as well as "King's widow, Coretta, US Attorney General Ramsey Clark and Tennessee governor Buford Ellington."[36]

It would have been impossible for the court not to have seen the unethical statements Foreman made in *Look* magazine right after Ray's sentencing. Foreman said in that article that it would have been his "duty" to take the witness stand against Ray, violate the attorney-client privilege, and betray Ray had he refused to accept the guilty plea. This statement is tantamount to a confession by Foreman that he coerced Ray into pleading guilty. Coercion is sufficient to void any contract, agreement, or plea that is alleged to be a voluntary act. What sort of "voluntary" plea could have been entered by Ray or any other criminal defendant when faced with the prospect that he would not only be deprived of legal counsel, but that his own attorney would offer testimony against him? If Foreman's threats failed to be considered coercion and duress, then it is difficult to understand the meaning of the right to a fair trial.

The greater tragedy was that the court actively obscured the truth of who really murdered King. The best way to "solve" the case was to put James Earl Ray on trial, but the Tennessee court system was more interested in expedient justice than it was in actual justice.

What insight did Judge Miller have that the Tennessee Supreme Court did not, when he said in subsequent years that Foreman's defense of Ray "reeks with ethical, moral, and professional irregularities?" Another time, Miller described Foreman's behavior as Ray's defense attorney as a "farce and a mockery of justice." How could Miller, a native Tennessean on the federal bench, see it, yet not a single Tennessee court system jurist could?

PART THREE: LOGICAL CONCLUSIONS

CHAPTER 9
The Work of a Two-Bit Felon?

Whoever murdered Rev. Martin Luther King Jr. knew where he was staying in Memphis and found a concealed place from where he could take a shot with a .30-06 rifle. We are told that the gunman was James Earl Ray and that he placed the rifle in front of Guy Canipe's store only a minute or two after firing the deadly shot. He miraculously escaped from the scene even though there were twenty-five to thirty Memphis police officers in the immediate vicinity at the time of the assassination.[1] A witness saw a white man in a white Mustang drive away from the scene, and the police issued an all-points bulletin.

Ray abandoned the car in Atlanta, took a bus north, and crossed into Canada. Using the legitimate birth certificate of a Toronto policeman, he obtained a passport. While waiting for it, he received telephone calls and visitors at both of the rooming houses in a run-down part of Toronto where he alternated staying, indicating that at least two people knew who and where he was. About a month later, he flew to London and then Portugal aboard a jetliner as a commercial passenger for the first time in his life. He entered the Canadian consulate in Lisbon to request that they reissue his passport because the last name, *Sneyd,* was misspelled as *Sneya.* Then he left the consulate with both old and new passports.

We do not know Ray's motivation to seek a revised passport. He had the Sneyd birth certificate in his possession and he knew it did not match the name on the passport. However, since Ray's objective in getting a passport in another person's name was to hide his identity, the error on his *Sneya* passport was golden, as it did not connect him with any other *real* person and would thus make it more difficult for the authorities to discover his true identity.

Customs authorities questioned Ray when he attempted to leave Portugal because the name on the new passport did not match the name of the one Ray had used to enter the country. Portuguese authorities

213

allowed him to board the flight back to London, where the police promptly arrested him.

RAY'S OTHER ALIASES

The aliases used by James Earl Ray from his first trip to Canada in July 1967 to the time he was apprehended in London a year later present the most baffling and complex aspect of the case. To some degree, they also give us a glimpse into the investigative process and agencies (including the HSCA), the attitudes of the four primary writers about Ray, and why, for the first time in his adult life, Ray had both freedom and money. Did Ray enjoy the best year of his life pretending at various times to be one of four Canadian men all by himself, or did he have a little help? The presence of the aliases has been overlooked—if not dismissed—in official investigations.

Years later, in his testimony to the HSCA, we learned that district attorney Canale left the conspiracy investigation entirely up to the FBI. However, the FBI never did much with the Canadian aliases because any leads they might have developed could have overturned the "lone gunman" position taken by its director, J. Edgar Hoover, and US attorney general Ramsey Clark the morning after King's assassination. The Haneses never looked into the aliases because the issue was not seen as critical to winning an acquittal.

The HSCA investigators were suspicious about the aliases, but did not or could not follow through to find the truth. At the same time, the HSCA had no subpoena power in Canada and could only interview Canadian witnesses who chose to cooperate, and even then it could only conduct interviews in the presence of Royal Canadian Mounted Police. The HSCA worked with budget, manpower, and time limitations. Political sensitivities, both within the committee and US House leadership, were ever present.

Ray's primary alias for the year preceding his capture was Eric S. Galt, used at various times as Eric Starvo Galt. It was the Galt alias that Ray used to purchase and register the white Mustang in Alabama, get an Alabama driver's license, send and receive correspondence, take bartending lessons, travel to Mexico, rent a room in Los Angeles during the winter of 1968, and do other normal things. Ray used four other aliases in addition to Galt. Two of those (Harvey Lowmeyer and John

Willard) were used only one time each before the King assassination. Two others (Paul E. Bridgeman and Ramon George Sneyd) were used exclusively after the assassination.

The Lowmeyer alias is the most easily explainable and the least sinister of Ray's aliases. James Earl Ray knew a man by that name who, like himself had been in a lot of trouble with the law back home in Quincy, Illinois. The real Lowmeyer served time in prison with Ray's older brother, John. Ray altered the spelling to suit himself, as the man's actual name was spelled with an "h" rather than a "w"— "Lohmeyer." Apparently, the only time Ray used this name was to purchase a .243 rifle at Aeromarine Supply Company in Birmingham, which he returned the next day to exchange for the Remington GameMaster .30-06.

Nothing is simple or innocuous about Ray's other four aliases. Unlike Lowmeyer, Ray did not know any of these men. They are the names of four real Canadian men. In 1967, all four of them lived within a five-mile radius of each other in the Toronto suburbs and shared similar physical descriptions and age, with those of each other and James Earl Ray.

In the summer of 1967, Ray took his first trip to Canada to visit Montreal. He did not travel to Toronto, where the men whose names he adopted lived (although he might have spent a night on the road in the area), until after King had been murdered. By that time, Ray had already been using the Galt alias for the better part of a year. The

James Earl Ray's Canadian aliases. Left to right: *Paul E. Bridgeman, Eric S. Galt, Ramon George Sneyd, and John Willard* (Courtesy HSCA *MLK Hearings*, vol. v, 11)

physical similarities of these four men to each other and to Ray, as well as their close proximity to each other, call into question whether Ray was provided these names by someone, and if so, by whom and for what purpose. The likelihood that Ray innocently created the identities of four, similar-looking Canadian men is infinitesimally small. Dreaming up a few make-believe names that are easy to remember is one thing. Dreaming up real men who have the same general description as yourself is quite another.

Two of the aliases bear particular scrutiny: Galt and Sneyd. The former was Ray's primary alias prior to escaping to Europe, and the latter was one to which he switched for the few weeks he was on the lam in Canada and Europe. The Galt alias is important because the real Eric S. Galt was an employee of a Canadian subsidiary of Union Carbide that conducted military work. Ray traveled to Mexico from the West Coast a couple of times, went to New Orleans, bought a car, and more, using the name of a man who held a Canadian top-secret clearance and worked at a facility where classified work for the US military was conducted.

A key clue in unraveling the mystery of Ray's assumption of Galt's identity is the signature. Pre-1966, the real Galt included an abbreviation of his middle name, St. Vincent, to "St. V." Galt used slightly open circles as periods after "St" and "V." The open and slightly ambiguous circles look somewhat like small, scribbled letters rather than periods and give an appearance that could easily be interpreted as the middle name *Starvo*.

The real Galt stopped signing his name in this manner in 1965, at which time James Earl Ray was in prison in Missouri, so he could not have known this. Galt had changed his signature prior to Ray's escape in 1967, but Ray's adoption of the name reflects the pre-1966 signature.

The real Eric S. Galt's signature (Courtesy HSCA, *Hearings*, vol. v, 11)

How is this possible? This seemingly miniscule detail was not resolved by the HSCA.

Both the real Galt and Ray had scars on their right palms and above the left eyebrow. The real Galt was a few years older than Ray, but they were alike in height and weight and had similar hair and eye colors and facial features. They easily could have passed as brothers if standing side by side or have impersonated the other with the proper papers.

The real Ramon George Sneyd was a Toronto policeman. In April 1968, Ray acquired a copy of Sneyd's Ontario birth certificate and applied for and received a Canadian passport in Sneyd's name but with his own picture on it.

Ray tried to obtain a passport when he was in Canada during the summer of 1967 but could not figure out how to do so. It is curious, then, that the official story is that he mastered the process the following year. When he returned to Canada after the assassination of King, with the police in every US city searching for him, Ray's passport application zipped through the system. Ray entered Canada by bus on either April 6 or 7, 1968. He obtained his passport photos on April 11, and his passport was issued on April 24, 1968. Strangely, this was the very same day the Province of Ontario provided an official copy of Sneyd's birth certificate. No investigation evaluated this coincidence, but it suggests intervention. The speed with which the passport was processed and issued as well as the fact that the birth certificate and the passport were issued on the very same day suggests that the process was expedited by someone who was in an official position to do so.

After Ray was apprehended in London, Toronto deputy police chief Bernard Simmons said that Ray "must have had some unusual sources of information" to complete the Sneyd passport application.[2] Chief Simmons believed that Ray was aided by a co-conspirator or conspirators, just as Harry Avery had suspected that one of the letters from Canada in his purloined evidence file pertained to Ray's passport.

A critical question is how Ray got Sneyd's name, a Toronto cop who was another Ray look-alike. In his testimony to the HSCA, Ray said that one of the first things he did when he got to Canada in April 1968 was go to the *Toronto Evening Telegram* and sift through newspapers from 1932, looking for birth announcements. According to Ray's typewritten statement incorporated into the HSCA record (with original errors and all capitals as submitted by Ray): "AFTER A TIME I CHOSED

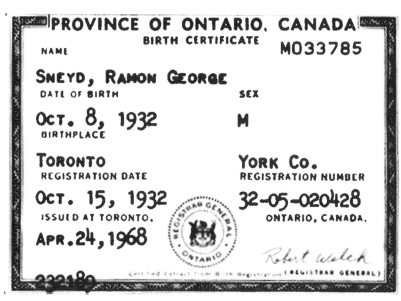

Ray's birth certificate as Ramon George Sneyd (Courtesy Shelby County Archives)

Ray's application for a Canadian passport as Ramon George Sneyd (Courtesy Shelby County Archives)

Ray posing as Ramon George Sneyd (Courtesy Shelby County Archives)

SEVERAE NAMES FROM THE FILMS; TWO OF THE NAMES WERE, RAMON GEORGE SNEYD & PAUL E. BRIDGMAN. MY PURPOSE IN OBTAINING THESE NAMES WAS TO APPLY FOR A PASSPORT UNDER ONE OF THE NAMES IF CONDITIONS WERE FAVORABLE."[3]

Ray couldn't have gotten luckier than finding, in the birth announcements published in a thirty-six-year-old newspaper, the name of someone who looked a lot like Ray as an adult. Incredibly, Ray picked out the names of *two men* whose likenesses were similar to his own.

Either of the people whose names he chose could have been crippled, or six feet four inches tall, or black, or had red hair or some other obvious visual characteristic that is quite different from those of Ray. But, like Ray, they were white men with similar height, build, hair, and eyes.

Ray's statement went on to say that he telephoned "several" of the people he had found in the newspaper, including Sneyd. He says he told them he was with the Register General's office and that he was investigating passport applications. When he spoke to Sneyd, whom he identified in the statement as "a Toronto policeman," he said Sneyd informed him that he had never previously applied for a passport.[4] This is what Ray needed to know in order to avoid applying for a passport that might have already been legitimately issued or associated with someone who was deceased.

The bizarre part of the history is that the HSCA investigators seemed completely uninterested in any of the details. They did not ask Ray to clarify whether he knew Sneyd was a policeman when he called him on the phone, or if Sneyd told Ray he was a cop. They didn't ask him why he indicated on the application that Sneyd's occupation was a "car salesman" if in fact he knew he was a cop.

There are problems, too, with the Galt alias. At Brushy Mountain Prison on March 28, 1977, the first general counsel of HSCA, Richard Sprague, asked Ray how he came to use the Galt name. Ray replied, "I have no idea. I just—just a name. I might have seen it in a phone book or something." Ray was not in Toronto on his 1967 trip to Canada, so it is unlikely that he found it in the Toronto phone book. Consequently, Sprague asked where Ray was when he saw the name Galt in a phone book. Ray replied, "I don't know if I saw it in a phone book. I just—I'm just trying to explain to you where I could have gotten these various names from."

Sprague was undeterred by Ray's obfuscation on the Galt alias: "Well, did anybody ever give you that name?"

"No, I don't—no one give it to me. I didn't get it from any Canadian sources or anything," Ray replied. If Ray had gotten the name from an American source, perhaps his comment about "Canadian sources" was his way of concealing the truth of the matter with a technically truthful caveat. Ray was a wily character in such matters and knew how to parse his words to achieve a certain nuance.

Ray and Sprague discussed whether the Galt alias came from a James Bond book or movie. Ray said it is possible he might have read the name in a book: "You can't explain these aliases, where you get them all at." Then Ray told Sprague that he had decided on the Galt alias when he left Chicago headed to Montreal in July 1967. But Ray quickly added, "It's possible I got the name when I was in Birmingham."[5] Of course, the real Eric St. Vincent Galt's name and telephone number were in the Toronto telephone book, not the one of Birmingham, Alabama. In any case, the real Eric St. Vincent Galt lived in Scarborough, Ontario, a Toronto suburb. Amazingly, the HSCA never interviewed him. The only investigator who actually interviewed the real Galt was author Philip H. Melanson in 1984.

Melanson concluded that James Jesus Angleton (the CIA supervisor of Richard Ober, who opened the 201 file on Ray) was responsible for providing the Galt alias. Part of Angleton's responsibility at the CIA was coordination with allied intelligence services, including those of Canada. The relationship between Ray's 201 file, Ober, and Angleton was not revealed until the declassification and release of previously concealed CIA documents in 1994, five years after Melanson's book was published.

Melanson found that Galt's Canadian employer, a subsidiary of Union Carbide, was working on a classified project for the US military. Angleton likely had access to Canadian security files and could have identified Galt as a Ray look-alike (including similar scars).[6]

Angleton's involvement is a plausible explanation as to how James Earl Ray replicated Eric Starvo Galt's signature from the way the genuine Eric St. Vincent Galt signed his name prior to 1966. If Ray was given this alias by his mysterious handler, Raoul, in July 1967 (as the HSCA clearly established that Ray was using the Galt alias at that time), Angleton would have been able to pull it out of the Canadian security-clearance system.

Angleton had the connections and credibility with the Canadian liaisons to accomplish this without raising suspicions. Melanson cited an example of Angleton's influence with the RCMP intelligence organization. Melanson wrote that Angleton was "outraged" in 1972 when he discovered that his counterpart in Canadian counter-intelligence, Leslie "Jim" Bennett, was being investigated as a possible Soviet double agent. Angleton subsequently "injected himself" into the RCMP investigation and even reviewed and analyzed the RCMP's findings.[7] Such was Angleton's influence, credibility, and power and the CIA's clout with Canadian authorities.

Once Angleton acquired Galt's information, he needed a way to pass the details to Ray. Raoul must have given Ray a photocopy of Galt's pre-1966 signature to show him how to sign his alias name—a similar signature would be another level of protection. Angleton could have easily lifted the signature from Galt's security clearance file, which had been last updated in 1961. After Ray received the signature, he likely studied the scribbled "St. V." and decided the middle name was "Starvo." There is no other way that Ray could have matched the look of Galt's pre-1966 signature and come up with the erroneous middle name.

William Pepper also suggested that the US intelligence community provided Ray with the Galt alias.[8] Pepper wrote that providing a patsy with an identity with security clearance (such as Galt's) is a means of avoiding trouble before it starts. If Ray, using the Galt alias, were to roll through a stop sign or get pulled over for some other minor violation, a routine police check of Eric S. Galt would run into a protected file. This would alert the intelligence team and give them leverage to urge the local law-enforcement agency to let their man go.[9] This might explain how James Earl Ray stayed out of trouble the year prior to King's death. For example, when Ray, using the Galt alias, went to the local police station to follow up on a jaywalking citation he had received on or about April 8, 1968, he was told there was no ticket on file.[10]

Paul E. Bridgeman, another of Ray's aliases, establishes a secondary connection to Galt. Both real men went to the same physician, Dr. Marvin Maxman, for annual physicals.[11] Unfortunately, however, HSCA investigators were unable to locate Bridgeman, and Dr. Maxman refused to be interviewed.[12]

Ray apparently used the alias John Willard only once, to check into Bessie Brewer's flophouse on South Main Street in Memphis the afternoon of the King assassination. Like the real Galt, the real Willard also traveled throughout the South in the 1960s.

When the HSCA investigated the matter of the Canadian aliases, it focused on only three issues "of primary investigative concern:"

• The relative ease with which Ray obtained a Canadian passport;

• Any criminal associates Ray may have had in Canada before or after the assassination; and

- Any financial transactions Ray may have made in Canada.[13]

Incredibly, the HSCA asked no questions about the amazing speed with which the passport was issued to Ray, just the "ease" in getting it. It asked no questions about Sneyd being a policeman and whether Ray knew that fact in advance.

The HSCA asked no questions about Galt's top-secret clearance or whether this fact was relevant to the case. It asked no questions as to how Ray came to use four names of real Canadian men, who lived near each other in the Toronto area, for nearly a year before Ray ever set foot there.[14] It asked no questions about whether another person or organization systematically provided these aliases to Ray.

The investigation into the three primary concerns is summed up by Edward Evans, chief investigator for HSCA MLK task force: "The staff found Ray's explanation for the aliases highly incredible. Yet, the investigation could uncover no evidence that he contacted an alias ring or received other assistance, despite the remarkable coincidences and possible sinister interpretations."[15]

Maybe Evans's statement was a cop-out or simply reflected a frustrated exhaustion. Maybe it was what the HSCA members wanted to hear. Maybe that analysis was as in-depth as HSCA committee members or investigators would dare go. Whatever the reason, the HSCA investigation came to rest, just like the FBI investigation before it, far short of the mark.

WHAT HUIE, MCMILLAN, POSNER, AND SIDES SAY

William Bradford Huie did not address the aliases in much detail. His attempt at an explanation was that Ray saw a sign for the town of Galt, Ontario, on the road near Toronto and adopted the name. Huie speculated that Ray simply thought up the first and middle names.[16] Huie ignored all the other impossible coincidences of physical similarities to Ray and the geographic proximity of all of the aliases.

Author George McMillan devoted only one paragraph in his work to the question of the Galt alias. He claimed that Ray got the name "Galt" from Ayn Rand's work *Atlas Shrugged*. This aligns with his larger view of the imprisoned and escaped Ray as a political activist attracted to right-wing candidates such as Barry Goldwater and George Wallace. McMillan also claimed that Ray thought of "Eric Starvo" as a manipulation of the character "Ernst Stavro Blofeld" of the James Bond film *From Russia With Love*. There is no supporting evidence for this speculation. The odds of James Earl Ray or anyone else coming up with the Galt alias as McMillan explained it and dreaming up an alias that actually corresponds to a real person with security clearance and physical similarities to Ray right down to the scars is unthinkably remote. In addition, McMillan did not mention the Bridgeman, Willard, or Sneyd aliases in any capacity.

In *Killing the Dream*, Posner addressed the Galt alias, claiming that the timing of Ray's initial use of it in July 1967 made it impossible for Raoul (who he believed was a product of Ray's imagination) to have provided the name. He also rejected both McMillan's explanation and Huie's explanation of the Galt alias. He claimed that the "only realistic alternatives" are that Ray thought it up by himself or, in a twist, his brothers provided it to him in Chicago.[17] But Jerry and John Ray would have brought no additional expertise to any such conspiracy, even if it had existed. None of them had participated in anything so sophisticated. Posner did not indicate that Jerry or John had anything to do with the other aliases.

Author Hampton Sides simply ignored the issue entirely. He mentioned the names of the Ray aliases in a matter-of-fact manner only a few times and gave no hint that there is anything mysterious or unsolved about the aliases in any way. This is not surprising, since the argument of Sides's book is that Ray stalked King due to compulsions of racial hatred and a desire to become famous. If those were truly Ray's motives, he would not have gone to Canada for several weeks after escaping from prison in 1967 in the first place.

RAY'S MYSTERIOUS CONTACTS IN TORONTO

Ray had two different rooming house addresses during his brief stay in Toronto in the spring of 1968. During a one-week period (April 25-May 2), at least two different visitors called (by telephone and in person), and at each location the visitors asked for Ray by the names of Bridgeman and Sneyd, the aliases he had used to rent the rooms and had just begun to use.

On April 25, a caller came looking for Bridgeman by name at the rooming house kept by Feliksa Szpakowska (also spelled Szpakowski) on Ossington Street. The caller was described as a "slight man," but Ray was not in the rooming house at the time.

Ray moved shortly thereafter to a rooming house on Dundas Street kept by Sun Fung Loo. He used his new alias, Ramon George Sneyd, to rent the room. On April 27, Loo answered a telephone call from a man who asked her to summon Sneyd to the phone. The caller did not ask whether Sneyd was staying there, making it apparent that he knew that he did.[18] Ray was not in at the time of the call.

Around noon on May 2, Ray received a caller in person at Loo's, whom she described as a "fat man." The man came to her door and asked if "Mr. Sneyd" was in, indicating that he knew Sneyd/Ray was renting there. She summoned Ray, who met the man at the door, spoke with him briefly, and received a white envelope.[19] That same afternoon, Ray went back to the Kennedy Travel Agency to pay in Canadian currency for and pick up a plane ticket and passport, which had been there for a week.

Canadian authorities determined that the "fat man," who was later identified by Loo, had not delivered cash to Ray but had visited as a good Samaritan. The man, whose name was not initially divulged to the public but known by the RCMP and later the Canadian press, told authorities he found the envelope, which he believed contained job applications, in a nearby telephone booth with Ray's alias and street address typed on it.

The FBI identified the "fat man" as Robert McDouldton (spelled McNaulton by the CIA), a "reputable citizen" who had no involvement with Ray, according to the Canadian authorities.[20]

Melanson tracked down McDouldton in 1984, though he was agitated that he had been found. He told Melanson that, at the time, he feared for his life.[21] If McDouldton were just a good Samaritan, why would he fear for his life for returning job applications? More importantly, however, Ray was on the lam and his true name was known by authorities worldwide. Even under an alias, why would be filling out job applications? These are questions unanswered by any official investigation.

Melanson pointed to other problems with the good Samaritan story. McDouldton told authorities that Ray's alias and street address (which was near the telephone booth) were typed on the envelope. Loo took a glance at the envelope and told authorities that she believed only a name was typed on it— no address to be found.[22] If the envelope in fact did not show both the name and the street address, how did McDouldton know where to find Ray?

Neither the FBI nor the HSCA interviewed Szpakowska, Loo, or McDouldton during their investigations.

What Do the Canadian Aliases Mean?

The entire situation of Ray's aliases speaks of professional intelligence and security expertise. The aliases were not the products of a ninth-grade dropout. Despite Ray's comments that no one gave him the aliases, it is clear he did not acquire them on his own. One might ask why Ray shrugged off questions about the involvement of others in developing these aliases. He might have thought them up himself. His brothers might have thought them up. Or, alternatively, he may have been afraid to acknowledge that someone provided them to him.

Ray could have been telling the truth when he stated that he saw the names in a telephone book or discovered them in some other innocuous way. But this explanation is extremely unlikely due to all of the coincidences and advantages of these aliases as previously explained. Equally unlikely is the possibility that Ray's brothers came up with these names.

That leaves us with the unavoidable conclusion that others provided Ray with these aliases. The most plausible explanation is that Ray's handler, Raoul, funneled the carefully screened aliases to him. Angleton and Ober, or someone who reported to them, chose the aliases as a means of facilitating the management and manipulation of Ray. Only an intelligence organization with access to security clearance files and other databases could find these four lookalikes and match them to Ray, right down to subtle scars.

It is likely that Ray deliberately obscured the truth about the aliases because he feared for the lives of his family members and himself. He was probably told just enough about the information they had on the whereabouts of his brothers, his sister, and parents—with just enough threats made against all of them—to convince him that if he ever uttered a word about getting the aliases from anyone, his family would be harmed. He was obligated to lie all the way to his grave because family members survived him. The truth died with Ray on April 23, 1998.

There are two final, important points about Ray's four Canadian aliases.

First, the fact that these aliases were real Canadians is not merely a geographic accident or due to proximity to the United States. Ray spoke only English, so running his aliases from Mexico (even with the use of Anglo-sounding names) was not an option. But if language alone was the controlling factor, then American aliases could have been used. The option of domestic aliases was not viable due to the relative ease of exposure of the entire conspiratorial enterprise by a routine police, credit, or employment inquiry. (Indeed, Ray was in various domestic databases such as Social Security, Internal Revenue Service, FBI, military service, and criminal records). Canadian aliases were chosen in order to minimize this risk. Also, if a later investigation were to trace Ray's steps across the border, investigators would encounter jurisdictional limitations and challenges and would not have subpoena power. It would be infinitely easier for the CIA to thwart an American investigation probing events in Canada than it would a domestic investigation.

Second, the four look-alike aliases were provided to Ray as part of up-front contingency planning. If the cover for the CIA's preferred alias Eric S. Galt were blown, Ray would have other look-alike aliases as fallbacks. As the conspiracy operated, the Galt alias was sufficient cover without using any of the other aliases for nearly a year. Ray used the Willard alias only once, to rent the room at Bessie Brewer's rooming house in Memphis. He did not use the Bridgeman alias until he rented the room on Ossington Street in Toronto. The Galt alias took Ray from Montreal in the summer of 1967 across the US, into Mexico, and back to Toronto by April 1968. This alias was jettisoned only when Ray escaped to Canada and on to Europe.

Did Ray Stalk Martin Luther King?

Part of the Ray's image concocted for the public included the allegation that James Earl Ray stalked King. This idea has been around since the early years of the case and is based almost entirely on three separate coincidences of Ray and King's schedules. The HSCA's final report noted that the first evidence of Ray's stalking was his decision to leave Los Angeles on March, 17 1968, and head for Atlanta, where King lived. Through its own analysis, the HSCA reported that there is no evidence as to whether Ray was stalking King during the first eleven months on the lam.

The HSCA also determined that Ray was in Selma, Alabama, on March 22, the day after King was there. The following week, Ray allegedly returned to Atlanta after purchasing a .243 rifle at Aeromarine Supply Company in Birmingham, Alabama, on March 29 and exchanging it the next day for the .30-06 he took to Memphis. HSCA investigators found an April 1 receipt supposedly signed by Ray as his Galt identity at an Atlanta laundry.

The stalking-theory advocates argue that Ray drove from Atlanta to Birmingham to buy a rifle and immediately returned. They say Ray spent the night of April 1 in Atlanta and quickly headed to Memphis on April 3 when the news broke that King would fly back to Memphis that morning. If Ray actually were stalking King, who was in Atlanta on April 1 and 2, and Ray already had the rifle in his possession, why not do the job right then and there? Yet there is no evidence of any sort that Ray attempted to locate King in Atlanta.

The third coincidence is Ray's trip to Memphis on April 3, the day King arrived and checked into the Lorraine Motel.

This allegation of Ray stalking King was revitalized in Hampton Sides's 2010 book, which features "stalking" in its title. Besides the title, however, Sides's book says almost nothing about Ray stalking King. Instead, the book focuses on the oddities and foibles of Ray's personality and habits and the plausibility of a four-time felon murdering the most prominent civil rights leader in the nation. Sides does not explain how he obtained intimate details about Ray, whom he never met or interviewed.

Sides and others who argue a stalking theory claim that Ray formulated a plan to murder King while he was in Los Angeles during the winter of 1967 to 1968. Ray got on the highway eastbound from California on March 17, 1968, with his newly conceived plan, and in a matter of eighteen days he picked up King's trail in Selma, bought the murder weapon in Birmingham, and accomplished the deed in Memphis on April 4.

None of this makes any sense because there is not a shred of evidence that Ray had King under any sort of surveillance or that their paths crossed prior to Memphis. Furthermore, if Ray was the racist they claimed, why did he not buy a high-powered rifle sooner? Ray's rifle was purchased just five days before the assassination. If Ray had been intent on stalking and killing King, he would have purchased the rifle weeks or months before. Ray was not the shooter because he had no motive to kill King, and no sane, behind-the-scenes moneyman would hire someone to take a sniper's shot who did not have the expertise.

The stalking theory just doesn't add up. An inept, four-time convict and high school dropout doesn't wake up one morning and decide to track down a prominent man and murder him from a concealed, remote location with a long-distance shot that he is ill-prepared to make. A hit man might pull it off, but not a petty property criminal. In addition, stalking is not an inexpensive endeavor. Ray would have needed to acquire funds before proceeding on such a mission, which would require the participation of at least one additional person.

How Did Ray Know Where King Would Be?

The week after accepting Ray's guilty plea sentencing him to ninety-nine years in prison, Judge Preston Battle rhetorically asked reporters, "Like others, I would truly like to know how Ray actually found the spot from which to fire. How did Ray know where Rev. King would be?"

The short answer is that Ray did not know where King was staying in Memphis. Information about where he was staying and his hotel room number were not readily available to the public. FBI Counterintelligence was actively manipulating the King entourage into staying at the Lorraine Motel, and FBI informants even reported the room number, 306, in advance. This information was undoubtedly shared with Angleton's CIA CI, but not even the Memphis police department knew until King arrived.

Since it is absolutely necessary for an assassin to know where to find his victim, it follows that Ray had no plans to murder King. As Hanes Jr. told me, King was not on James Earl Ray's radar. On the other hand, King was very much on the radar screen of the US intelligence community.

Wednesday, April 3, 1968, was the first day that James Earl Ray was ever in Memphis. Raoul had told him to buy the rifle in Birmingham, take it to Memphis, and meet him there. Ray stayed in the New Rebel Motel on Lamar Avenue in a scruffy part of town. Ray said that he gave Raoul the rifle that evening and it was the last time it was in his possession. Raoul told him to move the following day to Bessie Brewer's rooming house on South Main Street.

William Bradford Huie was the first person to offer an explanation for Ray's knowledge of King's whereabouts. According to Huie, the April 4 issue of the *Memphis Commercial Appeal* reported that King "was at the Lorraine Motel."[23] Posner's account in his own work coincides with Huie's.[24] This is a half-truth at best because it does not specify whether King was staying there or simply present at that location. What the *Memphis Commercial Appeal* actually reported on April 4 is that King had lunch on April 3 at the Lorraine Motel and was served with a court order by the US Marshals. The newspaper mentioned nothing about where the King entourage was staying overnight and thus could not have been the means by which Ray learned where to find King.

McMillan claimed in *The Making of an Assassin* that Memphis television stations broadcast a picture of King standing on the balcony in front of his room at the Lorraine and that the room number was plainly visible on the TV. When the HSCA issued its final report, it had no evidence of any local television coverage that might have included information as to where King was staying. Rather, it says that there were "reports" that an unidentified radio station announced that King was in room 306 of the Lorraine Motel.[25] In either case, there was no analysis as to whether Ray saw or heard any information about King's whereabouts from electronic media.

McMillan also claimed that the April 4 issue of the *Memphis Commercial Appeal* ran a photo of King on the balcony of the Lorraine. This too is inaccurate, as no such photo was in the edition that circulated in Memphis of the April 4 newspaper.

Hampton Sides states in his book that the *Memphis Commercial Appeal* "featured a page-one photograph of King standing in front of room 306 at the Lorraine."[26] This is grotesquely false. The *Memphis Commercial Appeal*'s archives do include two photos of King on the balcony at the Lorraine that were taken on April 3. Neither of those pictures were in the following day's newspaper, and they remained unpublished until after King's death. Sides noted that the error crept into his work because he "conflated statements from multiple accounts" instead of verifying the photographs in the newspaper archives. Sides admitted to me that specific citations that appeared in McMillan, Huie, and Posner's works "were wrong."[27]

If Ray were a lone, racist, assassin, he indeed would have had to know where to find King. But the fact is that Ray did not know, and there is no means of proving that he did. Previous writers offered faulty explanations that implicate Ray without evidence. The truth of the matter is that no one saw James Earl Ray or anyone else carry a rifle into the rooming house. Ray's fingerprints were not found in the bathroom, and no one saw him there. No one saw him pull the trigger and leave. No one saw him or anyone else carrying a rifle down the hallway. No one saw him leave the rooming house with a bundle. And no one saw him place the bundle in front of Guy Canipe's store. The twenty-five or thirty uniformed Memphis police officers "in the immediate vicinity" didn't see Ray either. In sum, someone arranged all this for the purpose of implicating James Earl Ray, who was perfect at only one thing: being someone else's pawn.

CHAPTER 10
Blakey vs. Blakey

As chief counsel for the HSCA, G. Robert Blakey was at the heart of the congressional investigation. He is primarily responsible for the conduct of that investigation and the HSCA *Final Report,* which lists its findings and conclusions "I wrote a book," Blakey told me, "the *Final Report.*"[1] He stands by those findings today and applied the word "irresponsible" to my dissent. Yet, in recent years, Blakey has introduced serious concerns that suggest his entire investigation was compromised.

It is clear that the CIA had an interest in keeping Ray from a full trial. The record is equally clear that the eleven months prior to Rev. Martin Luther King's assassination were the best months of James Earl Ray's life, from a financial standpoint. "After two years of investigation with a staff of several hundred and the expenditure of several million dollars," as Blakey noted, he was unable to counter Ray's explanation as to how he had money to burn: that Raoul gave it to him. The money was real, ergo Raoul was real. Blakey's "hundreds" of employees found no trace of another source of Ray's money. Because Blakey and his staff could never prove otherwise, they inadvertently confirmed Ray's assertion: someone gave Ray the money on which he comfortably lived.

Furthermore, the CIA (via James Jesus Angleton) almost certainly provided Ray with the Canadian aliases he used. Blakey and his staff knew that there was more to know about their acquisition, but because the four real Canadian men whose names Ray used as aliases were not in the jurisdiction of congressional subpoena, they could not pursue the investigation.

Blakey has since been bitterly critical of the CIA's "support" in the HSCA investigation. His criticism is focused on the CIA's liaison to the HSCA investigation, George Joannides.

Joannides was involved in a Miami-based CIA front organization that "identified" alleged JFK-murderer Lee Harvey Oswald as a Castro sympathizer. Joannides was the hidden hand guiding the Directorio Revolucionario Estudiantil (the Revolutionary Student Directorate, or DRE). It was the CIA's own front group that "outed" Oswald as a communist-leaning, pro-Castro activist. This fact was kept secret from both the Warren Commission and the HSCA.

Blakey justifiably felt betrayed when Joannides's actions were revealed in the mid-1990s by the Assassinations Records Review Board (ARRB). He said that, had he known at the time, he would have insisted that the CIA remove Joannides from his liaison role and that he would have considered him a material witness and interrogated him under oath. The Joannides situation indicates that the CIA deliberately manipulated both the Warren Commission and HSCA investigations. Blakey has stated publically that he no longer believes "anything" the CIA told the HSCA.

Why would the CIA manipulate and compromise the investigation about King's assassination? The answer to that question is concomitant to the CIA's interest that James Earl Ray not receive a full trial. Specifically, the CIA wanted to ensure that their scapegoat—Ray—remain in prison as the confessed murderer of Martin Luther King so that there would never be a trial where the evidence was tested in open court. Years later, Blakey has doubted the integrity of his own investigation while desperately holding on to its findings. This puts the Blakey of 1979 in conflict with the Blakey of the twenty-first century.

However, any regrets now don't change the past. If the CIA manipulated or even infiltrated the HSCA, how can anyone vouch for the integrity and credibility of the HSCA findings? Blakey wrote, "If a person lies to you on one point, you may reject all of his testimony."[2] According to Blakey, his personal standard relies on the fact that when a witness is caught lying, his entire testimony can be disregarded because its veracity is called into question. If one were to apply this standard to the HSCA *Final Report*, it would end up being dismissed as state propaganda, disinformation, myth, or simply error. Consequently, the application of his own standard would require that he abandon and repudiate the HSCA findings.

There are several areas of the HSCA investigation and/or the case against James Earl Ray that exemplify Blakey's conflict, including:

1. The existence of Ray's money and his explanation for its acquisition;
2. The green bundle of evidence " and Blakey's "improved witnesses;"

3. The HSCA's analysis of Ray's guilty plea and Percy Foreman's conduct and role; and

4. The alteration of the transcript by HSCA personnel.

RACE, MONEY, AND RAOUL

According to the HSCA's report, the "committee was convinced that while Ray's decision to assassinate Dr. King may have reflected a desire to participate in an important crime, his predominant motive lay in an expectation of monetary gain."[3]

The HSCA discovered that Ray was not the maniacal racist that writers Huie and McMillan asserted in the 1970s; thus, a less obvious motive needed to be proposed. Although Blakey has asserted that Ray's ego drove him to kill King, this statement does not coincide with what he confirmed in the HSCA's report. Blakey also told me that Ray's effort to elude identification and capture was not consistent with the theory that Ray wanted to gain notoriety from the assassination.

Furthermore, Blakey said that Ray expected to collect "a $50,000 bonus offered by a group of racists connected to the American Party that was circulating in St. Louis, Missouri." If Ray had suddenly become a successful robber and had the funds to support himself, why would he assassinate King for money? In addition, how could he hope to be paid for killing King without being in contact in advance of the crime with those who held the bounty?

There is no evidence that Ray was ever in contact with anyone who might have wanted King's death. Ray would have known that, without coordinating with the people who were offering the bounty, someone else would have tried to claim the money.

Blakey's explanations of post-assassination payoffs do not take into account how Ray received money to live on for the nine-month period that immediately preceded the King assassination. However, Judge Arthur Hanes Jr. told me that the government "was wedded" to the proposition that Ray did it alone.[4] The HSCA investigation was blinded from the start to any suggestion that Raoul actually existed. To admit his presence was to admit that the government's whole theory of the crime was wrong.

The question of the source of the money comes back time and time again. On November 30, 1978, the last month of the investigation, Blakey said,

> The committee gave careful consideration to the conspiratorial implication of Ray's accounts of his dealing with the mysterious Raoul, even though Ray himself was unable to provide further identification of this individual. All leads on Raoul were pursued on the assumption that such a man might indeed exist.
>
> Nevertheless, when you come down to it, the Raoul theory that seems best to fit, although the ultimate question is for the committee, is that the mysterious accomplice might actually be one of Ray's brothers, Jerry or John, or a composite of the two of them.[5]

The insurmountable problem in substituting Ray's brothers for Raoul is that Jerry and John were both broke at the time. Neither of them had the money to buy a one-year-old Mustang for their brother as well as give him money to drive back and forth across the country. Both brothers had served time in prison by 1968, and neither one had much ability to plan and organize a sophisticated, complex crime. Neither man could have supported their brother.

On the other hand, Ray was not broke during this period. It was the best year of his life. He had spending money, and it was not an "advance" from St. Louis-based George Wallace supporters on a non-existent bounty on King's life. Ray lived on hard, cold cash in amounts to which he was never previously accustomed.

The HSCA investigation began and ended with an attempt to identify any criminal named Raoul who was associated with James Earl Ray. They concluded that there was none.

But what if Ray was correct—that Raoul actually existed? Blakey's staff did not indicate that they considered whether Raoul was an intelligence operative who would not have shown up in any sort of criminal investigation. In order to find that kind of "Raoul," Blakey's staff would have had to look to George Joannides's organization, the CIA. Even if they had looked there, it would have been Joannides's job to deflect their investigation and divert their attention to other matters.

The truth of the matter is that the HSCA looked for Raoul in the wrong places. They ignored the existence of the money Ray had in his possession. They attempted to morph the issue of Ray's unexplained spending money into the $50,000 bounty he had allegedly hoped to collect after the fact, but they were unable to connect Ray with those who held the bounty. In fact, the HSCA *Final Report* does not identify any individual who supposedly held the bounty money or contain any evidence that any such bounty existed.

Ray, the man who was capable of so little during his life, was the man the government said accomplished so much. If their narrative had given any implication that Ray had outside help, then Blakey would not have been compelled to suggest Ray's brothers as Raoul. It was much easier to blame it all on Ray.

THE GREEN BUNDLE ACCORDING TO BLAKEY

Was the green bundle dropped by James Earl Ray as he fled the scene of King's murder, or was it planted to implicate him? If the former assertion is correct, the overwhelming implication is that Ray was the assassin. If the later assertion is correct, it is unavoidably clear that Ray was a pawn and King was murdered as the result of a conspiracy.

Blakey claimed that Ray dropped the bundle as he fled the scene of the crime just moments after firing the shot that killed King. This means that either Ray pulled the trigger and subsequently dropped the bundle, or someone else pulled the trigger and the bundle was dropped by a third person, only for the purpose of implicating Ray.

Guy Canipe, the owner of the store where the green bundle was placed, was prepared to testify at Ray's trial scheduled for November 12, 1968, that the bundle was dropped at his storefront before he heard the sound of the assassination shot. "If that were a fact," Blakey agreed, "it would mean that the dropping of the bundle was a witting or unwitting co-conspirator planting evidence against Ray." The November 1968 trial never occurred because Ray fired the Haneses the prior weekend and hired Percy Foreman instead.

According to Blakey, Bernell Finley, a black man who was shopping in Canipe's store at the time the bundle appeared, "told a different story" than Canipe to the FBI and HSCA investigators. Finley heard what sounded "like the backfire of an automobile," and, a short time later, he saw a man walking by the store, heard a noise on the sidewalk near the entrance, and saw a bundle there. He described the man as white male of average build wearing a dark suit. He heard the screech of tires and saw a white automobile pull away from the curb.

A friend of Finley's, Julius Leroy Graham III, was with him in Canipe's store. The signed statements each man gave to the Memphis police department the morning following King's murder did not contradict Canipe. Neither man's statement added much to Canipe's description of events. Furthermore, the FBI report of Finley's interview on April 7, 1968, does not establish the time sequence of events nor does it include any first person quotes.[6] It most certainly does not tell "a different story."

Blakey's HSCA staff had no suspects other than Ray. If Blakey determined that Ray was not the guilty party, he would have had to admit failure. Thus, the HSCA was stuck with Ray, and they could do nothing to question or discredit the evidence against him. Had they acted without other biases or influences in the 1970s, Ray would have gotten the full trial for which he was entitled. The case against Ray was too big to fail, and Blakey's job was to make it stick.

Blakey claimed that Finley and Canipe's statements to the FBI in 1977 supported the government's theory of Ray's guilt. Graham's statements were largely ignored because they did not contribute additional support to Blakey's timeline. In the HSCA *Final Report*, only a general summary of Finley and Canipe's statements about the timing of the shot and the appearance of the bundle (or vice versa) were included. There were no recorded first-person quotes from either man.

Blakey's investigation considered statements given to Memphis police within hours of the King assassination less valid than those given to the FBI nine years later. One of Blakey's senior staff attorneys, Peter G. Beeson, warned me about relying on the memory of eyewitnesses: "Even in the late 70s, it was clear that the recall of witnesses regarding a 1968 assassination had faded."[7]

Incredibly, Blakey did not even mention in the HSCA *Final Report* whether there was any conflict between these men's statements given to Memphis police and the statements they gave to the HSCA nine years later. Because the documents of the HSCA investigation are sealed, there is no way to know whether the investigators compared the two sets of statements.

In any case, it does not change the fact that Canipe was willing to testify under oath in 1968 that the bundle appeared prior to the gunshot. Certainly, it is possible that Canipe was mistaken, just as it is possible that Finley was mistaken. But if Canipe had testified that the bundle appeared before the shot was fired, it would have struck a devastating blow to the case against James Earl Ray, as it was the only "evidence" that connected him to the crime. The question stands as to whether Guy Canipe's detailed statement to police made two hours after the King assassination rings true. I believe it does. Do the statements of any other witnesses substantially dispute it? They do not. Canipe described walking out of the front door of his business to inspect the bundle and looking both ways down the street and seeing no one. Canipe's description of a quiet, vacant street with the green bundle already lying at his feet is corroborated by Memphis patrolman W. B. Richmond. Both Canipe and Richmond describe a quiet scene in the street prior to the assassination shot and bedlam afterwards due to police, guns drawn, running in every direction.

Does the story Blakey and the FBI stitched together nine years later make more sense than Canipe's? It does not. The *Final Report* includes only a summary or evaluation of witnesses' testimony without revealing the actual transcript of those interviews. As the documents themselves have been sealed, we don't know what the FBI or HSCA investigators asked, much less what the witnesses said in response.

Blakey claimed that Bernell Finley "told a different story" than Canipe's to the FBI. It is possible that Finley told a different story nine years later, but if he did, why didn't Blakey put the first-person quotes in the HSCA *Final Report*? Blakey never explained why he thought that Finley's story was more credible than Canipe's.

The most damning aspect is that the HSCA staff never considered the possibility that the evidence was planted, perhaps because they didn't want to find such evidence. Blakey and his staff saw themselves as prosecutors rather than investigators.

THE GUILTY PLEA ANALYSIS

Blakey's staff analyzed Ray's guilty plea in March 1979. This was two months after the HSCA terminated due to the Ninety-Fifth Congress's adjournment *sine die* on January 2, 1979. The "supplementary staff report" to the HSCA, *An Analysis of the Guilty Plea Entered by James Earl Ray; Criminal Court of Shelby County, Tenn., on March 10, 1969*, by senior staff counsel Ronald B. Adrine was not submitted until after the HSCA's findings were transmitted to the clerk of the US House of

Representatives and the committee terminated. When the newly elected Congress took office the following day, "a small number of us were asked to stay on after the HSCA's mandate to review all of the investigative materials and to collate, assemble, and write the final report," according to Adrine.[8]

Blakey told me that Ray's guilty plea was "legally voluntary," though it is doubtful that the HSCA had actually considered the question. (Ironically, Blakey used Ray's terminology to make this affirmation, as Ray had admitted that he was "legally guilty.") The HSCA was already gone by the time Adrine submitted his review of Ray's guilty plea. Blakey said: "In the law, 'voluntary' does not mean free from any pressure . . . Ray had a choice: plea and save your life, or go to trial, be convicted, and receive the death penalty . . . That [Ray] faced a hard choice is irrelevant; he exercised it, in light of the circumstances; that is what 'voluntary' means in the law." Blakey made other related statements to me, most importantly perhaps, "Ray did not need Foreman to tell him how bad were the risks he ran in a trial. He knew what the consequences might be of a trial for the murder of MLK." It is clear that Blakey did not believe that Foreman pressured Ray

It is equally clear that Blakey believed that Foreman provided Ray with competent legal advice:

> Nobody charged with the death penalty is "free of pressure." The issue is, was the plea a "counseled bargain." Foreman was not the only lawyer; he and the public defenders represented Ray. Collectively, they were "competent." "Competent" means, only half joking, that they could pass "the foggy mirror test." That is, alive with a JD. No one, including Ray, had any illusions about Foreman.

The Shelby County public defender, Hugh Stanton Sr., attempted to confer with James Earl Ray once and was rebuffed. The jail logs show that Stanton went to see Ray on January 20, 1969, and was in his cell for only five minutes. Ray did not trust Stanton and refused to discuss anything about the case with him. It is technically correct that Judge Battle appointed Stanton to the case, but only for the purpose of helping Foreman investigate. Ray never acknowledged or accepted Stanton's participation in his defense. These facts were all well known to the HSCA staff.

The report Adrine submitted does not entirely agree with Blakey's position, as the report was based on the altered transcript and contains words that James Earl Ray did not say in court when he entered his guilty plea. Adrine wrote: "The US Supreme Court has held that the voluntariness of a guilty plea can be determined only by considering all of the relevant circumstances surrounding it, and it is reversible error for a Federal court to accept a tendered guilty plea unless the record shows that the defendant voluntarily and understandingly entered it."[9]

Adrine noted in his report, as previously mentioned, it was "Foreman's decision to plead Ray guilty," not Ray's alone (or at all).[10] If Foreman made the decision instead of Ray, it is difficult to see Blakey's argument that the standard of "voluntariness" was met.

Blakey, who refused to comment at all on Adrine's report, said, "Ray knew enough law on his own. His lawyers were there, but they did not make much difference. You have to look at everything." Amazingly, Blakey suggests that Ray didn't need representation. Furthermore, Blakey suggests that Ray had ineffective counsel when he said that his lawyers "didn't make much difference."

In "look[ing] at everything," Foreman appears to have made the decision to plead Ray guilty. At least, that's what Foreman himself said— that Ray didn't need legal counsel to handle a routine assassination murder charge and that Ray's lawyers didn't make much difference anyway. From this picture it is difficult to see how one can argue that Ray's plea was voluntary and that justice was served.

However, Blakey also said that "Foreman—he was admittedly unethical. Frankly, I would not believe him about anything." So why did he see to it that Foreman's testimony before the HSCA went unchallenged on several points, including the charges Ray leveled at him for using coercive pressure to get him to plead guilty? The only logical answer is that the government had committed to the idea that Ray was the lone gunman. Blakey was not going to do anything to upset this construction.

Another glaring discrepancy between Blakey and Adrine's stories is their differing understandings of whether Ray "knowingly" entered a guilty plea. Adrine wrote in his report, "Statements made by James Earl Ray both prior to, and subsequent to, the guilty plea raise questions as to his grasp of its finality."[11] Adrine considers Ray's guilty plea "pretty much unfathomable," but he sticks with the conclusion that it was not coerced. One can imagine how the members of the HSCA might have grappled with this information had it been made in time for them to consider it. The *coup de grâce* in Adrine's supplementary report read,

"Ray stated that his main purpose in entering the guilty plea was to get rid of Foreman. He looked upon the plea as a mere technicality, designed to get him out of Memphis. He believed that Foreman planned to throw the case."[12]

How could any guilty plea be voluntary if the defendant believed his lawyer was going to throw the case? This threat was confirmed only a month after Ray entered his guilty plea when Foreman wrote in *Look* magazine that if Ray had not pleaded guilty, he was going to take the witness stand against him.

Adding all of the elements of Blakey's "whole picture" together, it seems that Foreman, not Ray, made the decision to plead guilty; that Ray allegedly didn't need legal counsel; that his lawyers didn't make much difference anyway; that Ray didn't grasp the finality of the guilty plea; that Ray entered the plea to get rid of Foreman and to get away from the dehumanizing conditions of the Shelby County jail in Memphis; and that Ray believed Foreman was going to throw the case.

Incredibly, Blakey doesn't recall Ronald Adrine by name or personality on his staff, instructing his staff to perform an analysis of Ray's guilty plea or any report that included such analysis. Blakey's apparent lack of interest in determining whether Ray's plea was coerced or valid is amazing.

The brief conclusion of Adrine's report further contradicts Blakey's argument that Ray's plea was constitutionally valid. Adrine points out that "the plea contained troubling issues," the literary contract first with the Haneses and then with Foreman constituted a "conflict of interest," and "Percy Foreman's personal investigation of the facts of the case should have been more thorough."

Adrine's written report does not explicitly conclude that Ray's guilty plea met constitutional requirements. Nor does it explicitly reject the notion that Foreman coerced Ray: "It *may be* concluded that Ray's plea surpassed the Constitution's minimum requirements" and "It *may be* concluded that . . . Ray was not coerced into entering [a guilty plea]." It does not explicitly say that Ray was not coerced.[13]

Adrine's use of the modal verb "may" reveals his opinion in contrast with that of his report on Ray's guilty plea and his conflict with Blakey. When Adrine wrote that "it may be concluded" that Ray's guilty plea was proper, he only expressed the possibility that it was proper. But if Ray's guilty plea "may be" proper, it is equally true that it "may be" improper, and this is where Blakey and Adrine butt heads. Blakey pointed out to me that Ray repudiated his plea "as soon as he made [it]." This in itself should raise questions. However, he revealed his baseline opinion when he noted that "No subsequent court thought it [the guilty plea] improper." Blakey did not approach the situation with an open mind. Likewise, Adrine's statement that it "may be" true that Ray was not coerced by Foreman expresses a possibility that he was, in fact, coerced.

There are other problems with Adrine's report as well as Blakey's statements about Ray's guilty plea and Foreman's conduct. Adrine specifically stated that it is reversible error "unless the record shows" that a guilty plea was entered voluntarily. The true record—Koster's unaltered transcript—shows that Ray didn't answer the question about pressure. Adrine's legal team, knowingly or unknowingly, based their analysis of Ray's guilty plea on the doctored transcript. The use of the legitimate Koster transcript most likely would have changed the conclusions of Adrine's report and with it the outcome of the entire HSCA investigation.

Blakey's policy regarding lies told by a witness, when applied to Percy Foreman's testimony before the HSCA, raises serious questions of veracity. Blakey plainly told me that he thought Foreman was "unethical" and that he "would not believe him about anything." Yet Blakey and his staff sided with Foreman on every point Ray argued regarding Foreman's coercion. Some of Ray's claims against Foreman were corroborated by events, circumstances, and other witnesses, yet Blakey sided with Foreman. Blakey's actions and the truth about Foreman seem irreconcilable. Adrine, now chief municipal judge in Cleveland, Ohio, recalled that he personally met Hanes Sr. "My general recollection about him is that he struck me as of sterling character and a very competent lawyer. I do not recall the details of the deal that Hanes worked out for Ray, but I do remember thinking that Ray would have been much better represented if he had allowed Hanes to handle his entire defense."

Blakey knew that Tennessee was one of the few states in the 1960s that had abandoned the death penalty insofar as the actual execution of condemned men is concerned. Two successive governors, Frank G. Clement and Buford Ellington, had commuted every death sentence to life behind bars. The overwhelming favorite for governor in 1970, John

Jay Hooker Jr., was a pitched opponent of the death penalty as well. It is fallacious of Blakey to have pretended that execution might actually have compelled Ray to plead guilty.

Finally, Blakey asserted that Ray "did not need Foreman to tell him how bad" it could get if he maintained his innocence and opted for a trial. He said that Ray was self-motivated and fearful of facing a trial by jury. Once again, Blakey misunderstood or deliberately misrepresented the situation. The fact is the Shelby County DA was highly motivated to offer a plea deal and avoid a trial that he feared could end in an acquittal or hung jury.

EVIDENCE ALTERED BY THE HSCA

It was certainly a problem that Blakey and his staff used the altered transcript throughout the HSCA investigation. They had the Koster transcript in their possession and could have discerned the differences between the two. An even thornier problem, however, is that Blakey's staff made numerous additional alterations of its own.

The altered transcript is quoted on page 316 of the HSCA *Final Report*. The exchange between Judge Battle and James Earl Ray also has a footnote, which reads, "A complete transcript of the guilty plea proceedings appears as MLK Exhibit F-80, III HSCA-MLK hearings, 52." This appendix contains no less than fourteen alterations to Koster's original transcript. Blakey refused to comment on these alterations or whether they constituted a federal crime.

Toward the end of Judge Battle's questioning of Ray, one discovers that the HSCA version of the transcript has two entire questions missing. The first question deleted is "Has anything else been promised to you by anyone?" The second deleted question is "Has any pressure of any kind by anyone in any way been used on you to get you to plead guilty?"[14]

Incredibly and in a very inartistic manner, the HSCA transcript modification noted Ray's reply to Battle's question about whether anything had been promised to him to get him to plead guilty as "No, no one has used pressure." This answer is not only entirely made up, it doesn't even answer the question.

The HSCA staff made other modifications to the transcript, including two incidences in which the word "guilty" was put in James Earl Ray's mouth. Both the Koster transcript and the audio recordings confirm that

Ray never used the word "guilty" at any time during the hearing. The HSCA also falsely claimed that Ray answered Battle's question about whether he killed King with, "Yes, legally guilty, un-huh."[15]

Battle was anxious to get Ray back in his seat to proceed with his guilty plea. Battle asked again whether Ray killed King. According to the HSCA version of the transcript, Ray replied, "Yes, sir, make me guilty on that."[16]

There are at least fourteen HSCA alterations to what is claimed to be the "complete transcript." Adrine told me that he was "not aware of the alterations you reference." Blakey needs to come clean on this issue and reveal whether he knew about or authorized these alterations or whether they were done by rogue staff members. With or without this additional input, the reliability of the HSCA *Final Report* is hopelessly dubious.

THE HSCA HAD THE TRUTH IN ITS GRASP

The fact is that the HSCA had it within its grasp in the late 1970s the ability to get to the bottom of the King assassination. Blakey knew that two questions were at the heart of the case: was the green bundle planted evidence, and did Foreman coerce Ray into pleading guilty.

Blakey's explanation of Ray's motive is irrelevant. Huie, McMillan, Posner, and Sides painted a false picture of Ray as a violent, Southern white racist. Blakey was forced to reject these writers' theses because their anecdotes were mostly propaganda and fiction. He has, over the years, begrudgingly acknowledged that "thoughtful people today, not just nuts, think that more people than James Earl Ray were involved."[17] I know of no credible writer today who gives serious consideration to the idea that Ray's help came only from his brothers. They were no more equipped to carry out the complex assassination of a famous figure than was James Earl Ray. But it was neither Blakey's nor the HSCA's failure alone.

Any number of courts had the authority to vacate Ray's guilty plea and order a full trial. Had any of them known that evidence was altered, the lawyers in the Shelby County DA's office and the Tennessee attorney general's office who introduced that evidence likely would have faced severe disciplinary action and perhaps criminal charges.

How could they all have missed the alterations? How could all of Ray's attorneys have missed them? How could Blakey and his staff have missed them? His staff had both Blair and Seigenthaler's/Squires's books in their possession. It is hard to believe that no one on the HSCA staff ever ran across these books and found the discrepancy. Furthermore, HSCA didn't seem to have referred to any of the audio recordings to check for consistency.

It is one thing to rely unknowingly on altered evidence to analyze the legality of Ray's guilty plea. It is quite another to know the truth and be unwilling to set the record straight. Blakey and his staff failed both Congress and the public in their inability to evaluate in-depth the discrepancies between numerous versions of material crucial to determining Ray's role in the assassination of Martin Luther King.

CHAPTER 11
The Red Flag of Conspiracy

James Earl Ray did not fit the profile of a sophisticated, professional criminal. Ray was a professional prisoner, and there is significant difference between the two. News stories, columns, and books written by individuals who met and knew Ray have described him as an inept thief, a petty street criminal, a stumblebum hood, a nitwit two-bit felon, a nobody, and a schmuck.

But Ray was human, and every person has the right to a trial. The established powers in Tennessee, from the governor's office to the court system to the Shelby County sheriff's office, saw to it that James Earl Ray never got one. As Judge Galbreath stated in his public letter, the executive and judicial branches of state government illegally deprived Ray of a trial. They failed to follow the constitutional limitations and mandates of their offices and the duly enacted laws that they were sworn to uphold.

Much of the present-day body of evidence was not available in the late 1960s at the time of Ray's sentencing or even in the late 1970s when the HSCA investigation took place. Indeed, much of the present-day evidence was not released to—or acknowledged by—the pubic until the mid- to late-1990s. Whether HSCA investigators were allowed to see all classified documents pertaining to the case is left up to speculation. The research that Philip Melanson conducted and published in the 1980s was not available to the HSCA. Additionally, the history of Harry Avery's investigation into Rev. Martin Luther King Jr.'s assassination and what he knew about the Ellington administration's involvement is only now being told.

A COMPLETE THEORY OF THE CRIME

The very first step in this long chain of events was the decision to murder Martin Luther King Jr.

247

Top intelligence and military officials feared that King would tell blacks in uniform in Vietnam to put down their weapons and refuse to patrol or fight. They also feared that he would pronounce compulsory military service as unjust and urge young blacks not to register for the draft or obey induction notices. This would have plunged the nation into social and political chaos, if not a race war. Military commanders believed that King was a communist and that his activities and much of the civil rights movement were funded by communist governments abroad in order to ferment internal chaos in America during war.

Whether the decision that King must die was made by President Johnson, Secretary of Defense Robert McNamara, or lower-level functionaries in the CIA or the Pentagon does not matter. Some official—or, more likely, an intelligence or national security committee with enough presumed authority—made and executed that decision. Once accomplished, senior government officials undoubtedly believed that they had no choice but to close ranks or risk blowing open the entire conspiracy.

James Jesus Angleton likely was ordered to run the operation, as indicated by his connections all around Ray and to many aspects of the case, both before and after the assassination. His subordinate at the CIA, Richard Ober, was called upon to provide security cover and intelligence on King. Ober was already working closely with the CIA's point of contact within the FBI, and they routinely shared intelligence reports on King and other civil rights leaders.

Angleton would have needed to develop a psychological profile for the perfect pawn and search databases for former or current servicemen, federal and state prisoners, and perhaps federal civil servants. There he found James Earl Ray.

Ray happened to be in prison in Missouri under the custody of Fred T. Wilkinson, then the Missouri director of prisons. Whether Ray's escape from Jeff City was assisted or not, the fact remains that the man in charge of the prison from which Ray escaped was well connected to Angleton.

Next, Angleton sought an appropriate alias (or multiple aliases) with which to provide Ray a cover. These he obtained from his search of Canadian security databases. He found one man with a top-secret clearance in Canada who was a ringer for Ray, right down to the same scars: Eric S. Galt. Other lookalike aliases were identified for use as needed.

After Ray's escape from Jeff City, his CIA field handler, Raoul, was tasked with recruiting Ray. Ray obtained an Alabama drivers license in Galt's name, and Raoul gave him money for a white Mustang and other expenses on an ongoing basis.

While Angleton's team planned the detailed assassination scenario, Raoul kept Ray busy with trips to Mexico, Los Angeles, and New Orleans. At some point well into their relationship, Ray was warned never to reveal anything about the origin of the aliases. This is why Ray offered one lie after another about them.

Ray was recalled from California in mid-March 1968 as the assassination planning began to take its final form. A site in Memphis was chosen because one of LBJ's closest and most trusted political allies and insiders, Tennessee governor Buford Ellington, could control the state's investigation and prosecution of the case. Ellington may not have known of the plot in advance because it was not necessary for him to know. He most likely was told after the fact and told only enough to obtain his support.

In the final three weeks before April 4, Raoul set Ray on a zigzag course across the South so that Ray nearly crossed paths with King in Memphis, Selma, and Atlanta. This was to obscure the truth in later investigations. Raoul gave Ray money to buy a deer rifle in Birmingham with instructions to bring it to Memphis. When Ray bought a .243 caliber rifle with a scope at Aeromarine Supply Company on March 29, Raoul sent him back the next day to get a .30-06 Remington GameMaster, also with a scope. Ray fired the rifle a few times in rural northeast Mississippi before heading to Memphis. He did not attempt to sight in the scope, as he was not familiar with that process.

The evening of April 3, Ray met Raoul in a motel in Memphis and turned over the rifle to him. Raoul told him to move the next day to Bessie Brewer's rooming house at 422 South Main Street. At around 3 p.m. the next afternoon, Ray looked at rooms and rented one on the second floor under the alias John Willard. Ray met with Raoul that afternoon before leaving the rooming house to purchase a pair of binoculars from York Arms.

Before Ray returned and only a couple of minutes before the shot rang out, someone placed a green bundle in front of Guy Canipe's storefront. It contained Ray's transistor radio, his shaving kit, two cans of beer, the April 4 final edition of the *Memphis Commercial Appeal*, and the Remington rifle.

When the sniper murdered King, all hell broke loose at the Lorraine Motel and on the street. The sniper team was extricated, the murder weapon never found, and no one saw the gun or the shooter.

As Ray returned from York Arms, he could see a lot of police activity and decided to get out of town. After crossing into Mississippi, he heard on the radio that Martin Luther King had been assassinated. At first, he had no idea that he had witnessed the post-shooting bedlam near his rooming house or that an entire nation was looking for him. This changed in only a few minutes when he heard that police were looking for a white man in a white Mustang. Ray then turned east on the first major road he encountered and headed for Atlanta. Miraculously, he was not picked up on the highway that night.

He ditched the car in Atlanta, took a bus to the Detroit area, and crossed into Canada at Windsor, Ontario. Authorities were soon looking for Galt, because the car registered in that name was discovered in Atlanta. Making his way to Toronto, he dropped the Galt alias and rented a room as Paul E. Bridgeman. A caller to this rooming house left a telephone message for Bridgeman.

Ray then applied for a passport under the name of Ramon George Sneyd. He switched rooming houses and aliases (to Sneyd), and, on May 2, another man asked for him by name and passed on an envelope. Ray paid for his plane ticket and picked up his passport. In a matter of days, Ray was on a flight to London, then Lisbon, and back to London, where he was promptly arrested.

His English barrister, Michael Eugene, wrote to Arthur Hanes Sr. through the Alabama Bar Association, and Hanes agreed to represent Ray. William Bradford Huie approached Hanes, with whom he negotiated a contract for exclusive access to Ray's story.

Ray was locked up in the Shelby County jail for nearly eight months under extremely harsh and inhumane conditions. Huie began writing articles sympathetic to Ray, generating limited public sympathy.

Meanwhile, Hanes and his son, Arthur Hanes Jr., turned down a plea bargain for a life sentence from district attorney Philip Canale. They began preparing for an innocent plea at a trial scheduled for November 12, 1968.

Huie was the CIA's front door into Ray's inner circle. On or about November 1, he deliberately spooked Jerry Ray into advising his brother that the Haneses could no longer be trusted. Percy Foreman was hired soon after.

Foreman came into the case believing that he would win acquittal for Ray, but within a few weeks, he had changed his mind and demanded a guilty plea. Ray, under Foreman's threats, marched into Judge Battle's court and entered a plea that made him "legally" guilty of the murder of King. He lied to every question Battle put to him in precisely the terms Foreman had demanded, except for a question about pressure, which he did not answer.

The next day, Ray was in Commissioner Harry Avery's custody at the main state prison in Nashville. Ray wrote to Judge Battle forty-eight hours later, renouncing his plea and advising him that he had fired Foreman. Late in March, Ray again wrote to Battle and asked him to consider the letter notice of a motion for a full trial.

Avery began his own investigation and concluded that Foreman had coerced Ray and that others were involved in King's murder. Governor Ellington warned Avery to drop the investigation, and when he refused, Ellington fired him.

Meanwhile, Judge Battle died suddenly at his desk in Memphis, leaving it unclear if he had considered Ray's letters an actual motion for a full trial. The case was transferred to the docket of Judge Arthur Faquin, who ruled that Ray's guilty plea was voluntary, based in part on the altered transcript of the March 10, 1969, hearing. The Court of Criminal Appeals and the Tennessee Supreme Court ruled likewise.

Ray's lawyers continued the effort to get a full trial in federal courts. Ray had some success at the US Court of Appeals, Sixth Circuit. Judge William Ernest Miller twice had ruled in favor of motions on behalf of Ray, once overruling federal district court. But Miller died unexpectedly in 1976 with a motion on the Ray case pending before his court. The US Supreme Court refused his petition.

The US House of Representatives reopened both the JFK and MLK investigations in 1976 by creating the House Select Committee on Assassinations. Richard Sprague, the original chief counsel, was forced out after he made it clear that he intended to gather whatever documents he believed were relevant from whatever agency that held them, including the FBI and the CIA.

Harry Avery advised Sprague that he had an evidence file of the early period of Ray's incarceration in the state penitentiary. When the investigators arrived at Avery's home in Tennessee on December 3, 1976, both his file and the duplicate file at his attorney's office in Nashville had disappeared. Once Sprague was forced out as chief counsel, the new HSCA chief counsel, G. Robert Blakey, was only interested in supporting the previous rulings against Ray.

In the 1980s and 1990s, Ray's attorneys repeatedly returned to state court in an attempt to have the rifle retested, which the state prosecutors opposed. Their petition succeeded in the 1990s, but the tests were once again inconclusive. Today, the alleged murder weapon is on display at the National Civil Rights Museum, the site of the former Lorraine Motel in Memphis.

Ray died on April 23, 1998, after Gov. Don Sundquist refused to cooperate with a privately sponsored effort to obtain a liver transplant.[1] The death penalty out of which Ray thought he had bargained in 1969 was effectively imposed in 1998. The legal petitions for a trial became moot, but the questions for history remain.

WAS RAOUL REAL?

Attorney General Canale, the FBI, the HSCA, and others have all claimed that Raoul was not real.

But the money on which Ray lived for fifteen months was real. The money with which he bought the white Mustang, expensive cameras, expensive audio equipment, and rifle was all real. He took dancing lessons during his winter in Los Angeles, had plastic surgery on his nose, and sat through several sessions with a professional psychologist. All of this was real—and Ray paid with real cash in every case. If Raoul didn't give Ray the money, who did?

Ray bought the wrong rifle when he first went to Aeromarine Supply on March 29, 1968. He took it back the next day and exchanged it for a .30-06. Ray didn't know anything about either rifle, according to Donald Wood, who had waited on him in the store. Raoul, Ray claimed, had told him to make the exchange. Obviously, Raoul wanted more than just a rifle with Ray's fingerprints on it. He wanted witnesses of Ray's purchase and Ray's fingerprints on a .30-06.

The aliases of four Canadian men who looked a lot like James Earl

Ray were also real. There is no chance that Ray invented the aliases out of his imagination only to find out years later that they coincidently corresponded to four real Canadians who lived within five miles of each other and looked a lot like Ray. Someone provided those aliases to Ray.

Ray had callers at both rooming houses in Canada in April 1968 when the police in the US were looking for him. Both callers used the correct alias, despite the fact that Ray changed his name when he moved from one rooming house to the next. Someone sent those callers to Ray.

There is also physical evidence that indicates Raoul's existence. A short, Hispanic man wearing an "army jacket" was seen in Bessie Brewer's rooming house near the time of the King assassination. This jacket was found in the trunk of James Earl Ray's car and was inventoried as evidence. Hanes Jr. told me that the discovery of the jacket was "electrifying," because it was far too small for Ray. He said that if Foreman had not taken over the case, he would have been the first to say, "if the jacket doesn't fit, you must acquit." If the jacket didn't belong to Ray, then whose was it?

Raoul was a real man. He was a professional handler and manipulator. He was also a buffer, shielding the rest of the participants' association with the assassination. Ray could not identify anyone other than Raoul, individually or organizationally. It was Raoul's job to make certain that Ray was given the blame, and he did his job very well.

EIGHT ELEMENTS OF CONSPIRACY

There are eight elements of the King assassination that indicate that Ray was not the triggerman or that he did not knowingly participate. Instead, they point towards the participation of one or more other individuals.

- The hit on King was professional. One shot was fired, there were no witnesses, and the shooter escaped.
- The evidence was planted. The green bundle (including the Remington GameMaster rifle) at Canipe's storefront shows that others were involved.
- Ray used the aliases of real Canadian men who shared similar physical features.
- Ray received money that he didn't steal or earn.
- The CIA lied about why it opened a 201 file on Ray, and many CIA officials, agents, and associates surrounded the Ray case.

- William Bradford Huie and Percy Foreman both changed their position on Ray's guilt and whether others were involved.
- The HSCA was unwilling to investigate Foreman's behavior.
- Ellington's administration had information about Ray's guilty plea and conducted itself improperly during the case.

1. A PROFESSIONAL HIT

The distance of approximately 207 feet (69 yards) from the shooter's concealed location to the catwalk of the Lorraine Motel was not a long shot for a .30-06 rifle. Its discharge creates a very loud report even in the open countryside, and more so in an urban setting such as Memphis.

The HSCA *Final Report* states that "the report of a high-powered rifle cracked the air."[2] But out of eight eyewitnesses just a few feet away from King when he was shot, only a single person had heard what he thought was a gunshot. Everyone else heard what he or she thought was a firecracker, a car or truck backfiring, or just a sound that was described nebulously as "something."

Rev. Ralph David Abernathy, who was twenty feet or less behind King inside the motel room, thought he heard a firecracker. Neither of two police officers in the courtyard of the Lorraine Motel just below and slightly in front of King interpreted the sound as a gunshot. Officer W. B. Richmond said that he heard a firecracker. Marrell McCullough, an undercover officer, said that he heard an "explosive sound." Likewise, Andrew Young was in the courtyard and he thought it was a firecracker. Another member of the King entourage, Chauncey Eskridge, also in the courtyard, told Memphis Police that he heard "something like a firecracker." King's chauffeur, Soloman Jones, told Memphis Police that he was ten feet away from King at the time of the shot and also thought he heard a "firecracker."[3] News reporter Joe Sweat, who was in the motel parking lot below King, told me that he thought it was a truck backfiring.

The FBI interviewed every Memphis police officer and every Shelby County sheriff's deputy who was on duty in the area and reported that no one actually heard a shot, though some of them heard "something." Why did no one hear the unmistakably loud discharge from a high-powered rifle fired across a relatively short distance between two-story buildings? The logical answer is that the rifle fired at King was fitted with a silencer.

A silencer does not eliminate the sound of a gunshot or reduce it to a faint thud. Rather, a silencer slows the release of the expanding gases at the end of the barrel, reducing the noise level and changing the sound of it. Every one of the eyewitnesses, even the one who had thought it was a gunshot, said that it wasn't until they saw that King was down that they knew what had happened.

This was the work of a professional sniper who had the skill to fire a single, fatal shot, and the training, temperament, and expertise to escape from the scene with the murder weapon.

The rifle recovered in the green bundle of evidence on South Main Street had a single, spent brass case in the chamber and no live rounds in the magazine.

James Earl Ray had neither the skills to accomplish the shot nor the ability to elude a squad of uniformed policeman. Ray also knew better than to load only a single round of ammunition into a rifle that would hold four rounds.

The murder of King was a professional hit. It was not lucky shot by an amateur or the undisciplined style of the White Knights of the Ku Klux Klan (WKKKK) or some hate group associated with Georgia white supremacist J. B. Stoner, as Wexler and Hancock argue. Those groups have a history of being bloody and imprecise. They could have murdered King almost anytime by blowing up his church, or blowing up half the Lorraine Motel with any number of people in their rooms. On the contrary, the hit on King was a precise job carried out by a professional.

2. PLANTED EVIDENCE

The evidence against James Earl Ray consists of the rifle and other items found with Ray's fingerprints on them in the green bundle. Without it, there was and is no case against James Earl Ray, or even a plausible argument that he was knowingly involved in a plot to kill King.

Canipe said that he heard someone drop the bundle, walked to his front door to see what had been dropped, and noticed a rifle barrel sticking out of the bundle. There were no police in the street yet. Then he stepped out to the street and saw a well-dressed white man walking away from his store headed south. The man got in a white Mustang and drove away. It was another couple of minutes before the police swarmed into the street.

The bundle was left behind and the white man in the white Mustang departed moments before the shot that killed King was fired. The rifle with James Earl Ray's fingerprints on it was not used to shoot King, because it was already at Guy Canipe's feet. And if it was James Earl Ray whom Canipe saw drop the bundle and drive away in the white Mustang, then Ray was gone before the shot was fired. He would have had no reason to drop the bundle because he could have made it to his car without being seen by the police.

It was planted evidence, just as J. Tony Serra suspected. Someone other than Ray fired the shot that killed King. Raoul maneuvered and manipulated Ray into the vicinity of the shooting, and the evidence was planted to incriminate him.

3. THE ALIASES

The odds of finding four men who have physical similarities to oneself are extremely remote. Can you name four people of your gender, age, build, and similar eye and hair color? It is difficult to find one such person, much less four. The real Galt and Ray even shared two visible scars in the same places on their bodies. This suggests that there was a carefully devised selection process. There was lots of information available on Ray's prison and military files about his personality, psychological profile, background, level of intelligence, etc., just as there was in the real Galt's security-clearance file.

Once Ray was selected, James Jesus Angleton or one of his subordinates matched him to Galt based on security file databases. All that was left was to allow Ray to escape and to recruit him.

Ray used the Galt alias during his first trip to Canada in the summer of 1967. He came back from Canada with cash in his pocket and told his brother Jerry that from then on, he would be working for a man named Raoul and would use the name of Eric S. Galt. Ray jettisoned the Galt alias in late April 1968, just as authorities were about to close in. He briefly took up the Bridgeman alias, followed by the Sneyd alias, and obtained a passport eight days after applying for it. Not only were the actual men of those names geographically close to each other and physically similar, but, while Ray was in Toronto waiting for his passport, someone asked for him by his alias on the telephone and at the doors of both of his rooming houses. Furthermore, Ray received his passport in an unusually short amount of time, giving rise to the suspicion that he had outside help.

The aliases allowed Raoul and his handlers to protect Ray from minor legal troubles that might otherwise send their asset back to prison before he had completed his mission. They could set him up and play him like a hand of cards without Ray ever knowing the game was on.

4. WHO GAVE RAY THE MONEY?

James Earl Ray grew up poor, and much of the money he had later in life, he stole. The same was true for his brothers John and Jerry. All three served time for felony robbery, including bank robbery. Ray bussed tables and washed dishes in Chicago for a few weeks prior to his first trip to Canada in July 1967. When he came back through Chicago that summer, Ray had money on him and treated his brothers to steak, whiskey, and prostitutes, according to Jerry Ray. Ray says the money came from the man named Raoul, whom he had met in Canada.

All four of Ray's biographers agree that *Ray did have money* when he got back from Canada. The Shelby County District Attorney knew Ray had money, as did HSCA investigators. Ray could have stolen a large amount of money or perpetrated a series of smaller crimes. Did he become a successful thief for the first time in his life, or did someone provide him with money? If someone gave Ray the money, then Ray was either the actual triggerman or a patsy. Either way it indicates that there was a conspiracy to murder King.

Authors McMillan and Posner both allege that Ray was a dope addict and pusher in prison and passed $7,000 in cash to Jerry during visits to Jeff City. McMillan added that Shelby County district attorney Phil Canale told him that Ray's sister, Carol, received the dope money from Jerry and doled it out to fund James Earl Ray's activities on the lam.[4] One would presume, however, that if prison officials suspected James Earl Ray of passing money to his brother, they would have ended "contact" visits. Furthermore, if Ray's sister was laundering dope money through her bank accounts, why didn't the FBI arrest her?

Another theory as to how Ray came into so much money is that he and his brother John robbed the Bank of Alton, Illinois, of more than

$27,000 on July 13, 1967. While it is true that both John and Jerry pulled bank robberies, none of the Ray brothers were ever suspects in the Alton job.

A particularly far-fetched theory is that Ray murdered King because he thought there was a large cash bounty on King's life. Blakey supports this theory, no doubt because he realizes the theory of the Alton Bank robbery is so weak. Wexler and Hancock also subscribe to this theory, as they believe it fits the style of the WKKKK. The theory may seem to establish a motive, but it fails to explain where Ray got the money he lived on prior to the assassination. Furthermore, considering Ray never made contact with the bounty holders, he would likely have had to stand in a long line of imposters attempting to take credit for the crime. More importantly, the FBI and HSCA investigators never found anyone who was offering a bounty, nor did they ever find the bounty itself.

The forty-nine-paragraph document Ray signed as part of his guilty plea is completely silent about his funds. There is no credible evidence that he earned the money or stole it. The most plausible explanation is that Raoul gave it to him in exchange for heeding instructions.

5. THE CIA'S 201 FILE

When Richard Ober opened a 201 file on Ray, the CIA said it was to assist the FBI to find Ray in countries where Ray might have fled.

Ray's 201 file shows no evidence that the CIA ever attempted to find him, and records no evidence of any CIA activity until Ray was already in custody. What it shows is the fact that the CIA did not want Ray to get a full trial.

The CIA had no reason to offer a phony explanation unless it had something to hide. Why would it monitor the progress of Ray's appeals process unless it feared exposure of someone or some operation, especially if a full trial were granted?

Furthermore, Ray's early biographer, Huie, had an unmistakable connection to the CIA. Huie came calling on Ray's first attorneys to get in the case from the get-go and was instrumental in bringing about Foreman's presence on the case.

Ray's attorney during the most sensitive part of his appeal process— when it seemed that the federal courts might overturn his sentence and order the State of Tennessee to grant him a full trial—was Bernard

Fensterwald Jr. Fensterwald represented at least three high-profile CIA agents (one presumes with the approval of the agency) and had his own connections to the CIA. He failed to recognize that the altered transcript had been entered as evidence.

Most of the known CIA connections to the Ray case lead back to James Jesus Angleton. Angleton was connected to author Priscilla Johnson McMillan, wife of early Ray biographer George McMillan, through the Oswald investigation. Angleton was also connected to Bernard Fensterwald Jr. through John A. Paisley, who interrogated Yuri Nosenko. He was Fensterwald's neighbor and friend, and eventually his widow hired Fensterwald to look into her husband's mysterious death.

Angleton was connected to Cord Meyer Jr., who was Priscilla Johnson McMillan's political ally from college long before he ran CIA's Operation MOCKINGBIRD.

Angleton had connections that also reached to King's inner circle of advisors. William Sloane Coffin Jr., who was a former CIA man and a fellow Yale skull and bonesman, publically supported King. Coffin's church in New York was the site of some of King's important anti-Vietnam War speeches.

Everywhere around James Earl Ray and the case against him were CIA operatives who had a vested interest in the outcome of Ray's case.

6. THE FLIP AND THE PROPAGANDA

It is a matter of public record that William Bradford Huie and Percy Foreman changed their positions on Ray's guilt and whether he was the assassin. Huie, as previously noted, had extensive experience with various CIA operatives. He contacted the Haneses and wanted in on the case.

Huie approached the case with the idea that there was a conspiracy to murder King and that Ray likely had some part in it, but perhaps not as the triggerman. Foreman initially approached the case with the view that there was no solid evidence to pin the crime on Ray, and he expected to win his acquittal.

Percy Foreman was a man at the pinnacle of his profession. He was flamboyant and obnoxiously adept at getting people acquitted in murder trials. He had taken many apparently hopeless cases and won. All it took was money to get Foreman on your legal team.

By November 1968, when Foreman came into the Ray case, Huie had published two lengthy articles in *Look* magazine that were sympathetic, if not downright favorable, to Ray. The day Foreman was permitted by the Criminal Court in Shelby County to represent Ray (November 12, 1968), Huie's second *Look* article hit the newsstands titled, "The Story of James Earl Ray and the Plot to Assassinate Martin Luther King."[5] When Huie met his deadline for this article, he still believed that if James Earl Ray did it at all, he did not do it alone.

We also know that at the time Foreman entered the case, he was preparing for a trial. He negotiated with the District Attorney's office and the court for time to prepare for a trial.

So why did both men change their minds? Were both ignorant of the evidence the state had against Ray prior to their involvement, and once they saw it they knew Ray had murdered King?

Hardly, because there was no real evidence against Ray no matter how you might reassess it. There were no eyewitnesses, and Percy Foreman could have torn up the hodge-podge of physical evidence. One can imagine the fun Foreman would have had with Lt. Ghormley and Inspector Zachary on the stand, each with a conflicting story about how the green bundle was found and who found it first.

The only way this double flip-flop could have occurred is if someone intervened. The intelligence community panicked as the original trial date approached and the Haneses still intended to have Ray enter a plea of innocent. The Haneses were preparing to shred the state's case, which would have put an end to the myth of Ray's guilt from the get-go. This would have led to a re-investigation of the assassination. An acquittal could have caused a race war right in the middle of the Vietnam War.

Huie had too much to lose by refusing to cooperate. Besides, Huie's initiative to join the case may have represented the CIA's entrance through the front door from the beginning. Either way, Huie would have jeopardized his connection to Ray's exclusive story had he not played along with the Haneses and gotten Ray some favorable publicity in the early days of the case. Whether he was the CIA's front door or was later approached, Huie was told enough about the money to be made on Ray if the story was switched to the lone-gunman theory, and perhaps he was threatened.

Huie was instructed to talk to Jerry Ray in order to undermine the Haneses and get Ray and his brothers to fire them. He deliberately insulted Jerry Ray and spooked the Ray brothers with the false idea that the Haneses took all of their instructions from him. When the CIA found out that the Haneses were out of the case and a Texas-based lawyer who had represented LBJ insiders had been hired, they must have thought it was a godsend. They would not only get a delay of the trial date, but also they would have a familiar personality with whom to work. Foreman, after a while, got the same visit that Huie had gotten, and the game was on to pressure Ray to accept a guilty plea.

In the subsequent propaganda campaign, Huie's 1970 book was the first with the "Ray is a racist" narrative. The title of his book had changed from the original "We Slew the Dreamer" to "*He* Slew the Dreamer."

As public skepticism about the King assassination grew and talk of a special congressional investigation swelled, the time for the next installment of "Ray is a racist" matured. George McMillan's *The Making of an Assassin* came out in 1976, just in time to provide additional material to argue against a new investigation. The book, and the now-famous McMillan, were not successful in stopping the US House of Representatives from funding the HSCA, but the allies of the lone-gunman theory succeeded in placing McMillan's book as the centerpiece on which the new investigation would be based. Almost nothing in McMillan's book was corroborated by the HSCA investigation—and much of it was disproven.

7. *The HSCA and the Truth about Foreman*

Foreman testified under oath before the HSCA on November 13, 1978, denied coercing Ray in any way, and claimed, contrary to Ray's assertions, that he put no pressure at all on his client. Assistant deputy chief counsel Peter G. Beeson accepted as true the story Foreman told under oath that his entire James Earl Ray case file was lost as a result of the untimely death of John Hooker Sr. Blakey told me he "did not make a judgment one way or the other" about the truthfulness of Foreman's claim about his lost file. He said his memory "is that the staff (not me) had extensive interaction with the Hooker people."[6] They apparently had no contact whatsoever.

Beeson could have called Foreman's Nashville attorney, Gareth Aden, who took up the case when Hooker Sr. died. Had they done so, they would have found that Foreman had lied, which would have destroyed his credibility.

To make matters worse, had Blakey conducted a legitimate investigation, he would have discovered that the Davidson County, Tennessee District Attorney's office conducted a routine criminal investigation in 1970 of Hooker Sr. vis-à-vis his legal representation of Foreman. The HSCA should have wanted to know whatever the Davidson County District Attorney had in his files regarding Foreman. The man who conducted that investigation was Hal D. Hardin, who noted that the HSCA never contacted him.

Why didn't Beeson and Blakey contact Gareth Aden and Hal Hardin? If the HSCA staff had been running a legitimate, competent investigation there is no excuse that they did not. If they had caught Foreman lying, it would have destroyed Foreman's credibility and opened a full trial for Ray. That is the last thing Blakey wanted. The government's case had grown too big to fail, and Blakey knew he had to leave it that way.

8. GOVERNOR ELLINGTON AND THE RAY CASE

Harry Avery overheard the Nashville end of a key telephone conversation originating in the governor's office. This conversation was intended to ensure high officials in the US Justice Department that there would be no trial for James Earl Ray and there would be no evidence tested in open court. In other words, someone in the governor's office assured federal officials that the case would be closed with no surprises.

The 1968 murder of King was a state crime, not a federal crime. The participation of the Justice Department and Ellington in the Ray case was not only highly improper, it was also an attempt to tamper with the judicial process. One of Governor Ellington's senior staff members told me he was aware such conversations were occurring.

Ellington probably knew in general terms some of the truth of what really happened, and certainly what was at stake in undertaking this cover-up. Ellington had his *bona fides* as part of LBJ's inner circle and knew how to be a good team player and keep his mouth shut. He proved this again when he fired Harry Avery. Avery was the only involved official of any level of government who expressed a belief that there was a conspiracy to murder King.

US Attorney General Ramsey Clark may or may not have known what really happened. But as a native Texan, Clark had known LBJ all his life and likely figured out enough to know that he did not want all of the facts.

The Red Flag of Conspiracy 263

Ray Was the Perfect Pawn

James Earl Ray was unqualified in skill, intellect, and temperament to assassinate Martin Luther King on his own as well as escape the scene relatively undetected. If the assassination had been a Jack Ruby-type job, where someone put a sub-nose revolver in King's torso and pulled the trigger, Ray could have conceived of the plan. There was ample opportunity to murder King in this manner almost any day. The crime that was committed and the ensuing flight from justice was a far more complex scenario. James Earl Ray's ability to accomplish it without help is not believable—Ray didn't have the expertise and he didn't have the money to do this on his own.

Just as Ray was manipulated before the shot was fired, he was manipulated equally after the fact. Ray was badgered and pressured by Percy Foreman, his lawyer, to plead guilty. Ray fought for many years for a full trial and for court permission to retest the rifle using more modern technology, and the state and federal government fought him all the way. If Ray had used that rifle to kill King, why would he have wanted it retested with more accurate techniques that might have proved it was the murder weapon?

Ray was the perfect scapegoat. It was quite believable that a ninth-grade dropout, four-time felon, white man who couldn't complete a two-year hitch in the Army without a less-than-honorable discharge would kill King. When Ray bolted from Memphis to Atlanta to Canada and then to Europe, it made it easier for police and prosecutors to blame him because his flight made him look guilty.

The Ugly Truth

Racism did not kill Martin Luther King Jr.—at least not through the gunshot of a single white man.

James Earl Ray was just a pawn, important only when manipulated into participating in other peoples' crimes. In the King assassination, Ray was sacrificed as part of a political gambit.

The ugly truth is that the government decided to silence King because he was considered a risk to national security. It effectively used the divisive issues of race and war in America to hide the truth of its crime.

The struggle for truth continues today. The HSCA had it within its power to reveal the truth but turned away to follow the path that was predictable from the outset. The CIA undermined the integrity of that investigation and may very well have been behind those who have loyally supported—or even constructed—the government's narrative about the case. The HSCA staff's alteration of evidence is a crime against history.

The government's case against James Earl Ray had to succeed. King had challenged the status quo, and the government decided that he had crossed the line.

Therefore, a scapegoat was needed to camouflage the most obvious element of this event: it was an assassination of a major political figure for political reasons carried out with professional precision.

After three minutes and forty-three seconds of scripted questioning, the government sealed the fate of James Earl Ray and placed their necessary pawn behind bars.

The CIA still has secret files on King and James Earl Ray. The US House of Representatives still has massive files from its HSCA investigation sealed until 2029.

Government at all levels has stood in the way of the American people's desire to know the truth. It is time for the government to open all of the files on King, Ray, and anyone or anything else related to the assassination or the cover-up. Only then can we know the full truth.

APPENDIX A
Glossary of Individuals

Gen. Creighton W. Abrams Jr. Commenced the US Army's modern program of spying on US citizens in 1963.

Gareth Aden. Attorney with the Hooker, Keeble, Dodson, and Harris firm in Nashville. Represented Percy Foreman in federal court after John Hooker Sr. died.

Hon. Ronald B. Adrine. Senior staff counsel of the MLK Task Force, US House Select Committee on Assassinations, 1976-79. Presiding judge of Cleveland, Ohio, municipal court.

James Jesus Angleton. CIA Counterintelligence chief, 1954-75.

Harry S. Avery. Tennessee commissioner of correction, 1963-69.

John Buchanan Avery Jr. Attorney and state senator approached by the *Nashville Tennessean* to represent James Earl Ray.

William L. "Dick" Barry. Chief of staff and legal counsel to Gov. Buford Ellington, 1967-71. Former Speaker of the Tennessee House of Representatives.

Hon. W. Preston Battle Jr. Criminal court judge appointed by Gov. Buford Ellington who conducted Ray's sentencing hearing and died twenty days later with the motion for a full trial before his court.

Hon. James C. Beasley Jr. Former assistant district attorney for Shelby County, Tennessee.

Peter G. Beeson. Assistant deputy chief counsel of the MLK Task Force, HSCA.

Howard Bingham. Film producer photographer, and biographer of Muhammad Ali.

James A. "Bubba" Blackwell. Former criminal court clerk, Shelby County, Tennessee.

G. Robert Blakey. Chief counsel and staff director of the House Select Committee on Assassinations, 1977-79.

Larry Brinton. Nashville journalist who wrote for the *Nashville (TN) Banner* for many years.

Hon. Hamilton S. Burnett. Chief justice of the Tennessee Supreme Court who publically commented on James Earl Ray's appeal.

Philip M. Canale Jr. State district attorney general, Shelby County, Tennessee.

Guy W. Canipe Jr. Received the green bundle of evidence on the doorstep of his business at 424 South Main Street, Memphis, Tennessee.

Hon. Anthony J. Celebrezze. Judge, US Court of Appeals, Sixth Circuit.

William Ramsey Clark. US attorney general in the Johnson Administration at the time of the King assassination and the manhunt for James Earl Ray, 1967-69.

Frank G. Clement. Governor of Tennessee, 1953-59 and 1963-67. Appointed Harry Avery as Commissioner of Correction.

Hudley Crockett. Press secretary for Gov. Buford Ellington, 1967-70. Democratic candidate for US Senate in 1970.

Buford Ellington. Governor of Tennessee, 1959-63 and 1967-71. Reappointed Harry Avery as Commissioner of Correction. Floor manager for Johnson at the 1960 Democratic Convention.

Hon. Arthur C. Faquin Jr. Criminal court judge who presided over the James Earl Ray case after the Battle's death in 1969.

Bernard Fensterwald Jr. Prominent Washington, DC, attorney who represented James Earl Ray in the mid-1970s.

Percy Foreman. Houston criminal defense attorney who represented James Earl Ray for four months from November 1968 through February 1969.

Hon. Charles Galbreath. Court of criminal appeals judge who publically questioned why James Earl Ray was illegally deprived of a trial.

William Henry Haile. Tennessee assistant attorney general who handled much of the appeals process in the Ray case.

Hon. Arthur Hanes Jr. Former circuit court judge in Birmingham, Alabama. Along with his father, the original attorney of James Earl Ray.

Arthur Hanes Sr. Former mayor of Birmingham, Alabama. Along with his son, the original attorney of James Earl Ray in 1968.

Hon. Hal Hardin. Former circuit court judge in Tennessee. As deputy district attorney for Davidson County, he conducted a criminal investigation of John Hooker Sr. in his representation of Percy Foreman.

Robert W. Hill Jr. Chattanooga attorney who represented Ray during the early appeal process in state courts.

Frank Holloman. Director of the Memphis Police Department during the King assassination.

John Jay Hooker Jr. Prominent Nashville, Tennessee, attorney, businessman, and newspaper publisher. Also the Democratic nominee for governor of Tennessee in 1970 and 1998.

John Jay Hooker Sr. Prominent Nashville, Tennessee, trial attorney who represented Percy Foreman in a federal suit by James Earl Ray.

J. Edgar Hoover. Director of the FBI, 1935-72.

W. E. "Bud" Hopton. Director of the Tennessee Bureau of Investigation at the time of King's assassination. Former FBI agent who gained fame in the fatal shootout with Pretty Boy Floyd.

William Bradford Huie. Journalist, screenwriter, and author of *He Slew the Dreamer,* among others.

Erby L. Jenkins. Knoxville, Tennessee, attorney who, as a special justice of the Tennessee Supreme Court, wrote the opinion denying Ray's appeal for a full trial in 1970.

Lyndon B. "LBJ" Johnson. President of the United States from 1963 to 1969.

Nicholas Katzenbach. US attorney general, 1964-66.

Rev. Martin Luther King Jr. Civil rights activist and clergyman. Assassinated on April 4, 1968, as he stood on the second-floor balcony of the Lorraine Motel in Memphis, Tennessee.

Charles E. Koster. Deputy clerk of criminal court of Shelby County, Tennessee, who typed the original March 10, 1969, sentencing hearing transcript.

Stonney Lane. Warden at Brushy Mountain Prison when James Earl Ray escaped in June 1977.

James H. "Jim" Lesar. One of Ray's attorneys during the federal appeal process in the 1970s.

Robert I. Livingston. Memphis attorney who represented Ray during the state appeal process in the 1970s.

George E. McMillan. Knoxville, Tennessee, native, propaganda writer during World War II, and author of *The Making of an Assassin: The Life of James Earl Ray.*

Priscilla Post Johnson McMillan. Author of *Marina and Lee,* wife of George McMillan, and alleged CIA asset.

Hon. Robert M. McRae Jr. Federal district court judge in Memphis who conducted an eight-day evidentiary hearing on Ray's appeal.

Cord Meyer Jr. Senior CIA official who ran Operation MOCKINGBIRD and close friend of Priscilla Johnson McMillan.

Hon. William Ernest Miller. Judge, US Court of Appeals, Sixth Circuit. Became the second judge to die with a motion from James Earl Ray pending before his court in 1976.

William N. "Bill" Morris. Sheriff of Shelby County, Tennessee, at the time of the King assassination.

Hon. L. Clure Morton. Federal district court judge in Nashville whose decision was reversed by the US Sixth Circuit Court of Appeals when he denied Ray's writ of habeas corpus.

Richard M. Nixon. President of the United States from 1969 to 1974.

Roy Nixon. Chief deputy of Shelby County, Tennessee, at the time of the King assassination. Succeeded Bill Morris as sheriff.

Richard Ober. CIA counterintelligence agent who reported to Angleton and ran Operation CHAOS. Opened the 201 file on James Earl Ray and tracked the progress of Ray's appeal for a full trial.

John A. Paisley. CIA agent who interrogated Soviet defector Yuri Nosenko and was a neighbor and friend of Bernard Fensterwald. Paisley's death was never solved.

Maryann Paisley. Former CIA agent and widow of John A. Paisley. Hired Bernard Fensterwald to investigate her husband's death.

Sam J. Papich. FBI agent and liaison to the CIA.

William F. Pepper. Ray's attorney in the 1990s, personal friend of Martin Luther King Jr. and the King family, and author of many books on the assassination.

Hon. Harry Phillips. Judge of the US Court of Appeals, Sixth Circuit.

Gerald Posner. Journalist, attorney, and author of *Killing the Dream: James Earl Ray and the Assassination of Martin Luther King Jr,* among others.

James Earl Ray. Pleaded guilty to the murder of Rev. Martin Luther King Jr. Also known under aliases as Paul E. Bridgeman, Eric Starvo Galt, Harvey Lowmeyer, Ramon George Sneyd, and John Willard.

Gerald William "Jerry" Ray. Brother of James Earl Ray.

Samuel H. "Bo" Roberts Jr. Senior staff member to Gov. Buford Ellington, 1967-71.

Hampton Sides. Author of *Hellhound on His Trail: The Stalking of Martin Luther King Jr. and the International Hunt for His Assassin.*

Stephen C. Small. Nashville, Tennessee, attorney who was appointed by the court to represent Ray and others in a prisoners' rights suit.

James D. "Jim" Squires. Co-author of *A Search for Justice.* Was present in the courtroom at Ray's sentencing hearing.

J. B. Stoner. Savannah, Georgia, attorney and self-styled white supremacist who briefly represented Ray during the state appeal process.

Joseph Sweat. Reporter for the *Memphis (TN) Commercial Appeal.* Was present at the Lorraine Motel when King was assassinated.

Harold R. Swenson. Warden at the Missouri State Penitentiary in 1967.

Stephen G. Tompkins. Reporter for the *Memphis (TN) Commercial Appeal* who, in 1993, broke the story of the US Army's presence in Memphis the day King was assassinated.

Mike Vinson. Journalist and screenwriter who wrote the last published interview of James Earl Ray the month before Ray died in 1998.

Fred T. Wilkinson. Director of Missouri Department of Corrections in the 1960s. Conducted the swap of Soviet spy Rudolf Abel for CIA U-2 pilot Francis Gary Powers.

Ernest Withers. Memphis photographer and member of King's inner circle. Also a paid informant for the FBI.

William P. Yarborough. US Army lieutenant general (ret.) and military intelligence officer in the 1960s.

APPENDIX B
Timeline

1928   *March 10.* James Earl Ray is born in Alton, Illinois.

1946   *March.* Ray joins the US Army.

1948   *December 23.* Ray receives a less-than-honorable discharge from the Army for ineptness.

1949   *December.* Ray is convicted of his first crime, burglary, in California.

1950   *May.* Ray is convicted of armed robbery in Illinois.

1955   *April.* Ray convicted of mail fraud and sentenced to three years in Leavenworth Federal Penitentiary, which he serves.

1959   Ray is convicted of armed robbery of a Kroger store and sentenced to twenty years in Missouri State Penitentiary in Jefferson City.

1967   *April 23.* Ray escapes from prison.

        July. Ray travels to Quebec, where he meets a man named Raoul. When Ray returns to the US later that month, he uses the alias Eric Starvo Galt, the name of a real Canadian man.

        October-November. Ray travels to Puerto Vallarta, Mexico, at Raoul's request.

        November-March 1968. Ray spends the winter in Los Angeles.

1968   *March 29.* Ray purchases a .243 rifle at Aeromarine Supply Company in Birmingham, Alabama, under the alias Harvey Lowmeyer. FBI counterintelligence begins its campaign to manipulate King's entourage into staying at the Lorraine Motel the following week in Memphis.

        March 30. Ray exchanges the rifle for a Remington .30-06 Gamemaster.

        April 3. Ray arrives in Memphis for the first time ever and turns the rifle over to Raoul.

        April 4. At about 3 p.m., Ray rents a room at 422½ South

Main Street in Memphis under the name John Willard, a real Canadian man. At or just moments before 6 p.m., a green bundle is deposited on the street in front of Guy Canipe's Memphis store at 424 South Main Street. At 6:02 p.m., Martin Luther King Jr. is murdered in Memphis.

April 8. Ray escapes to Toronto, Canada, and rents a room under the name of Paul E. Bridgeman, a real Canadian.

April 18. The CIA opens a 201 (person of interest) file on Ray. Ray rents a different room in Toronto under the name Ramon George Sneyd, a Toronto policeman.

May 2. A man calling for "Mr. Sneyd" gives Ray an envelope, and Ray pays cash that same afternoon for an air ticket to Europe. He picks up his passport, issued in the name of Ramon George Sneya (misspelled).

May 6. Ray takes his first commercial flight on a London-bound jetliner.

June 6. Ray enters the Canadian consulate in Lisbon to have his passport re-issued with the correctly spelled name, Sneyd.

June 8. Ray is arrested in London immediately after getting off the airplane.

June. Ray's British barrister writes to Arthor Hanes Sr.

June-July. Lights and cameras installed in Shelby County jail in anticipation of James Earl Ray.

July 8. Ray, Arthur Hanes, and William Bradford Huie create a three-party contract.

July 19. Ray is extradited and brought to the Shelby County, Tennessee, jail.

August-October. Ray refuses a plea bargain that would make him eligible for parole in thirteen years.

November 1. Jerry Ray visits Huie in Alabama and is told that he controls the Haneses.

November 10. Ray meets Percy Foreman, who convinces him to fire Arthur Hanes Sr.

November 12. Judge W. Preston Battle allows Foreman to participate in the Ray case.

1969   *February 3.* Ray transfers all the rights to his story to Foreman.

February 19. Ray reluctantly signs a letter authorizing Foreman to negotiate a guilty plea.

March 9. Foreman gives Ray two letters, both of which deal with money and contract rights that are subject to a guilty plea the next day. Foreman also presents Ray with the "script" he is to follow in court.

March 10. Ray pleads "legally" guilty to first degree murder of MLK. Battle sentences Ray to life and is transferred to state prison that evening.

March 13. Ray recants his guilty plea and writes Judge Battle that he has fired Percy Foreman.

March 24. Ray writes a second letter to Battle asking that the letter be considered notice of a motion for a new trial.

March 31. Battle is found dead at his desk in a darkened office.

March-May. Tennessee Commissioner of Correction Harry S. Avery conducts his own investigation with Ray at the main prison in Nashville.

April 15. Percy Foreman says in *Look* magazine that he was ready to take the stand and testify against Ray if he had not pleaded guilty.

May 26. Ray's motion for a full trial is rejected by Judge Arthur Faquin Jr.

May 29. Governor Ellington announces the firing of Commissioner Avery.

July 15. Ray's petition for full trial is denied by the Tennessee Court of Criminal Appeals.

1970   *January 9.* Ray's petition for full trial is denied by the Tennessee Supreme Court.

1972   *December 27.* Ray's appeal to the federal court system begins with *James Earl Ray v. J. H. Rose, Warden,* for a writ of habeas corpus, which is denied by Judge L. Clure Morton.

1974   *January 29.* US Court of Appeals, Sixth Circuit, reverses Morton's decision and orders a full evidentiary hearing.

October-November. Full evidentiary hearing conducted by Judge Robert M. McRae Jr. in Memphis federal court.

1976-79 HSCA re-opens the JFK and MLK assassinations.

1976   *April 12.* Judge William Ernest Miller becomes the second judge to die with motions from James Earl Ray pending before his court.

May 10. Ray's final appeal to the US Court of Appeals, Sixth

Circuit, is denied, as is his petition to the US Supreme Court.

December 3. House Select Committee on Assassinations investigators interview Harry Avery; they discover that Avery's original evidence file on Ray is missing along with a duplicate file.

1977   *March 30.* Richard Sprague is forced out of his position as chief counsel for the HSCA.

June. G. Robert Blakey is hired as chief counsel for the HSCA.

June 10-13. Ray escapes from Brushy Mountain Prison for forty-eight hours.

June 14. HSCA investigators re-interview Harry Avery.

1978   *November 13.* Percy Foreman lies to HSCA regarding how he got into the Ray case.

1979   *January 2.* HSCA issues its final report on the JFK and MLK assassinations on the penultimate day of the committee's existence.

March. The legal analysis of Ray's guilty plea by HSCA senior staff counsel Hon. Ronald B. Adrine is submitted after the committee's mandate had been terminated.

1990   *April 23.* Ray is interviewed for the first time by the author. Ray gives the author two sets of audiotapes.

1993   *March 21.*Reporter Steve Tompkins breaks the story that US Army intelligence personnel were in Memphis the day King died.

1994   Assassination Records Review Board releases Ray's CIA 201 file.

1998   *April 23.* James Earl Ray dies in Riverbend Maximum Security Institution in Nashville.

2000   Shelby County Archives turns over its original microfilms of all files pertaining to the MLK assassination and James Earl Ray to the National Civil Rights Museum.

2010   *September 10.* Congressman John Duncan requests the release of King-related documents from the clerk of the US House.

2011   Shelby County Archives makes all of its MLK/James Earl Ray documents available online.

August 24. Tennessee secretary of state Tre Hargett requests the release of Tennessee documents on the King assassination in the possession of the US House.

2012   *April 26.* US House clerk Karen Haas refuses to release any documents on the King assassination.

APPENDIX C
Acronyms and Terms

AP. Associated Press.

ARRB. Assassination Records Review Board.

CI. Counterintelligence.

CIA. Central Intelligence Agency.

CCF. Congress for Cultural Freedom, an organization partially funded by the CIA.

COINTELPRO. Counter Intelligence Program, an FBI operation to spy on Americans.

DCI. Director of Central Intelligence, head of the CIA.

FBI. Federal Bureau of Investigation.

HSCA. House Select Committee on Assassinations.

MIG. Military Intelligence Group.

NANA. North American Newspaper Alliance.

NARA. National Archives and Records Administration.

ONI. Office of Naval Intelligence.

Operation CHAOS. CIA operation to spy on Americans.

Operation MOCKINGBIRD. CIA operation that used American media to promote its propaganda.

OSS. Office of Strategic Services.

OWI. Office of War Information.

RCMP. Royal Canadian Mounted Police.

SOG. Special Operations Group, a CIA unit under control of Richard Ober during the 1960s.

TBI. Tennessee Bureau of Investigation.

UPI. United Press International.

USAINTC. United States Army Intelligence Command.

UWF. United World Federalists, a coalition of five small federalist organizations that merged in 1947.

Notes

Chapter One

1. Court Proceedings, March 10, 1969, Shelby County, Tennessee, Archives, http://register.shelby.tn.us/media/mlk/audio2/1969-03-10%20Court%20Proceedings--01.mp3, accessed November 20, 2011.
2. *James Earl Ray v. State of Tennessee*, 451 S.W.2d 854 (Tenn. 1970).
3. Larry Daughtrey, "Avery Says His Side Not Heard," *Nashville Tennessean*, May 30, 1969, 1.
4. House Select Committee on Assassinations, *Investigation of the Assassination of Martin Luther King, Jr.: Hearings*, 95th Cong., 2d sess., 1979, vol. IV, 236, 234. Memphis police director Frank C. Holloman stated to the Associated Press that there were thirty to forty officers in the vicinity of the Lorraine Motel to protect King. The *Memphis (TN) Press-Scimitar* reported that there were twenty-five to thirty officers in the vicinity. Holloman also said in his prepared statement to the HSCA that he sent a detail of police officers to the airport the morning King arrived, April 3, 1968, "for the purpose of offering police protection." Holloman said that King declined the offer and the Memphis police did not know he would be staying at the Lorraine Motel "until he arrived at that location."
5. Joe Sweat, telephone interview with the author, July 9, 2010.
6. From audiotapes given to the author by James Earl Ray.
7. Chester Higgins, "The Mystery behind [the] Murder of Dr. King," *JET*, June 22, 1968, 15.

Chapter Two

1. The term "scope" will henceforth be used when referring to a telescopic sight.

2.   This does not apply to shotgun ammunition, which has a completely different measurement system.

3.   US Federal Bureau of Investigation, *King Assassination (MURKIN) Files,* FBI Central Headquarters, 1968, sec. 52, 36.

4.   Ibid., 31.

5.   Reverend Abernathy and Ambassador Young gave written statements to the Memphis police department around 11 p.m. on April 4, 1968, approximately five hours after the assassination.

6.   Charles Stevens, signed statement to Memphis police, April 4, 1968, Shelby County, Tennessee, Archives.

7.   Arthur Hanes Jr., interview with the author, May 31, 2011.

8.   House Select Committee on Assassinations, *Investigation of the Assassination of Martin Luther King, Jr.: Final Report,* 95th cong., 2d sess., 1979, 311.

9.   Charles Stevens statement.

10.   Arthur Hanes Jr. interview.

11.   Ibid.

12.   HSCA, *MLK Hearings,* vol. XIII, 56.

13.   Ibid., 62; FBI, *MURKIN,* sec. 2, 92.

14.   HSCA, *MLK Hearings.,* vol. XIII, 55.

15.   Ibid., 55-59.

16.   G. Robert Blakey, e-mail to author, February 9, 2013.

17.   HSCA, *MLK Hearings,* vol. XIII, 57.

18.   Ibid., 61.

19.   Ibid., 63.

20.   Blakey email.

21.   HSCA, *MLK Hearings,* vol. XIII, 64.

22.   Ibid.

23.   Ibid.

24.   Ibid.

25.   Ibid., 64-65.

26.   Ibid., 65.

27.   William Bradford Huie, *He Slew the Dreamer* (New York: Delacorte, 1970), 115.

28.   Arthur Hanes Jr., e-mail to author, November 19, 2010.

29.   Huie, 113.

30.   HSCA, *MLK Hearings,* vol. II, 34.

31.   Ibid., 33-34.

32. George McMillan, *The Making of an Assassin* (Boston: Little, Brown, 1976), 298.

33. Gerald Posner, *Killing the Dream* (New York: Harcourt Brace, 1998), 92.

34. HSCA, *MLK Hearings,* vol. XIII, 65.

35. Posner, 222.

36. HSCA, *MLK Hearings,* vol. XIII, 113.

37. Ibid., 66.

38. Ibid., 111-12.

39. Ibid., 112.

40. Ibid., vol. II, 99.

41. Ibid., vol. XIII, 113.

42. Ibid., 117.

43. Ibid., vol. II, 99.

44. *Memphis Press-Scimitar,* "Palm Print on Rifle Being Used to Trace Identity of Suspect," April 5, 1968, 3.

45. Memphis Police Department, *Homicide Report,* Shelby County, Tennessee, Archives, http://register.shelby.tn.us/media/mlk/mlkviewimage.php?imgtype=pdf&local=Reports&image=Homicide%20Report.tif, accessed July 31, 2011.

46. HSCA, *MLK Hearings,* vol. IV, 285-86.

47. HSCA, *Final Report,* 287.

48. Memphis Police Department, *Statement of Guy Warren Canipe Jr.,* April 4, 1968, Shelby County, Tennessee, Archives, http://register.shelby.tn.us/media/mlk/mlkviewimage.php?imgtype=pdf&image=ray_material_2011-02-08/attorney_general_file/microfilm_images/001242ag09.tif#, accessed July 31, 2011.

49. HSCA, *Final Report,* 295.

50. FBI, *MURKIN,* sec. 6, 110-11.

51. The FBI interview of Guy Canipe from April 10, 1968, was designated "MLK Document 170141;" the HSCA interview of Canipe from May 11, 1977, was designated "MLK Document 030156." Both are held by the National Archives and Records Administration as property of the US House of Representatives.

52. Two separate transcripts with discrepancies to each other exist. One is located at HSCA, *MLK Hearings,* vol. III, 99-100, and the other at the Shelby County, Tennessee, Archives, at http://register.shelby.tn.us/media/mlk/mlkviewimage.

php?imgtype=pdf&local=Court%20Records&image=Ray%20 Guilty%20Plea%203-10-1969.tif.

53.   Bob Egelko, "Attorney Tony Serra Sentenced to Prison," *San Francisco Chronicle,* July 29, 2005.
54.   J. Tony Serra, e-mail to author, August 17, 2011.
55.   HSCA, *MLK Hearings,* vol. XIII, 97-98.
56.   Ibid., 98.
57.   Ibid., 100-101.
58.   Ibid., 106.

Chapter Three
1.   Jerry Ray, interview with the author, February 4, 2011.
2.   McMillan, 191.
3.   Ibid., 238.
4.   Posner, 324.
5.   Ibid.
6.   *Memphis Commercial Appeal,* "King Challenges Court Restraint, Vows to March," April 4, 1968, front page.
7.   *Memphis Press-Scimitar,* "King Offers March Plan to Court," April 4, 1968.
8.   McMillan, 100-102.
9.   HSCA, *MLK Hearings,* vol. XIII, 243. Strumm refused to speak to McMillan.
10.   Ibid., 244.
11.   Ibid., vol. IV, 112.
12.   Huie, 91, 101.
13.   Blakey email.
14.   HSCA, *Final Report,* 331.
15.   HSCA, *MLK Hearings,* vol. VIII, 244-45.
16.   Ibid., 245.
17.   Ibid.
18.   HSCA, *MLK Hearings,* vol. XIII, 249.
19.   McMillan, 202.
20.   HSCA, *MLK Hearings,* vol. XIII, 250.
21.   Ibid.
22.   James Earl Ray, *Who Killed Martin Luther King, Jr.?,* 2nd. ed. (New York: Marlowe, 1997), 169.
23.   HSCA, *MLK Hearings,* vol. XIII, 250.

24. Ibid., 250-51.
25. McMillan, 259.
26. Posner, 169.
27. Jerry Ray interview.
28. HSCA, *MLK Hearings,* vol. IV, 116.
29. Ibid., 116-17.
30. Huie and McMillan have interview notes that they claim were generated from conversations with Jerry Ray. Posner merely repeats their unsupported allegations.
31. McMillan, 238-39.
32. HSCA, *MLK Hearings,* vol. VII, 439.
33. Ibid., 499.
34. Jerry Ray interview.
35. Ibid.
36. McMillan, 299.
37. HSCA, *MLK Hearings,* vol. IV, 334.
38. Ibid., vol. VII, 450.
39. Jerry Ray interview.
40. HSCA, *MLK Hearings,* vol. IV, 113.
41. Huie, 45.
42. Posner, 163, 165.
43. HSCA, *MLK Hearings,* vol. IV, 117.
44. Ibid., 121.
45. Ibid., 123.
46. Ibid., 124.
47. Huie, 135.
48. FBI, *MURKIN,* sec. 33, 182; Ibid., sec. 54, 156.
49. Hampton Sides, *Hellhound on His Trail* (New York: Doubleday, 2010), 63.
50. HSCA, *MLK Hearings,* vol. XIII, 252-56.
51. Ibid., 252.
52. Ibid., 256.
53. Ibid., vol. VIII, 245.
54. Ibid., vol. VII, 178.
55. William F. Pepper, *Orders to Kill* (New York: Warner, 1995), 123.
56. HSCA, *MLK Hearings,* vol. XIII, 245.
57. John Jay Hooker Jr., interview with the author, Nashville, Tennessee, June 12, 2010.

58. Howard Bingham, telephone interview with the author, March 6, 2011.
59. Hooker interview.
60. Mike Vinson, telephone interview with the author, March 1, 2011.
61. Harry S. Avery, taped interview by Anna Sandhu Ray, September 1978.
62. Ibid.
63. Ibid.
64. Associated Press news story, as printed in the *Spokane (WA) Spokesman-Review,* June 9, 1977.
65. Douglas E. Kneeland, "FBI Hunt for Ray in Dr. King's Killing Stuns Prison Officials and Others Who Knew Him," *New York Times,* April 23, 1968.
66. Hanes interview.
67. HSCA, *Final Report,* 333.
68. HSCA, *MLK Hearings,* vol. IV, 112.

Chapter Four

1. Deborah Davis, *Katharine the Great: Katharine Graham and Her Washington Post Empire* (New York: Sheridan Square, 1992), 215.
2. HSCA Segregated CIA Collection (microfilm—reel 14), NARA 1994.04.06.11:02:24:430005, 2.
3. HSCA, *Final Report,* 288.
4. HSCA Segregated CIA Collection (microfilm—reel 14), NARA 1994.04.06.11:02:24:430005, 6.
5. Athan G. Theoharis et al., *The FBI: A Comprehensive Reference Guide* (Phoenix, AZ: Oryx, 1999), 347-48.
6. US Senate Select Committee to Study Governmental Operations with Respect to Intelligence Activities, *Supplementary Detailed Staff Reports,* 94th cong., 1st. sess., 1975, bk. III, 681.
7. Ibid., 725.
8. David Robarge, "'Cunning Passages, Contrived Corridors:' Wandering in the Angletonian Wilderness," *Studies in Intelligence* vol. 53, no. 4 (2009): 50-51.
9. Ibid., 50-52.
10. Hanes interview.
11. Hugh Wilford, *The Mighty Wurlitzer: How the CIA Played America* (Cambridge, MA: Harvard Press, 2008), 77-76, 103-4.

12. NARA, http://www.archives.gov/research/guides/catalog-tv-interviews-1951-to-1955.html, accessed February 27, 2012.

13. John M. Crewdson and Joseph B. Teaster, "CIA Established Many Links to Journalists in US and Abroad," *New York Times*, December 27, 1977.

14. *FBI National Academy* (Paducah, KY: Turner, 2000).

15. Pepper, 52.

16. Jerry Ray interview.

17. James DiEugenio and Lisa Pease, eds., *The Assassinations: Probe Magazine on JFK, MLK, RFK, and Malcolm X* (Port Townsend, Washington: Feral House, 2003), 305.

18. George McMillan, "Qualms about the House Assassination Investigation," *New York Times*, February 5, 1977.

19. DiEugenio and Pease, 305.

20. Carl Bernstein, "The CIA and the Media," originally published in *Rolling Stone*, October 20, 1977, http://www.carlbernstein.com/magazine_cia_and_media.php, accessed October 10, 2011.

21. *New York Times*, March 5, 1988.

22. Davis, 216-17.

23. Smith, 171.

24. HSCA, *Final Report*, 213-14.

25. Ibid.

26. David Talbot, *Brothers: The Hidden History of the Kennedy Years* (New York: Simon and Schuster, 2007), 381.

27. Anthony and Robby Summers, "The Ghosts of November," *Vanity Fair* (December 1994): 118.

28. Newman, 540.

29. The CIA's files that include Johnson McMillan can be found at the National Archives and Records Administration. For more specifics, here is a brief summary of what is available:

Date of Document	NARA Reference Number	Document Type
29 Nov. 1956	104-10173-10221	Contact report
19 July 1957	104-10173-10013	Official dispatch
24 July 1957	104-10173-10012	Results of name trace

26 Apr. 1958	104-10173-10220	Request for investigation and approval
29 Apr. 1958	104-10173-10219	Response to green list request
5 May 1958	104-10173-10239	Request of operational use of subject
7 May 1958	104-10173-10143	Special [redacted]
18 June 1958	1994.04.07.11:5210:030005	Fifty-six pages of relevant documents
19 June 1958	104-10173-10138	Routing slip and record sheet
25 May 1962	104-10173-10218	Request for approval or investigative action
11 Dec. 1962	104-10173-10215	Contact report, highly redacted
17 Dec. 1962	104-10173-10214	Request for approval or investigative report
6 Feb. 1964	104-10173-10228	Memo, highly redacted
3 Mar. 1964	104-10173-10212	Contact report
26 Apr. 1965	104-10173-10211	Memo, highly redacted
2 Dec. 1965	104-10173-10225	Memo, "Subject has been stationed in [redacted]"
13 Apr. 1978 (date created)	180-10144-10391	Twenty-eight pages of HSCA notes of CIA files from 1958 to 1969, many redactions.
No date	104-10173-10137	Form
No date	104-10173-10137	Memo

30.   Priscilla Johnson McMillan, e-mail to author, October 9, 2011.

31. DiEugenio and Pease, 304.
32. NARA 180-10144-10391.
33. David Miller, *The JFK Conspiracy* (Lincoln, Nebraska: iUniverse, 2002), 10.
34. J. Y. Smith, "Bernard Fensterwald, Lawyer for Watergate Burglar, Dies," *Washington Post,* April 4, 1991.
35. Richard E. Sprague asserts that Fensterwald represented Otto Otepka and Andrew St. George in his self-published book, *The Taking of America: 1-2-3,* 3rd. ed. (1985), 145. See also Anthony Summers, *Conspiracy* (New York: Paragon, 1989), 150-51.
36. Jim Hougan, *Spooks: The Haunting of America* (New York: Bantam, 1979), 114.
37. Warren Hinckle and William W. Turner, *The Fish Is Red: The Story of the Secret War against Castro* (New York: Harper and Row, 1981), 58.
38. Avery interview.

Chapter Five

1. *Life,* "How the U.S. Army Spies on Citizens," March 26, 1973.
2. Stephen G. Tompkins, "Army Feared King, Secretly Watched Him," *Memphis Commercial Appeal,* March 21, 1993.
3. Marc Perrusquia, "King Scrutiny a Myth, Say Agents Here in '68," *Memphis Commercial Appeal,* November 30, 1997.
4. Paul J. Scheips, "The Role of the Army in the Oxford, Mississippi, Incident, 1962-1963," Office of the Chief of Military History, Department of the Army, June 24, 1965. Declassified May 6, 1968.
5. Joan M. Jensen, *Army Surveillance in America, 1775-1980* (New Haven: Yale University Press, 1991), 239.
6. US Senate Committee on the Judiciary, Subcommittee on Constitutional Rights, *Military Surveillance of Civilian Politics* (Washington: Government Printing Office, 1973), 11.
7. Ibid., 11-12.
8. Ibid., 12-13.
9. US Senate, *Military Surveillance Hearings before the Subcommittee on Constitution Rights of the Committee on the Judiciary, April 9-10, 1974* (Washington: US Government Printing Office, 1974), 181.

10. Senate Committee on the Judiciary, 10.
11. Tompkins.
12. Jensen, 241.
13. US Senate, Subcommittee on Constitutional Rights, 22-23, 30.
14. Clay Risen, "Spies Among Us," *American Scholar,* accessed January 22, 2011, used by permission.
15. US Senate, Subcommittee on Constitutional Rights, 42, 51, 54, 64-65.
16. Ibid., 66.
17. Ibid., 68-72.
18. Ibid., 98-99.
19. Ibid., 111.
20. Tompkins.
21. Ibid.
22. Interfaith Communities United for Peace and Justice, http://icujp. org/king.shtml, accessed June 7, 2013.
23. Tompkins.
24. *Report to the President by the Commission on CIA Activities within the United States,* June 1975, Chapter 11, 130-150, available at http://www.aarclibrary.org/publib/contents/church/contents_ church_reports_rockcomm.htm.
25. President's Commission on CIA Activities within the U.S., Box 6. Index of testimony transcripts, Jan. 27, 1975, Ober, Richard. From the Gerald R. Ford Library, used by permission.
26. Wheaton B. Byers, interview, March 12, 1975, NARA 178-10002-10078.
27. Marc Perrusquia, "Photographer Ernest Withers Doubled as FBI Informant to Spy on Civil Rights Movement," *Memphis Commercial Appeal,* September 12, 2010.
28. HSCA, *MLK Hearings,* vol. VI, 589.
29. *Memphis Commercial Appeal,* "King Challenges Court Restraint, Vows to March," April 4, 1968.

Chapter Six

1. Evan Anders, "PARR, GEORGE BERHAM [1901-1975]," *Handbook of Texas Online* (Texas State Historical Association), http://www.tshaonline.org/handbook/online/articles/fpa36, accessed June 8, 2011.

2. *New York Times*, "Ray Lawyer Likens Panel to 'Harper Valley P.T.A.,'" October 16, 1968.

3. Hanes interview.

4. HSCA, *MLK Hearings*, vol. V, 75.

5. Kay Pittman Black, "New Ray Attorney Protests to FBI Chief," *Memphis Press-Scimitar*, November 13, 1968.

6. Deposition by Percy Foreman, November 11, 1969, in *Ray v. Foreman* lawsuit.

7. HSCA, *MLK Hearings*, vol. V, 75-76.

8. Ibid., 321.

9. Ibid., 149-50.

10. Ibid., vol. I, 109.

11. Sheriff William N. Morris Jr., statement, November 10, 1968, Shelby County, Tennessee, Archives.

12. Daily jail log for James Earl Ray, entry from November 10, 1968, Shelby County, Tennessee, Archives.

13. For many years, Memphis boasted that it had more churches than gas stations.

14. HSCA, *MLK Hearings*, vol. V, 78, as extracted from *Look*, "Ray Wanted to Win Recognition," April 15, 1969.

15. Ibid.

16. Ibid., 76.

17. Percy Foreman to Richard J. Ryan, letter, May 10, 1969, Shelby County, Tennessee, Archives.

18. Huie, 191-93.

19. *James Earl Ray v. J. H. Rose, Warden*, 491 F.2d 285.

20. *Transcript*, James Earl Ray Case 12-18-1968, Shelby County, Tennessee, Archives, 6.

21. Ibid., 26.

22. *Transcript*, James Earl Ray Case 02-07-1969, Shelby County, Tennessee, Archives, 21.

23. Anna McKenna, Office of the Chief Disciplinary Counsel, Texas Bar Association, e-mail to author, December 28, 2011.

24. Ray, 120.

25. Hanes interview.

26. Sidney Zion, "Ray of Truth In King Plot," *New York Daily News*, December 30, 1996.

27. Charles Edmonson, "Ray Security Called Danger to His

'Sanity'," *Memphis Commercial Appeal,* September 12, 1968.

28. Roy Nixon, telephone interview with the author, June 25, 2011.

29. *Transcript,* Criminal Court, September 30, 1968, Shelby County, Tennessee, Archives.

30. HSCA, *MLK Hearings,* vol. I, 110.

31. Pepper, 168.

32. James H. Lesar, telephone interview with the author, April 14, 2012.

33. John Avery Emison, "James Earl Ray Is Still Fighting to Clear Name," *Tennessee Oak Ridger,* April 25, 1990.

34. Ibid.

35. Hanes interview.

36. *Ray v. Rose,* 491 F.2d 285, footnote 4.

37. Deposition by Percy Foreman, November 11, 1969 in *Ray v. Foreman* lawsuit, 22. This document was "sealed" by the HSCA for fifty years (MLK Document 010050) and is available only through the Shelby County, Tennessee, archives. James Earl Ray was deposed the same day in the same lawsuit (*Ray v. Foreman*) and his deposition was likewise sealed for fifty years (MLK Document 030316). Unfortunately, it is not available in the Shelby County Archives.

38. Ibid., 26-27.

39. HSCA, *MLK Hearings,* vol. XIII, 226.

40. *Ray v. Rose,* 491 F.2d 285, paragraph 24, 26.

41. Harry S. Avery, taped interview by Anna Sandhu Ray, circa 1978.

42. Criminal Court transcript, March 10, 1969, Shelby County Archives.

43. *Ray v. Rose,* 491 F.2d 285, paragraph 24.

44. *Transcript,* Criminal Court, March 10, 1969, Shelby County Archives.

45. Weisberg, 107-8.

46. HSCA, *Martin Luther King Hearings,* vol. VII, 28.

47. Percy Foreman, "Ray Wanted to Win Recognition," *Look,* April 15, 1969, 112.

48. Nancy Petro, e-mail to author, March 21, 2013.

49. Hon. Hal D. Hardin, interview with the author, April 23, 2013. The case regarding Ronald Harries is reported at 594 F. Supp. 949 (1984).

50.   Hanes interview.

Chapter Seven

1.   James A. Blackwell, telephone interview with the author, June 25, 2012.
2.   Charles E. Koster, telephone interview with the author, June 25, 2012.
3.   James A. Blackwell, personal interview, April 17, 2013.
4.   Blair, 209-44.
5.   John Seighenthaler, et al., *A Search for Justice* (Nashville: Aurora, 1971) 183-87.
6.   James D. "Jim" Squires, telephone interview with the author, April 18, 2012.
7.   Transcript by Charles E. Koster, Shelby County, Tennessee, Archives.
8.   Respondent's Post-Hearing Memorandum, filed by the Tennessee Attorney General in Federal District Court in Memphis, *Ray v. Rose* (C-74-166), November 29, 1974.
9.   James H. Lesar, telephone interview with the author, April 14, 2012.
10.   Memorandum, *Ray v. Rose* 535 F.2d 966 (6th Cir. 1976).
11.   Lesar interview.
12.   Stephen C. Small, telephone interview with the author, June 4, 2012.
13.   William Henry Haile, telephone interview with the author, May 17, 2012.
14.   Koster interview.
15.   *Affidavit*, James A. Blackwell, April 19, 2013.
16.   *Affidavit*, Charles E. Koster, May 6, 2013.
17.   Memorandum Decision, *Ray v. Rose*, 535 F.2d 966 (6th Cir. 1976).
18.   *Ray v. Rose*, 535 F.2d 966 (6th Cir. 1976).
19.   Vincent Clark of the Shelby County, Tennessee, Archives, e-mails with the author, April and May 2012.
20.   HSCA, *MLK Hearings*, vol. XIII, 290-99.
21.   HSCA, *Final Report*, 316.

Chapter Eight

1.   Hudley Crockett, interview with the author, July 7, 2011.
2.   William L. "Dick" Barry, interview with the author, July 31, 2010.

3. Samuel "Bo" Roberts Jr., interview with the author, June 12, 2010.

4. Lyndon B. Johnson Library, Recordings and Transcripts of Conversations and Meetings, Tape WH6503.03, March 8, 1965, 8:10 a.m.

5. "Historical Timeline," Tennessee Department of Correction, 2006.

6. Avery interview.

7. Ibid., as are all of Avery's quotes in this section.

8. Larry Brinton, "Avery Writing Book On Ray," *Nashville Banner*, May 16, 1969.

9. John Haile, "Ray-Avery Ties Studied," *Nashville Tennessean*, May 21, 1969.

10. Crockett interview.

11. Larry Brinton, "Avery Quizzed 'At Length' By TBI Director," *Nashville Banner*, May 21, 1969.

12. John Haile, "Avery: No Resignation Plans," *Nashville Tennessean*, May 23, 1969.

13. Ibid.

14. Larry Brinton, "Ellington Boots Avery," *Nashville Banner*, May 29, 1969.

15. Avery interiew.

16. Crockett interview.

17. Barry interview.

18. Null Adams, "Prison Chief Fired Over Ray Case," *Memphis Press-Scimitar*, May 29, 1969.

19. William Bennett, "Ray Case Theory Is Labeled Reason for Avery Firing," *Memphis Commercial Appeal*, May 30, 1969.

20. Fred Travis, "Avery Dismissed, Correction Post to Lake Russell," *Chattanooga Times*, May 30, 1969.

21. Daughtrey.

22. Roberts interview.

23. This quote is paraphrased to the best of my recollection. The words may not be exact, but the topic of the conversation is captured precisely.

24. Avery interview.

25. Ibid.

26. Brief for Petitioner-Appellant, US Court of Appeals for the Sixth

Circuit, *Ray v. Rose*, 535 F.2d 966 (6th Cir. 1976), by James H. Lesar.

27.   John Seigenthaler with contributions from James Squires, John Hemphill, and Frank Ritter, *A Search for Justice* (Nashville: Aurora, 1971), 199.

28.   James C. Beasley was elected in 1970 to a newly created seat on the Criminal Court for Shelby County where he served for many years. Later, he served on the Tennessee Court of Criminal Appeals.

29.   Defendant's Brief, filed June 25, 1969 by Ray's attorneys with the Court of Criminal Appeals, Jackson, Tennessee.

30.   Affidavit of Harold Weisberg to US District Court Western District of Tennessee, October 7, 1974.

31.   Woodrow Paige, Jr., "Judge W. Preston Battle Found Fatally Stricken, Victim of Heart Attack," *Memphis Commercial Appeal*, April 1, 1969.

32.   *Nashville Tennessean*, June 22, 1998.

33.   *Time*, "Intelligence: Of Dart Guns and Poisons," September 29, 1975.

34.   "Order of the Court of Criminal Appeals of Tennessee, at Jackson" July 15, 1969. Also based on an in-person visit to the office of the Clerk of the Appellate Courts, Western Division, Jackson, Tennessee, January 2012, and subsequent telephone conversations.

35.   *James Earl Ray v. State of Tennessee*, 451 S.W.2d 854 (Tenn. 1970).

36.   Associated Press news story as printed in the *High Point Enterprise* (North Carolina), March 15, 1969.

Chapter Nine

1.   *Memphis Press-Scimitar*, "Palm Print on Rifle Being Used to Trace Identity of Suspect," April 5, 1968.

2.   *Montreal Gazette*, June 10, 1968.

3.   HSCA, *MLK Hearings*, vol. I, 141.

4.   Ibid., 141-42.

5.   Ibid., vol. IX, 280-82.

6.   Melanson, 37.

7.   Ibid.

8.   Pepper, 78.

9.   Ibid.
10. HSCA, *MLK Hearings*, vol. I, 141.
11. Melanson, Weisberg, and Pepper spell Bridgeman with an "e;" Ray and the HSCA spelled it without the "e," i.e., Bridgman.
12. HSCA, *MLK Hearings*, vol. V, 11.
13. Ibid., 10.
14. Ray might have spent one night in the Toronto area on the road to Montreal in July 1967.
15. HSCA, *MLK Hearings*, vol. V, 12.
16. Huie, 35.
17. Posner, 159; HSCA, *Final Report*, 336.
18. Melanson, 41.
19. Ibid., 58-59.
20. FBI, *MURKIN*, sec. 55, 145-46; HSCA, *MLK Hearings*, vol. V, 60.
21. Melanson, 60-61.
22. Ibid., 57.
23. Huie, 171.
24. Posner, 37.
25. HSCA, *Final Report*, 298-99.
26. Sides, 144.
27. Hampton Sides, e-mail to author, January 17, 2012.

Chapter Ten

1.   All of G. Robert Blakey's direct quotes in this chapter are attributed to a series of e-mails to the author from February 9, 2013, to June 1, 2013, unless otherwise specifically noted.
2.   PBS, *Frontline*, http://www.pbs.org/wgbh/pages/frontline/shows/oswald/interviews/blakey.html, accessed June 3, 2013.
3.   HSCA, *Final Report*, 333.
4.   Hanes interview.
5.   HSCA, *MLK Hearings*, vol. VII, 311-12.
6.   FBI, *MURKIN*, sec. 2, 178.
7.   Peter G. Beeson, e-mail to author, May 30, 2013.
8.   Ronald B. Adrine, e-mail to author, June 10, 2013. All subsequent quotes of Adrine in this chapter are thus attributed.
9.   HSCA, *MLK Hearings*, vol. XIII, 222.
10. Ibid., 226.
11. Ibid., 234.

12. Ibid., 235.
13. Ibid.
14. Ibid., vol. III, 58.
15. Ibid., 59.
16. Ibid., 77.
17. Jerry Mitchell, http://blogs.clarionledger.com/jmitchell/2013/04/03/former-justice-official-to-fbi-run-mlk-prints/, accessed May 22, 2013.

Chapter Eleven

1. Ray died of cirrhosis of the liver due to a hepatitis C that was contracted when he was stabbed multiple times in the prison library in 1977.
2. HSCA, *Final Report*, 284.
3. Bernard Lee, Rev. Ralph David Abernathy, W. B. Richmond, Marrell McCullough, Andrew Young, Chauncey Eskridge, Soloman Jones, *Statements to Memphis Police*, April 4, 1968.
4. McMillan, 239-41.
5. William Bradford Huie, "The Story of James Earl Ray and the Plot to Assassinate Martin Luther King," *Look*, November 12, 1968.
6. G. Robert Blakey, e-mail to author, June 1, 2013.

Index

A

Abel, Rudolf, 100
Abernathy, Ralph David, 42, 254
Abrams, Creighton W., Jr., 114-15, 129
Aden, Gareth, 137, 261-62
Adrine, Ronald B., 239-43
Aeromarine Supply Co., 38, 47, 53, 55-56, 58, 61, 215, 228, 249, 252
Alabama National Guard (ANG), 124-25
Alamo, Tennessee, 34, 197
Alaniz, Nago, 132
Alexander, Lamar, 30
Ali, Muhammad, 86
American Broadcasting Co. (ABC), 106
American Civil Liberties Union (ACLU), 118
American Committee for Cultural Freedom (ACCF), 102
American Mercury, The, 102
Angleton, James Jesus, 24, 95, 98-100, 107, 111, 233, 248-49, 256, 259
Anschutz, Willie, 43
army jacket, 44, 253
Assassination Records Review Board (ARRB), 23, 183, 234
assassinologist, 105
Avery, Harry S., 29-30, 34, 87-88, 112, 185, 188-91, 193-202, 204, 217, 247, 251-52, 262; fired by Ellington, 195-97; missing evidence file of, 200-201
Avery, John Buchanan "Buck," Jr., 34, 198
Avery, Robert Bruce, 34

B

Bank of Alton, Illinois, 257
Barry, William L. "Dick," 185, 195-96, 199-200
Battle, W. Preston, Jr., 26-27, 132-33, 139, 141-42, 144-45, 152, 154-59, 165-67, 170-71, 174-76, 178, 180-82, 189-200, 202-6, 229, 240, 244, 251; death of, 204-7; Ray's guilty plea and, 156-69
Beasley, James C. "Jim," 150, 204-5
Beeson, Peter G., 133, 135-37, 141-42, 238, 261-62
Billingslea, Charles, 121
Bingham, Howard, 86
Black, Kay Pittman, 133
Blackwell, James A., 165, 167-69, 171, 179
Blair, Clay, Jr., 170-71, 182, 245
Blakey, G. Robert, 24-25, 43, 48, 50, 81, 165, 182-84, 233-45, 252, 258, 261-62
Bridgeman, Paul E. *See* Ray, James Earl
Brinton, Larry, 191-92, 194-95, 198
Brushy Mountain Prison, 30, 32, 220
Buckley, William F., Jr., 102
Burnett, Hamilton, 203
Burnham, James, 102
Business International Corporation (BIC), 103
Byers, Russell G., 84
Byers, Wheaton B., 124